D1191553

PR5398.G4   1973

GERSON

DAUGHTER OF EARTH A

Daughter of Earth and Water

A Biography of
Mary Wollstonecraft Shelley

Other Morrow books by Noel B. Gerson

MIRROR, MIRROR
TALK SHOW
BECAUSE I LOVED HIM
THE SUNDAY HEROES

A miniature of Mary Shelley by Reginald Easton.
(Copyright Bodleian Library Oxford.)

Daughter of Earth and Water

A BIOGRAPHY OF MARY WOLLSTONECRAFT SHELLEY

Noel B. Gerson

William Morrow & Company, Inc.
NEW YORK 1973

For Noel-Anne

Gerson, Noel Bertram.
    Daughter of earth and water.

    Bibliography: p.
    1. Shelley, Mary Wollstonecraft (Godwin), 1797-1851.
I. Title.
PR5398.G4 1973   823'.7   76-182976

I am the daughter of Earth and Water,
    And the nursling of the Sky;
I pass through the pores of the ocean and shores;
    I change, but I cannot die.
For after the rain when with never a stain
    The pavilion of Heaven is bare,
And the winds and sunbeams with their convex gleams
    Build up the blue dome of air,
I silently laugh at my own cenotaph,
    And out of the caverns of rain,
Like a child from the womb, like a ghost from the tomb,
    I arise and unbuild it again.
                    —PERCY BYSSHE SHELLEY, "The Cloud"

I

MARY WOLLSTONECRAFT GODWIN was destined from her birth, on August 30, 1797, to be different, out of step in both thoughts and feelings with ordinary minds and mundane emotions. The very nature of her unorthodox, controversial parents guaranteed that the child of their union would be dissimilar to anyone else who came into the world at the turn of the nineteenth century.

William Godwin, who was forty-one years of age when Mary was born, was the son of a Nonconformist clergyman and was himself trained for the Calvinist ministry, but wore the cloth for only a few years. His first book, *Life of Chatham,* written after he had been exposed to the works of Voltaire and other French foes of organized religion, turned him in a new direction, and he became a philosopher-historian. Such works as his *History of the Commonwealth of England* were regarded as sound by contemporary scholars, but in others, among them a series of sermons he called *Sketches of History,* he showed signs of the attitudes that would win him renown as a radical thinker and ultraliberal. A violent foe of despotism, he wrote a line that made the *Sketches* the talk of intellectual and theological London: "God himself has no right to be a tyrant."

As a mature philosopher Godwin embodied the essence of the Age of Reason by carrying every thought, no matter how extreme, to its logically rational conclusion. Deeply influenced by Voltaire, he increasingly rejected organized religion, and there were strong hints of anarchistic leanings in his political references.

The most famous of his works was *Political Justice,* published four years before Mary's birth, and it won him a place, almost overnight, in the front ranks of his peers. All governments were corrupt, he wrote, and most of society's institutions were worthless. Man yearned for perfection, he declared, and was perfectible. This was the heart of his argument, but he stressed that the individual could attain perfection only by discarding the warped, prejudiced institutions of the religious and social order, and thereafter relying exclusively on his intellect. Man, he insisted, could achieve the heights by use of the intellect alone.

Demonstrating his versatility, Godwin wrote a number of novels and several plays, in addition to his heavier works. And when Mary was five years old he also set himself up in business as a publisher of children's books, the most noteworthy of which were his own *Life of Chaucer* and the *Tales from Shakespeare* by his friends Charles and Mary Lamb.

Godwin's greatest influence did not grow directly out of his own writing and editing, but his ideas were disseminated through the creative efforts of the brilliant disciples who made a cult of Godwinism, as they called his philosophy. Inadvertently and somewhat to his own discomfort, Godwin found himself the intellectual father of the new romantic movement that was to become all-pervasive in literature. His concepts appealed to men whose fame eventually far outshone his, among them Coleridge and Lamb, William Wordsworth, Robert Southey and William Hazlitt. The ideas Godwin expressed in *Political Justice* and many of his lesser works gripped the imagination of such younger men as Percy Bysshe Shelley, who not only expounded the themes of Godwinism in his poetry but tried to live according to their precepts.

William Godwin neither looked nor acted like someone responsible for altering the approach to life of millions. He was of medium height, and although slender and handsome in his youth, he became overweight, bald and myopic. Even his most devoted followers described him as cold, impersonal and ever remote. His private life was his own, and he drew a sharp line between it and the rational Utopia he envisioned. He ate to excess, borrowed money freely from anyone who would make him a loan, and the most Coleridge could say of his personal habits was that he drank little and rarely smoked a pipe.

It may have been Godwin's awe-inspiring intellectual austerity that caused his disciples to worship him. Grudging in his praise yet remarkably patient as a teacher, he was to them a father figure. Also, according to Coleridge and Lamb, many women found Godwin fascinating, but he seemed unaware of their existence, an attitude befitting one who was devoting his entire life to the cultivation and exercise of his formidable mind.

Then, in 1796, the forty-year-old Godwin met a woman of thirty-six who smashed all of his neat theories to bits, although he did not realize it at the time.

Wordsworth did not exaggerate when he said that Mary Wollstonecraft was the most influential of Enlightenment radicals with the possible exception of William Blake. The daughter of a nondescript Irish mother and a drunken, aristocratic father who failed at everything he tried, including farming, Mary Wollstonecraft was a free, blithe spirit of the breed that her future son-in-law, whom she never knew, believed to be nonexistent save in the imagination of man.

Striking out on her own in the world at the age of

twenty-one, she and her sisters opened a school and were befriended by the great Dr. Samuel Johnson. But the failure of the school sent her to Ireland for a time as a governess, and thereafter she worked for a London publisher, James Johnson. In 1792 she went off to France alone to see the great Revolution for herself, an act of independence remarkable in a woman of her era, and there she met Captain Gilbert Imlay, the master of an American merchant ship.

They lived together until she gave birth to a daughter, Fanny, to whom she gave Imlay's name; he deserted her, and Mary Wollstonecraft returned to England, where an attempted suicide failed. Again she went to work for James Johnson, augmenting her income with her own writing, which had earned her a considerable reputation and a small amount of money during the past decade.

She tried her hand at novels, political essays and history, but it was one work that won her lasting renown. It was entitled *A Vindication of the Rights of Woman,* and its publication in 1792 made her a pioneer, perhaps the first of prominence in the Anglo-Saxon world, in the struggle for women's rights that has continued down to the present. The core of her argument well could have been written almost two centuries later by an advocate of Women's Liberation: "Tyrants and sensualists are in the right when they endeavor to keep women in the dark, because the former only want slaves and the latter a plaything."

It was woman's femininity that made her strong, Mary Wollstonecraft held, and she who abandoned the fundamental traits of her sex in an attempt to copy the male fell between two poles and perished. In an ideal world men and women would be reared and educated as equals and companions, and would go through life together as partners. Marriage was a noble institution, she declared, provided the husband did not take unfair advantage of

[*4*]

his superior legal position and the wife did not succumb to the pressures of society and become a nonentity. But marriage, as she saw it, was not necessary for happiness. Those who felt sure of their places in the world were entitled to live together without benefit of clergy and rear their children out of wedlock.

Education was the tool that would set woman free, Mary Wollstonecraft argued. She was indifferent to politics and neither sought nor wanted the vote; equality in all things would grow out of equal educational rights, facilities and opportunities.

Unlike some of the lesser champions of women's rights who were her contemporaries, Mary Wollstonecraft believed it was the duty as well as the privilege of women to bear children, and she contended that the intelligent woman, using her intellect to the full, would make the perfect parent. She also said that "whatever tends to incapacitate the maternal character takes woman out of her sphere and debases her."

Mutual sympathy marked the first meeting of Mary Wollstonecraft and William Godwin, which took place at one of the social evenings regularly held at his home, 7 Evesham Buildings in Somers Town, on the outskirts of London. Within a short time, however, they began to dine, attend the theater, frequent coffeehouses and stroll through London together. Their budding romance was an inevitable outcome of their intellectual beliefs, so many of which they held in common, and it was Wordsworth who observed that if their love had not been created in heaven, it had originated simultaneously in their minds.

Mary Wollstonecraft was handsome, articulate and, perhaps, the most intelligent woman of her day, and Godwin, the intellectuals' intellectual, melted in her presence and dropped his aura of severity. They initiated an affair in the autumn of 1796, with neither thinking in terms of the

[5]

marriage they disliked, as a matter of principle, and Mary moved to lodgings only a few doors from his for the sake of mutual convenience.

To the amusement of their friends they took pains to preserve their own and each other's independence. Neither took the other for granted, each maintained a separate social life, and they went through an elaborate ritual of arranging an engagement prior to their almost daily meetings. They were practicing what they preached, and all was tidy in their mutual world, which they believed was ruled by their minds.

Then, in February, 1797, Mary Wollstonecraft discovered she was pregnant. To what extent she was responsible for their marriage on March 29 is unknown, but the later correspondence of Godwin's friends, which he did not deny, indicates that he was anxious to have the legal ceremony performed. He did not care for his own sake, he declared, and his own principles were unchanged. But Mary Wollstonecraft would be censured by a society that demanded the amenities, and her illegitimate child would be made to suffer. In addition, Godwin said, he had grown very fond of little Fanny, who was learning to read under his tutelage, and he wanted to give her his name, too.

So William Godwin, the incorruptible thinker, and Mary Wollstonecraft, who had argued that marriage was a mockery when men and women of intellect indulged in it, were joined in holy wedlock before the altar of Saint Pancras Church.

The couple went to extraordinary lengths to maintain at least the fiction of independence. They continued to live in their separate dwellings, exchanging several communications each day and dining together only when one or the other extended an express invitation for the purpose. It so happened that they always ate their noon and evening meals together at one house or the other, and it

[6]

did not occur to either that the outside world, including friends who admired and respected them, laughed at their exaggerated courtesy.

Godwin exhibited the customary symptoms of the uneasy father as his wife's time approached, and he could not concentrate on his work; consequently his notes to her became increasingly curt. Finally, in mid-August, he confessed to her that he was finding it difficult to concentrate on matters of the mind. At no time did Mary Wollstonecraft lose her poise, however, and her letters to Godwin were models of cool, orderly decorum.

The middle-aged father's fears proved to be justified, however, and Mary's labor was so difficult that three prominent physicians, a midwife and two ladies who were close friends attended her. The infant, a girl, was born late in the evening of August 30, and the mother was exhausted by her ordeal.

The following day Godwin proposed to his wife that the baby be given her name, and Mary Wollstonecraft agreed.

That night complications set in, and for the next week and a half the physicians were in almost constant attendance on their patient. Godwin left the sickroom only for very brief periods to comfort his stepdaughter. On September 9 Mary Wollstonecraft began to sink rapidly, losing what remained of her strength, and the following day she died.

One of the physicians, Dr. Anthony Carlisle, who was knighted some years later, wrote that Godwin dropped to his knees at his wife's bedside and wept. Many years later Mary Shelley observed in a letter that no one, since that day, had ever known her father to shed a tear.

No man was less suited temperamentally to the task of rearing a three-year-old girl and a newborn female infant than William Godwin, and no one realized it more acutely than Godwin himself. Mary Wollstonecraft's friends and the wives of his own pitched in to help; a serving maid, a cook and a housemaid were hired; and Godwin settled down in a semibachelor existence that would never again resemble the solitary life he had known before his affair with Mary Wollstonecraft.

He wanted to be a good father, he wrote to various friends, but he didn't know how to begin. Small children were illiterate creatures endowed with animal spirits, and he knew neither how to communicate with them nor how to tame them. "When Fanny interrupts my reading with a request to hold her on my knee and tell her a fanciful tale, I confess I must curb my temper," he wrote to Coleridge. "And when the wild cries of baby Mary fill the house, threatening to shatter the glass in the windows, I succumb to unreasoning panic."

Children, the harried philosopher soon decided, needed a mother to supervise their activities, care for them and take responsibility for their welfare. He discovered that housekeepers interrupted him repeatedly in his study, even though he issued firm instructions that he must not be disturbed when he was working. Nursemaids and serving maids took unfair advantage of a man who knew as little about housekeeping as he did about children, and cooks robbed a man, helping themselves to food from his larder as though it belonged to them. His work was suffering, his temper was short and he was doing little for Fanny and nothing for the new baby.

There was only one way to solve his problem, the champion of bachelordom decided: he would have to find another wife. A scant six months after Mary Wollstonecraft's death he began to propose to various ladies of his acquaintance, but without exception they rejected him. His income was irregular, he was burdened by two very small children and the good ladies knew him well enough to realize he was a cold, withdrawn man who would be other than an ideal companion. His panic mounting, Godwin looked farther afield.

In 1798 he met a woman of considerable intellectual prowess, a Miss Harriet Lee, who was the headmistress of a girl's school in Bath, and had written, in collaboration with her sister Sophia, a new children's version of the *Canterbury Tales*. The application of reason told Godwin that Miss Lee would make a perfect wife for someone in his circumstances; as an author she was familiar with at the least the rudiments of his vocational needs and routines, and as a schoolmistress she undoubtedly understood little girls and knew how to handle them. After an acquaintance of only a month and a half he proposed to Harriet Lee in a letter so impassioned it was sometimes incoherent. But the lady understood enough to become indignant at his presumptuous haste, which impelled her to terminate the relationship.

Some order was maintained in the Godwin household only because of the sympathetic exertions of Maria Reveley, the wife of a close friend, who supervised the work of the servants, and prevented Godwin from squandering every penny he earned on those who came to his house nightly for food and drink rather than conversation. Above all, Mrs. Reveley took charge of Fanny and the baby, saw that they were fed, bathed and clothed properly and gave them at least a measure of the maternal affection they were so sadly lacking.

One day early in 1800 Mrs. Reveley's husband died, but Godwin wasted little time mourning the loss of his friend and studied the widow in a new light. Maria lacked Mary Wollstonecraft's regal beauty, but she was a handsome woman, and the philosopher had learned enough of the opposite sex to appreciate beauty when he saw it. Maria was a woman of high spirits, with an exceptionally even disposition, and equally important, she was unconventional in many of her attitudes, decrying the spread of the stifling bourgeois mentality and morality that were transforming England from a land of heroes and geniuses into a nation of shopkeepers. Above all, Maria had already demonstrated to his eminent satisfaction that she had an affection for small children, his own in particular.

Waiting no more than a month after the loss of her husband, Godwin proposed to her. But Maria Reveley was endowed with yet another quality Godwin failed to recognize: she was a very good judge of character, and knew he was emotionally unstable, improvident and remarkably childish in human relations that did not rely on intellect alone. So she rejected him, and compounded the insult by marrying a mutual acquaintance, John Gisborne, a dull, plodding man who had little imagination and no inner drive.

It is one of the ironies of Mary Shelley's life that Maria Reveley Gisborne, who had comforted her in her infancy, should become her closest friend two decades later, in Italy, when her own sorrows were so great she needed an older woman in whom she could confide.

In any event, the unhappy Godwin felt lost. His friends tried to cheer him, but accomplished little. He knew he was writing nothing of significance, and his income was sinking to an alarming low that would force him to dismiss the servants unless he found a publisher willing to pay him a substantial advance royalty. Fanny was growing old enough to observe everything taking place under the maladjusted family's roof, including her stepfather's latest habit, the nightly consumption of a jar of sack.

To make matters still worse, Mary was beginning to talk, and was constantly underfoot. She was so lively that her exasperated father gave her the first nickname of her life, Mercury, and was forced to invent elaborate strata-

[*10*]

gems to keep the two-year-old out of his study when he was trying to write or read.

He admitted his defeat in a letter to William Hazlitt, a young disciple who was trying to learn portrait painting and had not yet turned to his pen. "Two little girls, the smaller of them scarcely able to walk or talk, are the death of me. I must find relief from the tyranny imposed upon me by these infants, or I shall perish!"

II

An admiring Robert Southey once wrote that William Godwin understood better than anyone else then alive the intricacies of man's mind. In 1801, when Mary was three and Fanny was six, his desperate need for someone to take care of the children compelled him to take a new wife, Mrs. Mary Jane Clairmont, and his choice—to the extent that he had a voice in the matter—indicated that his inability to understand the character of woman was abysmal.

Charles Lamb, the East India House clerk who had aspirations to become a writer and was one of Godwin's devoted young followers, wrote to his boyhood friend Coleridge that "our dear friend has squandered his substance on the most reprehensible of women." Rarely waspish in his criticisms of those who were dear to him, the man who would win recognition as the greatest of English letter writers declared, "Godwin was sober and in full possession of his mental faculties. So there can be no excuse for his conduct; as for me, I can imagine no fate worse than spending the rest of one's life with that termagant."

All of Godwin's friends, his children and even the widowed Mrs. Clairmont's children by her previous marriage came to share that opinion of her and of the mistake William Godwin made when he married her. She had moved into the neighborhood in 1801, taking lodgings in the house adjacent to that in which Mary Wollstonecraft had lived. She had no intellectual leanings, and knowing literally nothing of philosophy, literature or art, ordinarily would not have met Godwin.

But their paths crossed because he was obliged, particularly on weekends, to take Mary and Fanny for outings. Mrs. Clairmont took walks for the same purpose, escorting her son Charles, who was a trifle older than Fanny, and her daughter Jane, who was approximately Mary's age. The children often played hide-and-seek and other games together, leaving the adults behind to chat.

Whether Mary Jane Clairmont had ever heard of William Godwin is doubtful, but she soon discovered he was highly regarded in England and abroad as one of the great philosophers of the time. Shrewd and calculating, she knew better than to converse with him as an intellectual equal, and instead played on his sympathies—and his vanity. She portrayed the bewildered widow who had no one to advise her, and Godwin was flattered when she turned to him for help. Although she was inclined to be plump, she had not yet gained the weight that would make her physically gross, and even Lamb was forced to admit she was not totally lacking in physical charms.

His battered ego soothed by Mrs. Clairmont's carefully administered balm, Godwin could not help but observe her sympathy for his motherless daughter and stepdaughter, or the pleasure of all four youngsters as they romped in the fields. Mrs. Clairmont needed to use little of her cunning to ensnare the widower. Godwin, whose mind was dealing with distant, abstruse matters, knew only that the Lord whose existence he sometimes denied was being kind to him, and had found him a new wife. He failed to notice that Mrs. Clairmont was sharp whenever she addressed Charles or Jane; he did not hear the greed she could not conceal when she asked about his financial standing; and it did not cross his occupied mind that she regarded the sacred principles he preached as gibberish, that she was a dominating woman who ruled her home with an iron hand.

Obviously the impractical Godwin did not stop to realize, either, that he could not afford to add three more persons to his family. He had written nothing of consequence for years, and was virtually bankrupt, a serious position for one who lived in an age when debtors were thrown into prison and allowed to languish there for years. His inability to face the real problems of real life and to solve his problems in a pragmatic manner was one of Godwin's greatest failings.

His blindness to the new Mrs. Godwin's faults well may be the most astonishing example of his nearsighted approach to life. Having found a substitute mother for his children and a housekeeper who would look after the family, he placed all responsibility in her hands, then retreated behind the closed door of his study to enjoy what had so long been denied him: the peaceful contemplation of the abstract.

In all fairness to Mary Jane Clairmont Godwin, her life could not have been easy. She soon discovered that her husband's financial affairs were even more tangled than she had thought, and he seemed incapable of discussing ways and means to increase his income. Fanny and Mary, the latter in particular, were headstrong children who had been allowed to run wild and had no concept of discipline. Fanny, a gentle child who was developing a love for domesticity, soon was tamed, but little Mary was made of more combustible material. The genes she had inherited from William Godwin and Mary Wollstonecraft, combined with the disorganized life she had led, made her a defiant rebel who could not be cowed.

The hatred Mary developed for her stepmother persisted for the better part of her life, and much of it rubbed off on her stepsister Jane, who called herself Claire or Clara when she became an adult and, for a time, was the most notorious of living Englishwomen. But even Mary was willing to admit that the new Mrs. Godwin did not neglect the health or welfare of any of the four children, who were joined by a fifth, William, born of the new union in 1802. All were adequately clothed and ate well, physicians were summoned when a child fell ill and regular routines were established.

It was not surprising that Mrs. Godwin took her own daughter's part against both Fanny and Mary when the inevitable childhood disputes disturbed the serenity of the family's home. But Mary's intransigence brought her into constant disfavor, and she was not only whipped frequently, but was sent into the fields to cut her own switches for the purpose. Beatings had no more effect on her than hot-tempered lectures, however, and no punishment, no matter how severe, could break her spirit. She wept only in private, and her pride would not permit her to shed tears in the presence of her stepmother.

Unlike Fanny, Mary showed no interest in domestic pursuits and no talent for activities in what was regarded as woman's sphere. Although the family employed a cook, the girls were expected to learn at least the rudiments of the culinary arts, but Mary was so often engrossed in a book that she allowed meats to burn and water to boil over. She was so clumsy with a needle that Mary Jane Godwin abandoned all attempts to teach her how to sew, and she treated her singing lessons as such a joke that they were canceled. Even dusting and housecleaning were anathema to her, and she showed her father's fine disregard for money when she refused to learn to keep a household ledger of expenses.

Her father was the one person on earth who mattered to her, and his favor was all-important. Godwin decided to save money by teaching the children at home, and he discharged his role of instructor with a zeal he showed for few other endeavors. Mary was eager to emulate him and anxious to earn his approval, so she threw her energies into her studies with a ferocity that impressed her father's literary friends and caused Mary Jane Godwin to complain that it was not natural for any child to spend all of her waking hours reading.

Aside from giving his children their daily lessons, Godwin virtually ignored them, leaving their rearing in the pudgy hands of his new wife. An illuminating letter he sent to an old friend in 1808 hints at the guilts he felt:

> Your enquiries relate principally to the two daughters of Mary Wollstonecraft. They are neither of them being brought up with an exclusive attention to the theories of education for young females propounded by their mother.
>
> The present Mrs. Godwin has great strength and activity of mind, but is not exclusively a follower of their mother; and indeed, having formed a family establishment without having a previous provision for the support of a family, neither Mrs. Godwin nor I have leisure enough for reducing novel theories of education to practice, while we both of us honestly endeavor, as far as our opportunities will permit, to improve the minds and characters of the younger branches of our family.

The Godwins were so busy it is understandable that they had no time to experiment with Mary Wollstonecraft's theories. Godwin's income from his writing was undependable, and Mary Jane, who had five children to feed, suggested to her husband in 1805 that he establish himself in business as a publisher of children's books. He had no experience in the field, and was reluctant, but she pounded at him until he agreed. The enterprise was called M. J. Godwin and Company, with Mrs. Godwin as managing director, and the family moved into a small house on Hanway Street, where both offices and home were established. The quarters proved inadequate, so another move was made in 1807 to Skinner Street, Holborn, where the family remained for many years. The ground floor was used for business purposes and the two upper floors as living quarters.

The financial difficulties that beset the company for the next quarter of a century were caused, in the main, by Godwin's failure to understand either the principles or operations of a business enterprise. Posterity must judge him as a successful children's publisher, all the same, since his literary taste was impeccable. His publication of the *Tales from Shakespeare* by Charles and Mary Lamb would have won him a measure of immortality even if he had published nothing else. His own *Fables,* written under the pseudonym of Baldwin to protect his name as a philosopher, have endured to the present day. Hazlitt's *English Grammar* became a classic, and Godwin had the honor of publishing in 1815 the first English version of *The Swiss Family Robinson,* by Johann Rudolf Wyss, which was originally published in Zürich in 1812, and which the philosopher translated himself from the original German.

Life in a world of books appealed to Mary, and she thoroughly enjoyed the visits of her father's friends and disciples, many of whom were becoming famous and almost all of whom had known her mother. She and Fanny were so often the centers of attention on these evenings that Mary Jane privately confined them to their bedrooms on such occasions.

When Mary was six years old, she rebelled, and drew Fanny into a plan she made to meet the emergency. The girls concealed themselves behind living room furniture the next time guests came to the house. They were soon discovered, of course, and Mary Jane tried to send them away, but Godwin unexpectedly displayed the courage he rarely showed in a confrontation with his wife, and granted the girls permission to see guests at any time.

This privilege helped to make Mary socially mature at an early age. Unlike Fanny, who was so shy she became tongue-tied in the presence of adults, Mary learned to hold her own in adult conversations, and soon became adept in keeping up her end on almost any subject. The exposure had an added benefit: a child who was at home with the Wordsworths, Coleridge, Lamb and his sister, Hazlitt and Southey, not to mention distinguished lecturers from Oxford and Cambridge, notables from abroad and even members of the aristocracy who had intellectual and literary pretensions, lost all fear of renowned persons. As an adolescent, then as an adult, Mary stood in awe of no one, regardless of how great his reputation, and learned to judge individuals on the basis of what she read in their characters.

Seeing some of the most famous men of the day when they were relaxing over a jar of sack, a bottle of port or an occasional glass of whiskey also gave her an opportunity to observe their idiosyncrasies, and confirmed her belief that only the timid, the insecure and the ignorant conformed to the rules that society made. "My stepmother," she wrote more than a quarter of a century later, "was so determined to obey every unwritten law of middle-class society that I gained a contempt for every bourgeois virtue, failing to see, so bitter were my prejudices, that many of these rules were worthy of obedience."

Because of its long-lasting emotional effects perhaps the least healthy of the influences on a growing girl in the Godwin home was the interest that Mary, Fanny and Jane developed in the occult. Godwin, who had no superstitions, denied the existence of spiritualism in any form. But the intellectuals of the period were going through a spiritualist phase, and at many social gatherings there were discussions of ghosts, unexplained physical manifestations of spirits from other worlds and similar phenomena.

These discussions took place during Mary's sixth to eighth year, and made a profound impression on her, as they did on Jane. Mary ostensibly accepted her father's uncompromising dictum that ghosts, weird creatures and the like were strictly the outgrowth of man's own fantasies. All the same, she and Jane could not resist the temptation to engage in séances and make other experiments behind the closed door of the bedroom they shared.

Left to their own devices when they were not studying, not only did the children spend far more time than was good for them playing games centering on the occult, but Mary discovered there were many books on the subject in her father's extensive library. Godwin granted his children unlimited access to his books at all times, so Mary and Jane read avidly about the occult, which made a lasting impression on both of them.

It was at about this time that the intellectually precocious Mary was first introduced to the written works of her own mother. Despising Mary Jane, she endowed Mary Wollstonecraft with every known virtue, and regarded every word she wrote as inspired. By the time she was ten, Mary had absorbed all of her mother's works, which she read again and again, often committing long passages to memory.

She developed an understandable but unfortunate habit during these years that contributed nothing to her emotional stability. Finding the atmosphere at home oppressive, and hating the interruptions of her stepmother, who always found chores for her to attend, she began to take her books to the graveyard behind Saint Pancras Church. There, sitting beside Mary Wollstonecraft's grave, at least

[*19*]

partly shielded from the elements by a willow tree, she could read in peace about the freedom that all women someday would enjoy.

When a quarrel with her stepmother was particularly unpleasant, Mary took cold meats and bread from the larder and ate a meal near her mother's grave. On several occasions she stretched out on the grave and went to sleep there rather than return home for another harangue, and on a number of nights Godwin had to go there and bring her home. Had he been more severe, perhaps, Mary would have abandoned the habit that was creating temperamental disturbances within her, but William Godwin, himself sorely tried by a wife who gave him little peace of mind, lacked the heart to castigate a lonely little girl for reaching out to her dead mother.

As the children grew older, Mary and Fanny began to drift apart. The three-year difference in their ages contributed to their incompatibility, as did the marked difference in their temperaments. Charles was even older, of course, and had little to do with any of the young females in the house. So Mary and Jane were inseparable, loving each other one moment, then becoming violently jealous the next. Both girls enjoyed playing with William, sometimes acting as surrogate mothers, but neither became close to him. "I could escape from almost everyone in the family, including myself," Mary confided to Leigh Hunt almost thirty years later, "but there was no escape from Jane. Awake or asleep, she was there."

The one privileged sanctuary was Mary Wollstonecraft's grave, and Jane never followed Mary there, perhaps because her fear of ghosts was so intense she thought the dead mother of her stepsister might put a curse on her.

Early in Mary's relationship with Shelley she told him about her visits to the Saint Pancras graveyard, but instead of discouraging her he responded to the romance of the concept and frequently accompanied her there. It was during this period that she revealed one of her innermost secrets to him: when severely troubled, she knelt beside the tombstone and "spoke" to her mother. As an adult she overcame this macabre adolescent fancy, but it is significant that she was still indulging in it at the age of seventeen.

Constantly driven by her father toward greater intellectual attainment, Mary neglected her health and developed few of the interests that other girls enjoyed. It was true that she could boast of experiences that were unique; in 1806, before she was nine, she heard Coleridge read the most famous of his poems, *The Ancient Mariner;* she listened to the brilliant young Thomas de Quincey, considered by some of his elders as the most promising young writer in England, expound his theories allegedly proving the existence of an occult world; she read some of her own child's verse to a transatlantic visitor, Aaron Burr, the former Vice-President of the United States, then in disrepute at home.

As Mary entered her teens she began to develop a strong resemblance to her mother. She was tall, with dark-blond hair and eyes that, as Wordsworth remarked, no man would forget when she grew a little older. But her incessant reading had taken its toll, and she was a frail, almost ethereal girl who tired easily, became fretful and found it difficult to concentrate. The family physicians recommended a change of scene, preferably a protracted sojourn in country air.

So Mary was sent off, in early June, to board in Ramsgate with a Miss Petman. The sea air helped the girl, who learned to enjoy long walks along the shore, and her physical condition improved. Her family's lack of funds, a chronic state in the Godwin household, made it necessary to bring her home again in December of the same year, but her father quickly made other plans for her.

He arranged with a Scottish friend named Baxter, who lived in Dundee, for Mary to join his family, which included his daughters Isabel and Christy, who were more or less Mary's age. Mary Jane, who longed to have her stepdaughter out of her house, endorsed her husband's scheme.

Mary departed for Scotland by ship in early June, 1812, and the same day Godwin sent off a letter to Baxter that paints a vivid picture of a father-daughter relationship, and describes his aspirations on her behalf:

> I daresay Mary will arrive more dead than alive, as she is extremely subject to sea-sickness, and the voyage will, not improbably, last nearly a week. Mr. Cline, the surgeon, however, decided that a sea voyage would probably be of more service to her than anything.
>
> There never can be a perfect equality between father and child, and if he has other objects and avocations to fill up the greater part of his time, the ordinary resource is for him to proclaim his wishes and commands in a way somewhat sententious and authoritative, and occasionally to utter his censures with seriousness and emphasis.
>
> It can, therefore, seldom happen that he is the confidant of his child, or that the child does not feel some degree of awe or restraint in intercourse with him. I am not, therefore, a perfect judge of Mary's character.
>
> I believe she has nothing of what is commonly called vices, and that she has considerable talent, which she willingly exhibits without embarrassment. I am anxious that she should be brought up like a philosopher, even like a cynic. It will add greatly to the strength and worth of her character.
>
> I should also observe that she has no love of dissipation, and will be perfectly satisfied with your woods and

mountains. I wish, too, that she should be *excited* to industry. She has occasionally great perseverance, especially when her interest has been aroused, but occasionally, too, she demonstrates a torpor I find disturbing.

The Baxter family offered Mary insights into the home life of well-adjusted, loving people, and her stay there was the happiest period she had ever known. She and Isabel Baxter immediately became inseparable friends who confided all of their adolescent thoughts and yearnings to each other, and their relationship lasted for several years, until it was terminated during the time of Mary's affair with Shelley by forces beyond the control of either girl. The young intellectual from London became friendly with Christy, too, as well as with the parents of the Baxter girls, and she was sufficiently chameleonlike to become a member of the family.

The woods and mountains opened her eyes to the beauty of Nature, and the teen-aged city girl marveled at views that Isabel regarded as commonplace. At the beginning of Mary's sojourn she was inclined to take a book to a rustic place with a view, then spend hours there alone, reading, brooding and daydreaming. But she soon learned that woods and mountains were made for hiking, and thereafter she rarely took a book with her on her daily excursions into the outdoors.

In her introduction to the edition of *Frankenstein* published in 1831, Mary candidly described her situation and her reactions to the new world in which she found herself at Dundee:

> It is not singular that, as the daughter of two persons of distinguished literary celebrity, I should very early in life have thought of writing. As a child I scribbled; and my favorite pastime, during the hours given me for recreation, was to "write stories." Still I had a dearer

pleasure than this, which was the formation of castles in the air—the indulging in waking dreams—the following up trains of thought, which had for their subject the formation of a succession of imaginary incidents.

My dreams were at once more fantastic and agreeable than my writings. In the latter I was a close imitator—rather doing as others had done, than putting down the suggestions of my own mind. What I wrote was intended at least for one other eye—my childhood's companion and friend; but my dreams were all my own; I accounted for them to nobody; they were my refuge when annoyed —my dearest pleasure when free.

It was beneath the trees of the grounds belonging to our house, or on the bleak sides of the woodless mountains near, that my true compositions, the airy flights of my imagination, were born and fostered. I did not make myself the heroine of my tales. Life appeared to me too commonplace an affair as regarded myself. I could not figure to myself that romantic woes or wonderful events would ever be my lot; but I was not confined to my own identity, and I could people the hours with creations far more interesting to me at that age, than in my own sensations.

For the first time in her fourteen years, Mary knew genuine happiness at Dundee. The Baxters were kind, sensible people who treated an adolescent as though she were an adult. Isabel was a wonderful, sensitive friend. Long walks in the bracing air of the mountains and woods restored the health of a girl who had been sliding deeper into gloom. Mary could write when she pleased, and be certain that Isabel—and sometimes Christy—would read and admire her efforts. Best of all, she could engage in the carefree prerogative of youth, the indulgence in fanciful daydreams, without being told by her father to return to her studies or by her stepmother to help the cook prepare dinner.

Above all, Mary was tasting real freedom for the first

time. It was not enough that she vividly recalled some of the words her mother had written on the subject of liberty; she felt compelled to read excerpts aloud after dinner. If the Baxters were unable to accept these radical doctrines, they were too kind to reveal their reactions, so Mary was able to convince herself that she was making converts to her mother's philosophy of life.

III

WHILE MARY WOLLSTONECRAFT GODWIN reveled in the earthly paradise she had discovered in Scotland, life on Skinner Street in London was unchanged. William Godwin suffered from his usual financial embarrassments, his business affairs were in a muddle and his wife, who was growing heavier with each passing year, became more vociferous in her attempts to push him deeper into the world of commerce for which he was unsuited.

Godwin's circle of young admirers continued to grow, and it appeared that his disciples were indifferent to his failures. They believed, as he did, in the purity of spirit that man himself made perfect, and they listened to him at his nightly social gatherings with a reverence that verged on idolatry.

One of Godwin's newest, most enthusiastic followers in 1812 was a young aristocrat, the heir-once-removed to his grandfather's baronetcy and fortune. Percy Bysshe Shelley, who was only twenty years of age, was tall and a trifle ungainly, with blond hair and eyes so blue that his direct gaze sometimes startled people. His background was anything but distinguished. At the secondary schools he had attended, including Eton, the most noted academy for young gentlemen in England, he had been such a misfit that other boys teased him unmercifully. At Oxford, where his love of reading and soaring intellectual prowess had held promise of great success, his academic career had been cut short after only a few months of undergraduate life.

Shelley and his close friend, Thomas Jefferson Hogg, who sometimes accompanied him to the Godwin house, had gone too far when they had abandoned Christianity and espoused the cause of atheism; no one would have cared had they kept their radical opinions to themselves, but they had written an anonymous pamphlet, and when the authorship had been discovered, they had been expelled.

Still an omnivorous reader, young Shelley had come to London, where he had lived precariously on the pittance his disappointed father had allowed him. A year before he had joined Godwin's circle he had eloped with a friend of his sisters', Harriet Westbrook, the daughter of a retired merchant, and jaded London was still whispering about the union of these children. The Shelleys lived on allowances paid by their parents, and although society disapproved of the match, many people agreed they made the most beautiful couple in London.

Harriet, who was almost breathtakingly lovely, looked and acted like a child of Mary Godwin's age; in actuality she was only a few years older. For her husband's sake she tried to read the stacks of books he gave her, but she was no intellectual, and the effort was too great. When she went with her husband to Godwin's house, she rarely said a word as the discussion raged around her. Instead she stared into the fire, a teen-aged girl lost in her daydreams, and she made such a charming picture that, according to Coleridge, men who happened to glance in her direction sometimes forgot what they were saying. Only her husband took her beauty for granted, and occasionally he was heard to complain that although she demanded affection, she rarely gave of herself.

Shelley called himself a poet, although he had written very little, and only a few people were familiar with what he had done. One was a somewhat older Godwin disciple, Robert Southey, who was not impressed with his work. But no one who listened to him discourse at the Godwin house could deny that here was a young man of incandescent intellect. He accepted all of William Godwin's theories, and managed to explain them in terms more pungent than those of the master himself. At times it was difficult to determine which was the instructor and which the pupil.

Aware of Godwin's ever-present financial plight, Shelley, out of gratitude, began to advance him money that he could ill afford to pay out of his own slender purse. But Shelley was like Godwin, and money meant very little to him.

According to a time-honored myth, Mary Godwin and Percy Bysshe Shelley first met when she returned home from Scotland at the age of seventeen, and immediately fell in love. This romantic tale was perpetuated by scores of Shelley's late nineteenth- and early twentieth-century biographers, but it is a figment of an imagination as lively as those of Shelley and Mary.

It is probable that the initial meeting took place in the summer of 1813, when Mary, who was approaching her sixteenth birthday, came home for a visit. The Shelleys were also in London at that time, and as Harriet was pregnant their traveling was limited. They were frequent visitors at the Godwin house on Skinner Street, sometimes making daily calls, and it is unlikely that Mary and Shelley consistently missed each other.

Logic would indicate that the adolescent girl and the married man of twenty-one had little in common that they recognized, and paid scant attention to each other. Jane Clairmont—who now called herself Claire, and was referred to by other members of the family as Clara, Clare and Clary, names they used indiscriminately—was also home from a boarding school operated by a French lady. Only a few months younger than Mary, Claire had become a compulsive talker, and often dragged her stepsister to a corner of the parlor for a confidential schoolgirl chat. Neither would have paid much attention to a man who gave every evidence of being devoted to a wife who was an expectant mother.

Late in May, 1814, Mary Godwin returned to Skinner Street to stay, and family and friends alike were astonished by the changes that had taken place in a year. She was no longer a gawky, giggling schoolgirl, but had blossomed into a radiantly attractive young woman. Her hazel eyes, as her father said in a note to Coleridge, who had inquired after her, had doubled their size, and her mind had become that of a woman. She seemed indifferent to her beauty, however, taking it for granted, even though she dressed with as much care as the limited family budget could tolerate.

Her social poise was still remarkable, but her intellect had deepened, and she seemed to have acquired a new self-confidence. Even her stepmother's most penetrating barbs appeared to leave her untouched. Thomas Lawrence, the most prominent and successful portrait painter of the day, who would be knighted the following year by the prince regent, often escaped from his fashionable clientele by spending an evening at the Godwin home, and was one of the first to notice Mary's great beauty.

"You look like a Madonna," he is alleged to have told her, and offered to paint her portrait.

Mary, disappointing posterity, rejected the offer. "You would be wasting your time, sir," she is supposed to have replied. "A countess will pay you two hundred guineas for her likeness, but I can give you nothing other than a smile of gratitude. No, Mr. Lawrence, I cannot sit for you. I am the daughter of an artist, and I know that a man of talent has no commodity to sell other than his time."

In many ways the Godwin household had changed

through the years. Fanny managed the household now, setting her stepmother free to work in the publishing office downstairs, and did the marketing, supervised the efforts of the cook and herself attended to many of the cleaning chores. Charles, who had accepted a position in a printing firm and was expected to join his stepfather someday, no longer lived at home. Claire announced her intention of becoming an actress, took singing lessons, and after reading some of Lord Byron's poetry, declared that she was madly in love with him, even though she had never seen him. Her attitude displeased Godwin and Mary Jane, as Byron had acquired a reputation as a seducer of women, so they tried to coax Claire out of her fancy by indulging her whims. She needed no other excuse to sleep late every morning, and was so expert in shirking her share of the housework that Mary took pity on her own half-sister, Fanny, and did more than she was asked.

William, who attended a day school, was a solemn boy who peppered Mary with questions about the nature of God, man and the universe, and seemed disappointed when he could not win a debate with her. He was genuinely fond of her, however, which was more than could be said of his mother. Mrs. Godwin's hatred for her beautiful, intellectual stepdaughter was unabated, and nothing Mary said or did escaped criticism. If she saw Mary dusting the furniture, she insisted the task had been performed sloppily, and needed to be done again; when she found Mary reading in Greek or Latin, in order to improve her proficiency, she swore that the girl was too lazy to work.

Mary Jane's temper exploded daily when Godwin invited Mary to join him in his study for an after-dinner chat. There, beneath a portrait of Mary Wollstonecraft to which her daughter bore such a close resemblance, father and daughter held their own philosophical discourses. No matter how angry his wife became, Godwin refused to give up these daily meetings. He freely admitted that Mary was his favorite; she had the finest mind in the family, he declared, and with guidance she would achieve a reputation in the literary world even more formidable than her mother's. In his eyes the girl of seventeen could do no wrong, and he frequently strained the marital ties by ordering Mary Jane to leave his study.

Mary felt closer to her father than ever before, perhaps because her other family relationships were so unsatisfactory. She tried to establish a rapport with the painfully withdrawn Fanny, but they had nothing in common except Fanny's hazy memories of their mother. Now twenty years of age, Fanny showed little interest in the life around her, cared nothing about the famous and near-famous men who visited the house and was lethargic in her reading. Although no one, Mary included, realized it, Fanny was showing symptoms of a depression similar to that which had prompted Mary Wollstonecraft to attempt suicide.

Claire's antics sometimes amused Mary, sometimes exasperated her. Claire had been exposed to matters of the mind for her entire life, and was clever enough, when it suited her purposes, to parrot the thoughts of others in conversation. She could be good company when she was in the mood, and on occasion was so lively and gay that it was impossible to refrain from laughing. But her mind was shallow, she had become so narcissistic that she trampled on the rights of others, and did not hesitate to "borrow" any item of clothing or jewelry in the house that struck her fancy of the moment. Mary frequently became annoyed with her, and tried in vain to persuade her to accept greater responsibility, but she felt rather sorry for Claire and made valiant attempts to protect her from Mrs. Godwin's rages.

There was one aspect of life on Skinner Street that was kept a secret from all of William Godwin's children and stepchildren. His financial situation was so precarious that only the generosity of his young disciple, Percy Bysshe Shelley, kept him from bankruptcy. Shelley felt so indebted to the older man that he carelessly engaged in the ruinous practice of selling what were known as post-obits in order to keep Godwin supplied with funds. Money brokers charged exorbitant rates for these promissory notes, and the heir to a fortune who allowed himself to fall into the hands of these dealers sometimes was sent off to a debtors' prison himself.

The system employed in the sale of post-obits was as simple as it was outrageous. It was known, for example, that Shelley one day would inherit a comfortable fortune. So he could sell a note, payable when he came into his inheritance, and in return for receipt of one thousand pounds in cash immediately promised to repay three thousand.

Timothy Shelley had not yet learned that his eldest son and principal heir was engaging in the practice, and would have become even more disgusted with Percy had he learned of it. Harriet had given birth to a daughter, Eliza Ianthe, in June, 1813, and again was pregnant, so Shelley had cause to be concerned about his own finances. His situation was further complicated by the fact that he and Harriet had just separated, so he was obliged to pay the expenses of two households. The deterioration of the marriage, which shocked friends who regarded it as sudden, became a major contributing factor to the unsavory reputation Shelley was acquiring. The actual circumstances were muddled, and for the better part of two centuries Shelley and Harriet have both had their violent partisans, so it has been difficult for an impartial posterity to clarify the question.

Most authorities agree that Shelley was at fault. Harriet, who loved him to the best of her limited ability, was an adolescent who needed affection and found it difficult to demonstrate her feelings for others. Her attempts to improve her mind had foundered, in spite of Shelley's efforts to spur her, and he could not understand that she was incapable of exceeding the bounds of her own capabilities. As a disciple of the Godwin philosophy, he was convinced that any individual's growth toward perfection depended exclusively on desire and willingness to work.

So Shelley, needing a wife who could discuss and admire his work, felt lost. The marriage was further weakened by his distaste for Harriet's brand of domesticity. As a romantic who believed that passion, more intellectual than physical, was the essence of true love, he was bored by a wife who was concentrating on her own concerns, devoting much of her attention to their daughter and planning for the baby yet unborn. Certainly Shelley felt great affection for Ianthe, but she occupied only one small portion of his life, and his own needs were not being fulfilled.

Harriet was sojourning in Bath, and she shared the belief of many friends that the separation was temporary. But she undoubtedly feared the worst, as her apprehension over his possible interest in other women indicates. He was himself still so young, so emotionally immature and so immersed in Godwin's theories that he truly believed it was the privilege of every man and woman to seek, find and accept love anywhere.

In June and July of 1814 Shelley was a constant visitor to the Godwin house and ate most of his meals there. It has been suggested that Mary Jane made no objection because she envisioned the possibility, however remote, that Claire one day might become the wife of a handsome, wealthy baronet.

It was during this period that Hogg, Shelley's good friend who, for a short time, had imagined himself in love with Harriet, caught his first glimpse of Mary. He accom-

[33]

panied Shelley to the Godwin house one day, and while they waited for the philosopher in the parlor, a girl with a "thrilling" voice called, "Shelley." It was Mary, who was fair-haired, with skin so fair it was almost pale, and she was dressed in a Scottish tartan, which Hogg thought odd. Shelley conferred with her for a moment in another room, returning to announce that Godwin had gone out, and the two young men resumed their stroll. Identifying Mary for Hogg, Shelley did not indicate any particular interest in her.

Mary's first written reference to Shelley was made in the same early summer, when she scribbled in a notebook she was using for compositions in Latin: "Shall I write a poem on receiving a cordial shake of the hand from an esteemed and excellent person? Ah, I cannot write poetry."

She read poetry frequently, however, as did other members of the household, and she made an intensive study of Shelley's first major work, *Queen Mab*, which had been published recently. It was a radical treatise, often abstruse in form as well as in philosophical content, and hence was not easy to follow. Mary's copy was filled with underlined words and phrases, check marks and other symbols she used to help her better understand the poem.

It was almost inevitable that an attractive young man, even though married, should create a stir in a household filled with attractive young women. For a short time William and Mary Jane Godwin were afraid that Fanny, whose interest in males had always been so slight, might become involved with the poet. So, without telling anyone their true reason, they sent her off on a visit to friends in Wales.

Soon thereafter the Godwins became apprehensive again. Shelley seemed to be paying a great deal of attention to Mary, and his gallantry toward her was disturbing. Godwin took his disciple into his study for a chat, and bluntly remarked that he appeared to be involving himself with

[*34*]

Mary. Shelley replied that he behaved in precisely the same way to all young ladies, which was true. Godwin accepted his explanation.

There were influences pulling in the opposite direction, however, not the least of them Shelley's loneliness and Mary's feeling that she was not advancing her own goals as a writer. A major factor in drawing Mary and Shelley together—Harriet later called it decisive—was the poet's genuine admiration for the works of Mary Wollstonecraft.

He showed a familiarity with her writing almost as great as Mary's, and he often stood before the portrait in Godwin's study, commenting on what he called the serenity of her beauty. It was only natural for Mary to invite him to accompany her to the graveyard of Saint Pancras Church, which she herself had been visiting regularly once again since her return to London. Shelley soon became her constant escort on these excursions, and proximity under emotional circumstances, combined with a rare intellectual kinship, did the rest.

It was not strange that Mary and Shelley should think alike, since they were the most ardent of Godwin's followers and had absorbed even the most remote fine points of his philosophy. Mary had found a man who not only treated her as a complete equal, thus fulfilling the demands of the mother she still adored, but he treated her opinions with the gravity she believed they deserved. As for Shelley, he was ecstatic, and his frustrations over his inability to engage in a meaningful discussion with Harriet on any level but her own were forgotten. Here was a young woman with a mind as incisive and a grasp as broad as his own, and her appreciation of purity and beauty so closely resembled his feelings that he could scarcely believe it.

The relationship developed quickly, and the couple were soon in love, although Shelley was confused and found rationalizations for his feelings. It was on a visit to the

Saint Pancras graveyard that they first admitted their feelings; according to what both Mary and Shelley later told Godwin, the scene took place on Sunday, June 26, 1814.

It was Mary who could not tolerate an atmosphere that was becoming increasingly tense, and speaking with a bluntness that would characterize her relationship with Shelley for the rest of his life, she told him flatly and in so many words that she loved him. Writing to Hogg soon thereafter, Shelley described his own reactions:

> No expressions can convey the remotest conceptions of the *manner* in which she dispelled my illusions. The sublime and rapturous moment when she confessed herself mine, who had so long been hers in secret, cannot be painted to mortal imagination.

Within a week he wrote the first of his many poems to her, and in it he admitted that he had been badly upset because of his growing recognition of his love for her, which he had determined to keep from her because it had not occurred to him that his feelings might be reciprocated. The disclosure of her love had filled him with unspeakable, unprecedented joy, he declared, and he concluded the poem with three burning stanzas that could not have failed to sear the girl who had not yet reached her seventeenth birthday:

> Upon my heart your accents sweet
> Of peace and pity fell like dew
> On flowers half-dead;—thy lips did meet
> Mine tremblingly; thy dark eyes threw
> Their soft persuasion on my brain,
> Charming away its dream of pain.
>
> We are not happy, sweet ! our state
> Is strange and full of doubt and fear;
> More need of words that ills abate;—
> Reserve or censure come not near

Our sacred friendship, lest there be
No solace left for you and me.

Gentle and good and mild thou art,
   Nor can I live if thou appear
Aught but thyself, or turn thine heart
   Away from me, or stoop to wear
The mask of scorn, although it be
To hide the love you feel'st for me.

It is not surprising that, at the same time, Shelley stopped writing to Harriet, who became increasingly alarmed by his silence. He gave Mary a copy of *Queen Mab,* and apparently thought it neither strange nor ironic that he inscribed it to her on the page that contained his printed dedication to Harriet. Mary, believing that no one else would ever set eyes on the volume, wrote an inscription of her own:

> I have pledged myself to thee, and sacred is the gift. I remember your words: "You are now, Mary, going to mix with many, and for a moment I shall depart, but in the solitude of your chamber I shall be with you." Yes, you are ever with me, sacred vision.

The increasingly disturbed Harriet wrote to various friends in London, who replied that Shelley seemed to be enamored of Mary, and she accused him of infidelity in a short, angry note.

Shelley, living in the dream world of his own imagination, replied that he had formed a pure affection for Mary, but that he thought no less highly of Harriet, whom he now regarded as something of a celestial sister. Perhaps the logical solution, he declared, would be to bring Mary with him to Bath.

Harriet was shocked, and not only sent him a hasty rejection, but poured out her feelings in a longer letter to a friend:

Mary was determined to seduce him. She is to blame. She heated his imagination by talking of her mother and going to her grave with him every day, till at last she told him she was dying in love for him, accompanied with the most violent gestures and vehement expostulations. He thought of me and my sufferings, and begged her to get the better of a passion as degrading to him as to herself. She then told him that she would die—he had rejected her, and what appeared to her as the sublimest virtue was to him a crime. Why could we not all live together? I as his sister, she as his wife?

Unable to believe that the idea of establishing a *ménage à trois* had been Shelley's, Harriet attributed it to her rival. Shelley made no attempt to correct the impression when he received her rejection, which brought him back to earth with a crash from the dream world into which he had propelled himself. His one feeling was that of relief.

Harriet was prepared to fight for her marriage, and, returning to her husband, came to London on July 15, paying a visit to Godwin the same day. As far as is known, Mary was not at home, and in any event did not see either husband or wife. Later that day, while Shelley went out on an errand, Godwin returned the call and spent an hour alone with Harriet. The following day the Shelleys went for a long carriage ride with Godwin, and the two men continued for another hour or more after dropping Harriet off. Mary took no part in any of these conferences.

At some time over the weekend, according to the correspondence of Mary Jane Godwin, Harriet came alone to the house on Skinner Street and had a meeting with her rival's father and stepmother. She wept a great deal, Mrs. Godwin wrote, and indicated that she did not really blame Mary for what was happening, as she, too, had been young and impressionable. There was only one way to solve the dilemma, she insisted: the Godwins should close their door to Shelley.

Immediately thereafter Mary was summoned to a parental council, and was informed of their decision. Shelley would not be admitted to their home again, and she was forbidden to see him elsewhere. According to Mary Jane's correspondence, Mary "behaved as well as possible—and approved our renouncing his acquaintance."

Claire, who knew of all the various developments and actually made copies of her mother's letters, added other information on the weekend's activities in correspondence of her own. She accompanied Mary on a visit to Harriet Shelley, and herself heard her stepsister declare unequivocally that she was renouncing Shelley and would have no more to do with him.

Mary was strong enough to keep her word, and tranquillity was restored, at least for the moment. Godwin continued to hold meetings with his protégé to discuss philosophy, these sessions prudently taking place elsewhere than under the Godwin roof. The facts readily explain the situation: Shelley had just sold a large post-obit, and had given his mentor a considerable sum. Apparently neither man saw any connection between money matters and affairs of the heart.

Mary was in a torment, but had made her decision and was determined to abide by it. She respected her father and had given her pledge not to see Shelley again, so that was that, no matter how great her suffering. Her precise thoughts and feelings over a ten-day period are unknown for the simple reason that she kept them to herself and reduced none of them to paper; meanwhile the other members of her family were being kept busy by Shelley's histrionics.

Early one morning, soon after Godwin left the house

on an errand, a wild Shelley burst into the family's living room, his eyes red and his clothes badly crumpled. According to almost identical accounts written by Mrs. Godwin and Claire, he handed Mary a bottle of laudanum, a crude but powerful opiate. "They wish to separate us, my beloved, but we shall be united in death," he shouted. "Drink this and you shall escape their tyranny!"

Then he reached into an inner pocket and drew out a small pistol. "This," he exclaimed, "shall enable me to join you, and we shall be reunited for all time!"

Mary made no move and did not speak, but had turned very pale.

Claire screamed and dropped to the floor in what was perhaps a genuine faint; no one bothered to find out.

Mrs. Godwin was more practical, and with the aid of a Mr. Marshall, a friend who had dropped in for a cup of tea, managed to wrest the weapon from the poet, calm him and send him on his way.

Mary poured out the potent laudanum and refused to discuss the incident. Godwin felt sure she realized that Shelley was creating dramatic scenes for the sole purpose of winning her sympathy, but his wife was less certain. The girl was so young and inexperienced that she probably failed to understand her would-be lover's motives.

A few days later Shelley tried again. A messenger aroused the Godwins late one night to inform them that Shelley had taken an overdose of laudanum and wanted to see Mary before he died. Her father and stepmother had no intention of subjecting her to such an ordeal, and went in her stead. Shelley, who was already under the care of a physician, answered questions in curt monosyllables and would offer no explanation for his supposed suicide attempt. His complete recovery within a few hours indicates that he was indulging in play-acting.

The shrewd Mary Jane Godwin suspected he had staged

the scene because he had again been rejected by Mary. The older woman surmised that a note had been smuggled to Mary, asking her to meet him, and that she had refused. Some of the more prominent authorities on the life of Shelley have agreed with this opinion.

There can be little doubt that Mary and Shelley were corresponding, and in all probability Claire was acting as the go-between. On the afternoon of July 26 Mary and Claire went for a walk, and a short time later met Shelley in a park. While Claire paced up and down, the estranged couple talked privately. The precise nature of what they said was never disclosed, but Charles Clairmont later referred to the incident in his correspondence.

Shelley, he wrote, informed Mary that under no circumstances could he return to Harriet, having learned she was engaging in an affair with a Major Ryan, who had just arrived in London from Dublin. Shelley's earnest, pained recital convinced Mary he was telling the truth, but Charles wrote that he made up the tale out of whole cloth, generously conceding that Shelley's need for Mary was so great he himself believed the story as he told it.

Mary, who was already badly torn, hesitated no longer and agreed to elope with the poet whose weaknesses she already recognized but whom she still loved.

IV

ON THE EVENING of July 27, 1814, Mary and Claire both announced they were suffering from headaches and retired. Then, after the rest of the family went to sleep they rose again and hastily packed a few belongings. Perhaps the most astonishing aspect of the elopement was the agreement that Claire would accompany the runaway couple. The reasons later given by Mary and Shelley were almost pathetically inadequate: they were planning to go off to France, they said, and Claire was expert in the language; also, they wanted to give Claire the opportunity to escape from tyranny, too.

Few aspects of the Mary Godwin–Percy Shelley story have puzzled literary detectives more than the presence of of Claire Clairmont on the couple's illicit honeymoon. Only one explanation makes complete sense and has won general acceptance: Mary and Shelley knew that the elopement of a future baronet, who was a married man and a father, with a girl not yet seventeen, the daughter of one of England's most renowned philosophers, would create a national scandal. Both were so naive, however, that they believed they would ward off unsavory gossip if Claire accompanied them as a chaperone. It did not occur to any of the trio, it would seem, that the horrified whispers would become louder and more insistent when it was discovered that Shelley had disappeared with two girls not yet of age.

The escape was marred by last-minute disasters that threatened to transform it into a comedy of errors. Shelley had rented a chaise and it had been arranged that he would meet his beloved and her stepsister at the entrance to Hatton Garden, a short distance from the Skinner Street house. The appointed hour was four o'clock in the morning, and Shelley was on time. But the girls, unable to decide what clothes to take, were about fifteen minutes behind schedule. Then, as they were sneaking out of the house, Claire broke a heel and had to return for another pair of shoes. They started a second time, but had to turn back so Mary could write a note to her father, a detail that had slipped her mind in the excitement.

It was almost five in the morning and day was breaking when the lovers, escorted by their sixteen-year-old chaperone, pulled away from the curb and started off on the cobblestones toward the English Channel. There was no breeze that day, the sun was almost unbearably hot, and Mary, who was suffering from excitement, guilt and anxiety, was so ill it was necessary to make frequent stops in order to revive her. All three runaways took it for granted they would be pursued, so they held their halts to a minimum.

No journey could have been less romantic. The travelers perspired all day, and the dust of the road clung to their skins and clothes. Shelley and Claire were hungry and thirsty, but Mary felt too ill to eat or drink. At Dartford they finally dined on bread, cheese and ale while the horses were being changed, and at four in the afternoon, after a journey of eleven hours, they reached Dover.

The sea looked so inviting that Mary, who had learned to swim in Scotland, immediately went off for a dip. Neither Shelley nor Claire felt at home in the water, so they went to make arrangements for passage to France. The sky overhead was clear and the English Channel looked like a placid lake, but the calm was deceptive, and few vessels were planning to sail that night because of an impending storm. But Shelley knew they would be caught if they tarried, so he persisted until he found a captain willing to give the trio a small cabin.

Claire warned Shelley that Mary could not tolerate a ship's motion, so he refrained from mentioning the storm threat to his beloved when she rejoined them. Mary had been refreshed by her swim, looked radiant and was in high spirits as the trio boarded the Channel schooner. The ship weighed anchor, and after watching the white cliffs for a short time, all three repaired to the cabin to eat the rest of the bread and cheese they had purchased that afternoon. Claire, it seemed, planned to spend the night on deck and leave the cabin for the exclusive use of the honeymooners, but her thoughtful gesture proved unnecessary.

A diary in which both Mary and Shelley thereafter made faithful entries, and which they called a journal, tells the story of that night, which the poet repeated in one of his prose works, *History of a Six Weeks' Tour*. Mary described her agony in prosaic terms:

> . . . the moon rose, and night came on, and with the night a slow, heavy swell and a fresh breeze, which soon produced a sea so violent as to toss the boat very much. I was dreadfully sea-sick, and as is usually my custom when thus affected, I slept during the greater part of the night, awakening only from time to time to ask where we were, and to receive the dismal answer each time, "Not quite halfway."
>
> The wind was violent and contrary. If we could not reach Calais the sailors proposed making for Boulogne. They promised only two hours' sail from shore, yet hour after hour passed, and we were still far distant, when the moon sunk in the red and stormy horizon and the fast-flashing lightning became pale in the breaking day.

We were proceeding slowly against the wind, when suddenly a thunder-squall struck the sail, and the waves rushed into the boat; but they succeeded in reefing the sail; the wind was now changed, and we drove before the gale directly to Calais.

Shelley's addition to the *Journal* was more graphic and far more dramatic:

Mary did not know our danger. She was resting between my knees, that were unable to support her; she did not speak or look, but I felt she was there. I had time in that moment to reflect, and even to reason upon death; it was a thing of discomfort and disappointment rather than horror to me. We should never be separated, but in death we might not know and feel our union as now. I hope, but my hopes are not unmixed with fear for what may befall this inestimable spirit when we appear to die.

The morning broke, the lightning died away, the violence of the wind abated. We arrived at Calais, whilst Mary still slept; we drove upon the sands. Suddenly the broad sun rose over France.

The streets of Calais were lined with lodging houses, and Claire used her knowledge of the language to bargain for quarters that were clean but inexpensive. She engaged a room for Mary and Shelley and another for herself, and the exhausted travelers rested. Presumably Mary and Shelley consummated their love that day.

While dining early that evening at their lodging house the runaways assumed they were safe, but quickly discovered they were mistaken. The master of the ship that had carried them to France, a Captain Davidson, came to tell them that "a fat lady" was looking for them, and was claiming that Shelley had abducted her daughter.

A few moments later a tired and belligerent Mrs. Godwin arrived at the lodging house. Mary refused to see her, and retreated upstairs, and Shelley told Claire, who waited below, to think for an hour or more before agreeing to any offer her mother made.

The weather having turned fine that day, many visitors to France had crossed the Channel, the English taking advantage of the unaccustomed state of peace that the exile of the Emperor Napoleon I to Elba had brought their country and France. So there were few rooms available in the city, and Claire tried to placate her mother by offering to share her bed with her.

Mrs. Godwin agreed, and sitting down to dinner, only with Claire, immediately began a long harangue. When it became obvious that Mary had no intention of listening to her or even seeing her, she concentrated on Claire, and talking far into the night, tried to persuade her to return to England. She returned to her arguments before breakfast, and Claire went off alone for an hour to ponder.

She returned to announce that she had decided to continue the journey with Mary and Shelley. Mrs. Godwin silently turned away and departed without addressing her.

Later that morning the lovers and their chaperone left Calais for Paris, where they also found adequate quarters. They looked up a woman who had been a friend of Mary Wollstonecraft and Godwin, and met a minor French poet, Rouve de Savy, with whose work Shelley was acquainted. Making the belated discovery that they had left London short of funds for a prolonged journey, they also called on a business agent who handled French matters for the Shelley family, and after several long, unfruitful sessions, managed to obtain a grudging loan from him.

While Claire roamed the city alone, her companions made a discovery that seemed original to them: Paris was a city that existed exclusively for lovers. They went sightseeing and walked the streets until their feet and legs ached. They sat in coffeehouses, watching the world pass, and became especially fond of a place with a long tradition of literary patronage, the Procopé, which had achieved its original luster eighty years earlier, when Voltaire had been a regular patron.

They dined on French food for the first time in their lives, and were mildly astonished to find that English cooking was inferior to that of Paris. When not otherwise occupied they sat outdoors, overlooking the Seine, and there they read together, concentrating on some of Shelley's poems, which they had brought with them, and on various papers Godwin had written and given to his daughter.

They also spent a number of hours discussing and dissecting a novel Mary had almost completed. It was called *Hate*, and appears to have been the first sample of her writing Shelley ever saw. Neither mentioned his opinion of the work in what was later published as Mary's *Journal*, and no one has ever learned what happened to the manuscript. There were no copies, the original vanished and literally nothing is known of the story; its theme, plot and characters have been a mystery, down to the present day.

Most of the *Journal* entries were made by Mary, and Claire, not to be outdone, kept her own diary, while Shelley contented himself with jotting observations in a small notebook for future use. The trio ambitiously decided to walk from Paris to Switzerland, carrying their belongings on a donkey Shelley purchased in the Paris market, and they were a bizarre sight as they started out, the girls in their prim dresses of black silk, while Shelley was dressed in the conservative brown tailcoat, fawn waistcoat and matching trousers of an English gentleman. They quickly discovered that the poet knew literally nothing about animals, even though he had spent his earliest years on his father's country estate. He had been cheated when buying the donkey, and the beast was so weak that Shelley literally carried him to Charenton. There they traded him for a

[*47*]

mule, paying additional hard cash to bind the transaction, and the girls took turns riding the beast, which was a blessed relief. Then Shelley sprained an ankle, and had to ride in embarrassed ignominy while the girls trudged beside him.

But there were innumerable compensations. They ate most of their meals in the open beside the road, they paused whenever they wished to admire a view, they meandered aimlessly through small towns and villages. Mary's *Journal* and Claire's diary read like the wide-eyed accounts of innocent adolescents making a pastoral journey, and it is sometimes difficult to keep in mind that Mary was a young woman openly living with someone who was a married man and father.

Her attitude was completely unfeigned, however, and Shelley's joy was equally natural. They had taken the writings of William Godwin completely to heart, they believed implicitly in the theories he had expounded, and they were free spirits who were living in accord with those precepts. It did not occur to them that Godwin had not been offering practical advice to his readers, but rather had envisioned a new Utopia that man-made-perfect might someday create. The romantic young lovers and their equally starry-eyed companion had no desire to separate reality from the dream world of their own creation. They wandered on to Switzerland, three children enjoying an unending picnic, eating when they were hungry, sleeping when they tired and thrilling to the majesty of the Swiss Alps.

At this time they had no idea of the havoc they had left behind them. Harriet Westbrook Shelley was stunned, angry and resigned in turn, and it was small comfort that virtually all of Shelley's friends offered her their sympathy and support. Timothy Shelley was so disgusted by his son's behavior that he took steps to cut off his son's support, and was dissuaded only by Mrs. Shelley, who argued that even worse things might happen if Percy were rendered penniless.

William Godwin was livid, and regarded the elopement of his favorite child and most loyal student as a crass betrayal of all he cherished. Nothing in his attitude indicated that he saw the slightest connection between his teachings and their unquestioning acceptance by his daughter and her lover. He announced that he was closing his door to Mary and Shelley, and declared that nothing would persuade him to change his mind. But by implication he left one small opening in his sweeping dictum: he would continue to accept additional loans that Shelley had promised him.

The shock was equally great in English literary and social circles. Shelley was universally branded as a cad, and Mary was regarded as a wanton, far beneath a courtesan in standing and little better than the streetwalkers who were the curse of the London slums. The presence of Claire Clairmont in the party puzzled the gossips, but they soon invented a story that satisfied them, and within days it was accepted as fact everywhere in England. Shelley, according to the rumor, had "bought" both girls from Godwin, paying eight hundred pounds for Mary and seven hundred pounds for Claire. In brief, the reputations of all three were destroyed.

The wanderers received no mail, since no one knew where to reach them, so they learned nothing of their disgrace at home. Mary knew as a result of Mrs. Godwin's appearance in Calais that the family was upset, but nothing she wrote in her *Journal* indicates even a hint that she wondered what people in England might be saying or thinking about her. She was in love for the first time in her life, she was giving free rein to her poetic feelings, and she was reveling in pleasure unlike anything she had ever experienced.

Papa was angry, to be sure, but she knew she was his favorite and blithely assumed he would grow calmer and accept her situation. After all, she was doing nothing that he himself had not advocated, and she could quote him verbatim on the subject. The works of her beloved mother convinced her that Mary Wollstonecraft would have approved, too. In her ecstatic affair with Shelley, Mary lacked a social conscience; she had never been taught right from wrong by her father, at least in the sense that it had been drilled into most children of the age. Her stepmother had lectured her, to be sure, but Mary had learned when she had been very small not to listen to Mary Jane.

So her holiday was sublime. She encouraged Shelley, and he, in turn, urged her to try her hand at poetry as well as prose. They wandered from town to town and village to village throughout Switzerland, sometimes walking, sometimes renting horses or a carriage, occasionally traveling by public conveyance. The ever-present Claire was an intruder in the lover's paradise, but they had invited her to accompany them and felt responsible for her, so they made the best of the situation. When there were breathtaking views and rides on Lake Lucerne to enjoy, when there was poetry to recite and unaccustomed but delicious food to eat, they could ask for no more.

On August 24 they rented a tiny chalet on the shore of Lake Lucerne. The house and view enchanted them, and Shelley, who was writing a romantic novel, *The Assassins,* which he never finished, said the conditions were ideal for his work. Mary proposed that they take the house for six months, and the others agreed; they had found heaven on earth, and would remain there for the winter.

But the following morning, when they were preparing to visit their landlord and pay the rent in advance, as he had demanded, the harsh realities of the world destroyed their dream. Between them the trio had only twenty-eight pounds, which was scarcely enough money to take them back to London, provided they were careful of every ha'penny. The girls knew no one on the Continent from whom they could borrow, and Shelley, whose credit was exhausted, could obtain no additional funds until he returned to England.

So they started for home that day, deciding that the cheapest and most direct route would be by way of the Rhine River. Between August 27, when they left Brunnen, in Switzerland, and September 8, when they finally reached Amsterdam, they traveled by virtually every kind of conveyance known to the age. They enjoyed the snug little passenger ships known as water-diligences, where they slept on comfortable bunks and were served simple but edible meals. The freight boats, including one that carried a load of hogs, were less pleasant, and the worst was a flat-bottomed, unpainted barge that leaked badly, not only wetting their shoes but convincing them it would fall apart in the middle of the Rhine, whose swift currents were tearing at it.

When they could not find a boat they traveled by land, and one day they rented a coach for so small a sum that they congratulated themselves, but the vehicle soon broke down, and they were forced to continue on foot. By now such inconveniences no longer bothered them, and they walked without bothering to complain. They went from Bonn to Cologne by post coaches, which were remarkably inexpensive, but these carriages made so many stops that Mary estimated they traveled at a speed of no more than one and one-half miles per hour. They could have made better time had they walked, but she was tired, as was Claire, and Shelley was inclined to become irritable if he had to spend long hours on his feet. The lark was still an experience to be savored and remembered for the rest of one's life, but paradise was becoming a trifle tarnished, and faint strains of an adult attitude began to appear in Mary's *Journal* entries.

Suddenly, and for reasons beyond her understanding, Mary was seized with a desire to reach England as soon as possible. The joys of crude travel had dissipated, and she wanted to hear English voices, eat English food and sleep in an English bed. Her mood communicated itself to Shelley, then to Claire, but they would have denied that adventure had palled and that they were suffering from a common ailment of the young, homesickness.

The last portion of the journey to Rotterdam was so frustratingly slow it became a nightmare. The boats had lost their charm, and Mary was not only aware of the dirt, but found the odors offensive. The faces of other passengers, she recorded in her *Journal,* were "horrid and slimy." These people drank, smoked, sang, ate sausages redolent of garlic and "made jokes of a most disagreeable nature." The young English trio huddled together in a corner of the deck, deploring the habits and manners of barbaric foreigners.

Everything changed for the better when they reached the Dutch border, where they rented places in public coaches that swept down the cobbled roads with the speed, grace and comfort of "a good English carriage." Arriving in Rotterdam at sundown on September 8, they found their funds so badly depleted they could not afford to stay overnight, but had to arrange an immediate passage. After a search of the waterfront they found a captain who was sailing immediately, and he agreed to take them on board for the exorbitant sum of three guineas each. Shelley, who identified himself, managed "with great difficulty" to persuade the bark's master to wait for his payment until they reached England.

They set sail the same night, but heavy winds and contrary currents kept them at sea until September 13, when they finally landed at Gravesend. They had been traveling for a month and a half, and except for the period of almost a week they had spent in Paris, had never paused for more than two nights in any one place. Although problems that more mature people would have found insurmountable awaited them, they behaved and wrote in their notebooks as though they didn't have a care.

V

In the autumn of 1814 the seventeen-year-old Mary Godwin outgrew her girlhood and became a woman. She and Shelley set up housekeeping in a small London apartment, and were forced to take Claire in with them because she had nowhere else to go. William Godwin not only refused to see them or communicate with them other than through his attorney, but issued an edict forbidding other members of the family to have social intercourse with them. Shelley's father was silent, and even the poet's gentle, forgiving mother wanted no more to do with him. His publisher sided with Harriet, who was refusing her husband's offers of "friendship," and insisted he return to her. Virtually everyone Mary and Shelley knew in London shunned them, and she was dealt another blow when she received a letter from her dear friend, Isabel Baxter, who denounced her and terminated their relationship.

Financial problems worse than Mary had ever known created additional burdens. Shelley was hounded not only by the many people to whom he owed money, but by Harriet's creditors, who had learned that the marriage had broken up. Money was so tight that the couple, still accompanied by Claire, had to move to a less expensive flat, and finally took two rooms in a cheap hotel. No one called on them, all doors were closed to them and they knew that any visitor was certain to be a bill collector.

The crowning blow was Mary's discovery that she was

pregnant, and that her child would be born soon after Harriet brought her new baby into the world.

It was astonishing that a girl who had never known real trouble or hardship could have maintained such a cheerful equanimity. But Mary's love and admiration for Shelley were unfaltering, and not only sustained her but gave her new strength. Together they formed patterns that would remain unbroken for the rest of their lives together: no matter what difficulties beset them, they spent several hours each day reading and studying, and in the evenings Shelley read aloud to her.

Mary kept pace with her intellectual lover, and her reading was eclectic and omnivorous. She enjoyed literature and history, biography and contemporary works, the classics and drama. After teaching herself enough Latin to read Terence and Seneca, she mastered Greek. Like Shelley, who consistently encouraged her, she dipped into everything that interested her, and soon was reading as many as ten books per week, an average she maintained for many years.

Shelley and Claire found a measure of emotional relief in the occult. One evening, after Mary retired early, they sat up late, chatting, and when Shelley remarked that the witching hour had come, they talked about mysterious, psychic phenomena at such length that, through the powers of autosuggestion, they became thoroughly frightened and stayed awake for the rest of the night. Another night Claire became hysterical, and Shelley had to awaken Mary for help in soothing her. Eventually the poet's common sense enabled him to put the occult out of his mind, but Claire persisted, and her lively, infantile imagination kept the household in an uproar.

But Mary didn't lose her sense of humor, and after one particularly harrowing night she made a typical entry in her *Journal:* "The next morning the chimney board in

Jane's [Claire's] room is found to have walked leisurely into the middle of the room, accompanied by the pillow, who, being very sleepy, tried to get into bed again, but sat down on his back."

Charles Clairmont defied his stepfather's ban, and not only came to see the principals in the scandal, but tried to persuade Godwin to adopt a less severe attitude. Mary's attitude toward her half-sister Fanny Imlay was a crack in her facade that indicated she might not be as serene in the face of criticism as she seemed. She was bitter because her half-sister refused to speak to them, and even when Fanny relented to the extent of sending them a curt note informing them that Shelley's publisher had turned against them, Mary did not budge. Shelley and Claire tried to see Fanny to thank her, but she would not receive them, so Mary gave her no credit for her attempt to help them.

Shelley's attorney abandoned his client, refusing to represent him, and Mary was convinced that Harriet was at the root of what she considered deliberate persecution. Harriet more or less admitted the charge when Shelley confronted her, and insisted that her husband had been debauched by the philosophy of Godwin in *Political Justice*. This made Mary doubly indignant because she continued to admire her father's doctrines. Her own financial difficulties gave her no concern, but she was badly worried by Godwin's continuing financial plight, which Shelley was in no position to ease. She made several attempts by correspondence to become reconciled with her father, and when she was rebuffed she placed all of the blame on her stepmother.

By late October the many unpleasantnesses of the situation were gnawing at Mary. Claire's giddiness was an annoyance to her and to Shelley, and both were somewhat relieved when it appeared that the younger girl might be making up her differences with the Godwins. Then a new complication arose, and to someone less courageous than Mary it might have been the final straw.

Shelley was expecting a payment of funds at the end of the first week in November that would ease his financial burden, but his creditors were tired of waiting, and bailiffs armed with warrants for his arrest began to search for him. Hoping to elude them, he disappeared on the evening of October 23. For the next two weeks he and Mary met in secret, changing the place of their daily rendezvous from coffeehouse to public park, from Mary Wollstonecraft's grave to the steps of Saint Paul's.

The couple's financial situation was desperate, and they literally went hungry until Shelley sold his microscope for five pounds. When that money vanished Mary pawned some of her own belongings, and for two days ate only small quantities of bread. Claire, who had no romantic association to sustain her, spoke more loudly of going home, quarreled with her stepsister and contributed appreciably to Mary's tensions.

Shelley's good friend Hogg came to London, and did not help improve the atmosphere. He teased the poet about his "two wives," and when Shelley made the mistake of repeating the conversation to Mary, she felt hurt. But Shelley was convinced that his mistress and his friend would grow to like each other, and repeatedly invited Hogg to their lodgings. He was proved right, even though Mary was self-conscious for a time because Hogg long had been close to Harriet. Mary and Hogg soon became good friends, often spending hours in debate, and Hogg, whose ideas she thought "sadly perverted," quickly discovered he could not win an argument with this brilliant young woman.

On November 30 Harriet gave birth to a son, whom she named Charles, and notified Shelley in a letter she signed, "Your deserted wife." He was so pleased to be the father of a son that, his complex and embarrassing domestic situation notwithstanding, he immediately began to send announcements he wrote himself to all of his relatives, friends and acquaintances.

His reaction was too much for Mary, and her proud composure crumbled. More aware than ever of her own precarious situation, she revealed her true feelings in a brief *Journal* entry that said far more than the lip service she paid to the theories of William Godwin. The birth of Harriet's baby, she declared, should be announced with the ringing of every church bell in England because "it is the son of his *wife*."

Soon thereafter Mary's own pregnancy began to cause her acute physical distress, and the physician summoned by Shelley ordered her to spend several hours each day in bed. Hogg, of whom she was becoming genuinely fond, often sat at her bedside and kept her company, sometimes reading to her, sometimes engaging in his futile debates with her, occasionally helping her polish her Latin.

Thomas Jefferson Hogg was a curious young man. Having decided at one time that he had been enamored of Harriet, he now made up his mind that he was in love with Mary, and after first informing Shelley of his feelings, he wrote her a love letter.

Here was a situation for those who believed in living according to the doctrine William Godwin had enunciated in *Political Justice*. In the perfect world the philosopher had envisioned, there would be no need for monogamy because all human sexual and emotional jealousies would disappear.

But Mary was in no physical or mental state to appreciate her father's concept of Utopia. Her own reputation had been shattered, she was ill and in a few months she would give birth to an illegitimate child. But, even in this thoroughly unpleasant situation, she thought first of Shelley, who had little to sustain him other than his philo-sophical convictions. Also, she had no desire to hurt Hogg, whom she liked. So she answered his note with one of her own that was a diplomatic gem. Calling him "Dearest Hogg," she told him that he was so generous she could not help loving him. She regarded him with deep affection, she said, and delicately admitted the possibility, to which she referred in vague terms, that the day might come when she would return the passionate love he felt for her.

In her own mind, at least, she had protected Shelley, she had not hurt or ridiculed Hogg and she had won for her-self some small measure of temporary peace. Her confine-ment was becoming so difficult that she could think of little else, and on February 22, 1815, she gave birth, two months prematurely, to a daughter.

The infant was so small and sickly that the physician doubted she could survive. Mary was exhausted and Shel-ley did not leave her bedside. Godwin and his wife relented slightly, and although they still refused to call on Mary, they nevertheless sent her a gift of linens.

On March 6 the baby died, and Mary became so de-pressed she was either unable or unwilling to speak for forty-eight hours. Shelley wore himself out taking care of her, Claire proving to be of little help and often spending a few days at a time with her mother and stepfather. Then Shelley convinced himself he was dying of consumption, and Hogg moved in with the couple, cooking for them, nursing them and acting as their housekeeper. There was no more talk of a romance between Mary and Hogg, how-ever, Mary's retreat having seen to that.

In the midst of this travail there was one bright beam of financial sunshine. Shelley's grandfather had died, leav-ing an estate of more than a quarter of a million pounds. The old man's will had been badly drawn, and Shelley could lay claim to a portion of his inheritance immediately; although he had little chance of winning a court fight, the situation suited the purposes of his father, now Sir Timothy. Hoping to terminate all relations with the family black sheep, the older Shelley proposed to give Percy enough money to pay off his post-obits, and to establish a trust fund that would guarantee him an income of one thousand pounds per year for life.

Shelley, who was interested in the present and was more than willing to let the distant future take care of itself, promptly agreed. But the negotiations took months to conclude, and in the meantime the bailiffs were renewing their demands on Shelley for the payment of various debts. As Mary's physical health gradually improved, Claire returned to live with the couple, and her presence became a never-ending irritation to her stepsister, who was shouldering more than her fair share of burdens.

Mary's entries in her *Journal* reflect her exasperation with the girl who would not permit her to live alone and in peace with Shelley: "Talk about Clara's going away; nothing settled; I fear it is hopeless. She will not go to Skinner Street; then our house is the only remaining place, I see plainly. What is to be done?"

The next day's entry was even more barbed: "Very quiet in the morning, and happy, as Clara does not get up till 4."

Mary and Shelley discussed the problem every day, but neither knew how to solve it. Claire was imperious one day, clinging the next; she gave them no peace, she interfered constantly in their lives, and she behaved as though they were in her debt. But they felt they could not turn her out into the street, as she had nowhere else to go. Shelley, who had been slow to share Mary's feelings, was now convinced, too, that they would not know any real happiness until she left.

Even if Claire had been willing to return to Skinner

Street, that door was closed by a new complication. Two of Mary Wollstonecraft's sisters operated a highly successful school for girls in Dublin and were contemplating employing Fanny Imlay as a teacher there. But they made it plain she would not be welcome under their roof if the notorious Claire were permitted to return to the home of her mother and stepfather. At Mary's suggestion Claire advertised in the newspapers for a position as a governess, but there were no replies, in part because many respectable people knew Claire's identity and wanted nothing to do with a girl so closely associated with Mary Godwin and Percy Bysshe Shelley.

In spite of all the difficulties and distractions, Mary kept up the pace of her incessant reading. Her devotion to learning for its own sake was as genuine as Shelley's, and she permitted nothing to interfere with the studies that, at this stage of her life, were her only pleasure and hope for the future. She could do almost no writing at this time, but her reading gave her a sense of accomplishment, making her feel she was not merely existing from day to day.

Perhaps the most significant fact in Mary's life during these trials was the steadfastness of her love for Shelley. The ardor of a lesser woman might have been diminished by his lack of reliability, erratic behavior, hypochondria and occasional infantilism, but his weaknesses caused her to appreciate him more, not less. A very few of his friends still had faith in him, and if Mary was not the first to become aware of his genius, she nevertheless not only recognized it but knew it had to be nurtured if he was to do the work she believed him capable of producing. No matter what her own problems, she put him first, as she would continue to until the day she died, with the exception of one notable period of a few months. She was not yet eighteen years of age, but her love for him was already that of a mature woman, and was unfaltering.

The promise of a drastic improvement in Shelley's situation, combined with the reappearance of the bailiffs, impelled the couple to think in terms of leaving London for a time, and they began a search for a home in the country they could rent. They thought of themselves as logical people who did not believe in chance, but their views on luck were shaken when, just at this time in the spring of 1815, sheer happenstance drastically changed their domestic situation. Claire Clairmont won a substantial sum of money in a lottery, and decided to go off to Lynmouth for a long holiday. Mary and Shelley were freed of any responsibility for her, and could go where they pleased.

They immediately rented a small cottage in the country near London, and Shelley, who was still avoiding the bailiffs, preceded Mary there. While they were settling into the place they received the good news that Shelley's financial affairs had been settled. Sir Timothy paid off his son's debts and redeemed his post-obits, making Shelley solvent for the first time in years. The young poet also received a lump sum in cash, which enabled him to give Harriet two hundred pounds for her support and that of their two children. He remembered his promise of financial aid to Godwin, too, even though the philosopher still would not speak to him, and Shelley sent him, via an attorney, the sum of one thousand pounds.

"I begin a new Journal with our regeneration," Mary wrote in mid-May of 1815. She sensed that she and Shelley were entering a new period in their lives, and she was not mistaken. The months that followed the couple's move to the country were among the happiest they ever knew, and contributed materially to the firm foundation of their joint life.

VI

THE MOST IMMEDIATE DRAMATIC CHANGE caused by life in a rural cottage, fresh air and ample food was the improvement in the health of both Mary and Shelley. She had been painfully thin since the loss of her baby, but she regained her beauty "in a day and a night," as Shelley told her. He became far stronger, too, and forgetting his imaginary ailments, which frequently distracted him, he plunged back into his long-neglected work with a determination that elated Mary, who had been worried by his lack of interest in his writing.

They formed a routine they would follow permanently. Shelley arose at about eight in the morning, and sat down at his desk for an hour of work. Mary usually awakened around nine, and after they ate a light breakfast together they went their separate ways. They stayed at their respective desks until two in the afternoon, with Shelley working on manuscripts and writing letters, while Mary either wrote or read. At two they ate the first of the day's large meals, which usually consisted of soup, a roast with vegetables, and a dessert of fresh fruits and cheese. Both were orthodox in their food tastes, and Shelley gradually lost his desire for rich sweets, developing a liking for the simpler fruits and cheeses that Mary enjoyed.

At least two hours of every afternoon were devoted to long, rambling walks similar to their meanderings during their six-week journey to France and Switzerland. Both were acutely aware of flowers, trees and shrubs, of changes in the seasons and of hour-by-hour shifts in the weather. They wore stout walking shoes, but made no other concessions to the pastime; in accordance with the custom of the day, Mary was dressed in ankle-length skirts and petticoats, and Shelley wore the town attire of a gentleman.

They came home in time for tea, then returned to their reading and writing until eight, when they dined, usually .eating a meal much like that which they had enjoyed earlier in the day. Even in later years, when they took up full-time residence on the Continent, they remained English in their likes and dislikes for food. Like so many of their fellow countrymen who have lived abroad through the centuries, they rarely tried native dishes, and preferred, as Robert Browning said a few decades later, to bring the aura of their homeland to the table with them.

At nine or thereabouts they chatted with friends who dropped in, or, if they were alone, Shelley usually read to Mary from works of poetry or prose with which she was not familiar. Sometimes, when he thought it might help her understanding, he interjected comments of his own. Mary, who needed her sleep, usually retired around eleven, and rarely stayed up past midnight. Shelley, who lost all count of time when he became engrossed in a book, frequently read until dawn, but always arose at eight, regardless of his bedtime. Ladies and gentlemen, no matter how great their poverty, always hired servants, so there were few household chores to attend to.

Mary usually allowed her cooks to prepare what they pleased, and insisted only that food purchases remain within the limits of the budget she had set. The couple usually drank a little wine with their evening meal, but Shelley seldom touched strong liquor, and Mary actively disliked whiskey, gin and brandy. Neither smoked or used snuff, and the thousands of their compatriots who, in 1815,

still regarded them as depraved, would have been astonished to learn they lived within the bounds of modest
decorum that ruled the lives of other upper middle-class
people. They avoided heavy drinking, coarse companions
and, with the exception of Lord Byron, whose lechery they
deplored and disapproved, their few friends were also
quiet and home-oriented.

It amused Mary to condone what she called Shelley's
"secret vice"—the sailing of paper boats on ponds, lakes
and small streams. He could not look at a body of water
without tearing a sheet from the ever-present notebook he
carried, making a toy boat and sailing it. This fascination
continued to absorb him long after he could indulge an
adult version of the same sport, the sailing of real boats on
large lakes and the open sea.

After spending the summer of 1815 on the southern
coast of Devonshire, the couple rented a house at Bishopsgate, near London, moving in after taking a ten-day excur-
sion by boat up the Thames. They were so absorbed in
themselves and their own problems that they were scarcely
aware of the events taking place in the world around them
—the escape of Napoleon from his Elba exile in March,
the One Hundred Days that followed and his shattering,
final defeat by the Duke of Wellington at Waterloo. Mary's
Journal took no note of current history in the making, and
Shelley's only comments were written in a single sonnet
in which he, as a self-proclaimed republican, regretted that
the fall of Napoleon gave rise to an even greater tyranny
in the restoration of the Bourbons.

In the autumn Shelley was at work again, writing *Alastor*,
which was destined to become one of his major poems.
Mary, who quickly recognized the merit of the poem,
shielded him from outside intrusions, kept at arm's length
people who might annoy him and otherwise made certain
that nothing interrupted the smooth tenor of his life.

She could not prevent Harriet from getting in touch with him in November, however, the first time he had heard from her since spring. His wife demanded an increase in the two hundred pounds per year payment he was giving her, but Shelley refused, proposing instead that he take Ianthe and Charles under his own roof. Mary accepted his suggestion, and was willing to bring up the children as her own, but Harriet rejected the idea with such acrimony that Shelley threatened to cut off her entire allowance.

There were other irritations that made life less than ideal, but both Mary and Shelley were beginning to realize that it was almost impossible to attain perfection. Claire paid visits to the house in Bishopsgate, behaved disagreeably and then complained when Mary and Shelley failed to invite her to make her permanent home with them. But it was Mary's father who caused the young couple their greatest pain. Still adamant in his refusal to see them, he nevertheless continued to badger Shelley for money, often accompanying his coldly written requests with new, dubious ideas for money-raising schemes. Shelley had done everything within his financial power for the older man, at least for the present, and was reluctant to try to raise more money for him.

Mary was convinced, as was Shelley, that Godwin's attitude toward them was responsible for their social ostracism. If her father accepted their situation, she felt, other people would do the same, but they could not expect society to condone their life together when he advertised his disapproval to anyone who would listen to him.

On January 24, 1816, Mary gave birth to her second child at the Bishopsgate house after an easy confinement. The baby was a healthy boy, and the happy parents immediately named him William, after Mary's father. Godwin neither thanked them nor recognized the arrival of his grandson in any other way.

Mary grieved in silence, allowing no outsider to know how she felt, but Shelley's patience was growing short. He managed to find several hundred pounds for Godwin during the spring of 1816, when the older man gave him no respite from the demands for money, and although he still had a great intellectual regard for Godwin as a philosopher, and wanted his admiration, he nevertheless was able to see the flaws in Mary's father as a human being.

The humility that had been a characteristic in all of Shelley's letters to Godwin gave way to increasingly sharp bursts of temper, and after Godwin failed to acknowledge the birth of little William, the proud young father's indignation was boundless. Removing his velvet glove with a flourish, he wrote his true thoughts:

> In my judgment, neither I, nor your daughter, nor her offspring, ought to encounter the treatment which we receive on every side. It has perpetually appeared to me to have been your especial duty to see that, as far as mankind value your good opinion, we were dealt justly by, and that a young family innocent and benevolent and united, should not be confounded with prostitutes and seducers. . . .
>
> I have lamented also over my ruined hopes, hopes of all that your genius once taught me to expect from your virtue, when I found that for yourself, your family, and your creditors, you would submit to that communication with me which you once rejected and abhorred, and which no pity for my poverty or sufferings, assumed willingly for you, could avail to extort.
>
> Do not talk of *forgiveness* again to me, for my blood boils in my veins, and my gall rises against all that bears the human form, when I think of what I, their benefactor and ardent lover, have endured of enmity and contempt. . . .

Godwin loftily ignored the outburst, and made no reply. Shelley had relieved his own feelings by expressing them on paper, but Mary had to be patient, remain silent and wait for time or outside influences to change her father's opinion. Meanwhile she had her new baby, her books and —above all—Shelley to keep her occupied. But the girl who was not yet nineteen and the young man of twenty-three had lived longer at Bishopsgate than they had ever spent together in any one place. Relishing travel for its own sake, they were growing restless, so an unexpected opportunity that arose in May, 1816, seemed a godsend to a couple who were still being snubbed by most Englishmen of standing.

They learned, out of nowhere, and from Claire, of all people, that they had an opportunity to meet the glittering Lord Byron, perhaps to become well acquainted with him. The prospect filled both of them with a sense of keen anticipation, and Shelley in particular was anxious to form a relationship with his noted peer.

The sixth Baron Byron may have been the only person in England with a reputation worse than that of Mary and Shelley. At the age of twenty-eight he was recognized as a poet of dazzling talents and a wicked seducer of women. The most handsome man of his era, yet hampered by a clubfoot, his activities in the House of Lords and else-where had made him the idol of the Whig Party. He lived at the center of London society, and was regarded as being so attractive that no woman could resist him; his name was linked with that of almost every prominent lady in England, and many of the stories were true.

In spite of his reputation, however, his accomplishments in poetry and his work on behalf of liberal issues were real, and he had won the genuine respect of other literary men as well as of statesmen and politicians of high standing. Many men and most women were willing to ignore his sexual excesses and the carelessness with which he con-ducted his affairs.

But he had finally gone too far. In 1815, in order to

escape from a complicated liaison, he had married, but had not settled down, and now, scarcely a year later, the socially prominent Lady Byron had returned to the home of her parents with her baby. She would not go back to her husband, and London was filled with rumors, the most scandalous of which insisted he had long been enjoying an affair with his half-sister. Lady Byron's father threatened to bring the story into the open, so Byron signed legal separation papers, and after providing financially for his wife and daughter, left England.

He was on the verge of departure when Claire Clairmont came to Mary and Shelley with the suggestion that they take a little villa on Lake Geneva in Switzerland and spend the summer there—near the spot where Byron was intending to sojourn. Mary accepted the idea at face value and was delighted. It did not occur to her that Claire might have become personally involved with Byron, and it is probable that Shelley was also in the dark, although he learned the truth of the matter before Mary heard the story.

The facts were simple enough. Claire, like hundreds of other romantic young women, had conceived a grand passion for Byron, whom she had never met, and bombarded him with letters. Byron received large quantities of such mail, and usually ignored it, but Claire was clever, and the man who took pride in being the greatest wit of his day became intrigued. According to one account Claire auditioned as a singer at Drury Lane, where Byron was one of the directors, and flirted with him outrageously. In any event, and in whatever the manner that she accomplished her goal, Claire threw herself at Byron with great gusto, pretending to be endowed with the submissive qualities he allegedly wanted in a woman.

For a time Byron resisted her advances, but he was bored, his life was in the process of vast upheaval, and Claire's campaign succeeded, with Byron perhaps failing to realize that it was he who had been seduced. By the time he left England forever in April, Claire was his mistress. She was afraid she might never see him again unless she took matters into her own hands, and therefore came to the unsuspecting Mary and Shelley with her proposal that they go to Geneva—and that she accompany them. At this time they knew only that Claire had become acquainted with Byron.

Responding enthusiastically to the idea, Shelley and Mary planned to leave England at once, and even proposed that Hogg join the party as an escort for Claire. It is probable that this development is what caused Claire to reveal her secret to Shelley, who did not repeat it as yet to Mary, and Hogg was informed that a change in plans would make it impossible to include him as a member of the party. Claire was relieved, wanting no ostensible suitor on hand who would discourage Byron's attentions.

Just before leaving England, Claire wrote to Byron, who was already on the Continent, saying that she would meet him in Geneva. Meanwhile she presented a far different picture to her mother and stepfather, telling the Godwins that Mary and Shelley again wanted her to act as their chaperone. They objected strenuously but, of course, in vain.

On May 8 the Shelley party reached Paris, and a week later, after encountering snowstorms in the mountains, they were basking in the warm sun of Sécheron, a suburb of Geneva, where they took temporary quarters in a hotel. Mary appears to have known nothing of Claire's real relationship with Byron at the time of the Paris stop, but learned the truth by the time they reached Switzerland. The news stunned and horrified her, but she was powerless to intervene, and it was too late to return home in protest, so she was forced to accept the situation.

The intolerant attitude Mary and Shelley habitually displayed when confronted with sexual license is an irony that, at first glance, makes no sense. Shelley had deserted his wife and two children for Mary, and they were living together with their illegitimate child, but they were quick to condemn others for doing the same thing. According to their own standards, however, they were not inconsistent, and Mary, even more than Shelley, upheld the middle-class concepts of morality. Their own situation was different, they believed, because they were acting according to the principles of Godwin's philosophy. They were not wallowing in a cheap affair, nor was their primary purpose that of seeking sensual pleasures.

On the contrary, they were convinced that their love created an indissoluble bond, and although they had not been united in a ceremony that would give them legal standing or religious approval, they were nevertheless married to each other in their own eyes, and that was what mattered. So Mary believed her own situation in no way resembled that of Claire, who was a vulgar sensation-seeker in her affair with Byron.

One of the most curious aspects of this attitude is that Mary and Shelley apparently failed to realize their condemnation of promiscuity placed them firmly in the camp of the bourgeois moralists whose standards they professed to reject. They thought of themselves as rebels against the tyranny of their age, and their genuine love of human freedom, combined with their compassion for their fellow humans, led them to believe they were pioneers in the establishment of new moral codes. But, in their confusion, they fooled themselves as much as they outraged the society whose institutions they thought were outmoded.

Mary would have been shocked to learn that she was as much a prisoner of propriety as her own parents had been in a time of crisis. She and Shelley were like two small children who thumbed their noses at the world, but hastened to conform to that world's rules when given cause. Claire, who appears to have had at least some understanding of Mary's morality, was afraid the summer would be miserable for the entire party. What she could not have known was that the meeting of Mary and Shelley with Byron would produce results that would make her stepsister as notorious, in her own lifetime, as were the two celebrated poets.

VII

Lord Byron, who was traveling with a young physician friend, Dr. John Polidori, reached Sécheron on May 25, and not only established an almost immediate rapport with Shelley, but soon became Mary's good friend, too. Although Mary and Shelley believed he carried sexual license to excess, they adhered to the principle that every man's private life was his own business. They and Byron shared the same love of beauty, the same concern for human dignity and the same passionate conviction that all men deserved to be equal and free. That was enough to cement the friendship, and if anyone was the real outsider it was Claire, whose shallow mind was incapable of grasping the concepts that the others considered of primary importance. She was satisfied to renew her affair with Byron.

A few days after the newcomer's arrival, Mary and Shelley, together with their baby and several servants, moved into a rented house called Montalègre on the opposite side of the lake. Claire went with them, presumably to salvage whatever might have been left of her reputation. A few days later Byron and Dr. Polidori moved into an adjoining house, the Villa Diodati, that was separated from Montalègre by connecting vineyards. The two couples and the physician soon became inseparable companions.

Shelley bought a sailboat, and every evening that weather permitted, the entire party went out for a sail, usually leaving around six o'clock and returning at ten. Byron shared Shelley's enthusiasm for sailing, and Claire did not care what they were doing, provided she could be near Byron. Mary, who had good reason to dread sea voyages, soon discovered that the sailboat did not make her ill, and she developed a love for sailing almost as great as Shelley's.

After spending an evening on the lake the group usually went to the Villa Diodati, where they talked until the early hours of the morning, settling the problems of the world, after the manner of young people through the centuries. When Mary and Shelley returned to their own house through the vineyards, Claire did not accompany them.

The members of the two households saw little of each other during daylight hours. Mary and Shelley observed their usual routines, writing, eating and taking walks in accordance with their established custom. Byron followed his own schedules, and the entire party settled down comfortably.

Tourists who sometimes spied on them with telescopes were something of a nuisance, but their curiosity was a small price to pay for tranquillity. It did not occur to Mary and Shelley, although the more cynical and experienced Byron might have guessed, that the tourists were carrying lurid, wildly exaggerated tales of their activities back to England. The move into the two houses was made early in June, and by the middle of July stories were being told everywhere in England to the effect that Mary, Shelley, Claire and Byron were engaging in daily orgies, changing their partners indiscriminately. Byron, who may no longer have cared what was said about him, shrugged off the gossip when he finally heard the stories. Mary and Shelley were indignant, but by now they were resigned to what they regarded as inevitable misinterpretation, and wearily put the talk out of their minds.

The most wicked pastime the party developed was the

holding of séances, and Claire, whose love and fear of the occult was so pronounced, joined in these games with vigor. It is not surprising that some of the most imaginative people on earth should have started telling ghost stories of their own after holding a séance, and only Byron remained amused and detached. Even Dr. Polidori admitted he occasionally became perturbed.

Mary sometimes managed to upset herself, while Claire and Shelley reacted far more violently. On a number of occasions Claire became hysterical, and one night Shelley so completely lost his self-control that he ran through the villa, screaming in terror. The others were forced to chase and catch him, and Byron, with Dr. Polidori's aid, tied his feet and ankles and thrust a gag into his mouth. Mary was required to spend the next hour soothing him, and only when he became calm did she remove his bonds.

It was decided, by mutual consent, that the sport was too dangerous, and Byron proposed that they hold a contest: each would write a story based on the supernatural. The two poets and Claire began stories the following day, but soon became bored by the pastime and abandoned their efforts. Dr. Polidori persisted, and with Byron's aid completed a small book called *The Vampyre,* which was published in 1819. It achieved considerable popularity because it was generally believed that Byron was the author.

Mary, who treated the idea of the contest seriously, could not think of an idea, and therefore was unable to begin work. Each morning Shelley asked, "Have you started your story?" It soon began to annoy her because her mind remained blank.

The men and Mary sometimes went swimming, and the party visited the house in Lausanne where Gibbon had written the final chapters of *The Decline and Fall.* On weekends they climbed into the mountains, and a visit to the Castle of Chillon inspired two immortal poems, Byron's

"Prisoner of Chillon" and Shelley's "Hymn to Intellectual Beauty."

Mary's admiration of the poets' facility and talent caused her to wonder whether she should give up all pretense of becoming an author, but she refused to give in to her occasional despair, and one night a conversation between Shelley and Byron gave her the spark she needed. She told the story herself in the introduction to the 1831 edition of *Frankenstein:*

> . . . various philosophical doctrines were discussed, and among others the nature of the principle of life, and whether there was any probability of its ever being discovered and communicated. They talked of the experiments of Dr. Darwin (I speak not of what the Doctor really did, or said that he did, but, as more to my purpose, of what was then spoken of as having been done by him) who preserved a piece of vermicelli in a glass case, till by some extraordinary means it began to move with voluntary motion. Not thus, after all, would life be given. Perhaps a corpse would be re-animated; galvanism had given token of such things: perhaps the component parts of a creature might be manufactured, brought together, and endued with vital warmth.
>
> Night waned upon this talk, and even the witching hour had gone by, before we retired. When I placed my head on my pillow, I did not sleep, nor could I be said to think. My imagination, unbidden, possessed and guided me, gifting the successive images that arose in my mind with a vividness far beyond the usual bounds of reverie. I saw, with shut eyes but acute mental vision, —I saw the pale student of unhallowed arts kneeling beside the thing he had put together. I saw the hideous phantasm of a man stretched out, and then, on the working of some powerful engine, show signs of life, and stir with an uneasy, half vital motion. Frightful must it be; for supremely frightful would be the effect

of any human endeavor to mock the stupendous mechanism of the Creator of the world. His success would terrify the artist; he would rush away from his odious handiwork, horror-stricken. He would hope that, left to itself, the slight spark of life which he had communicated would fade; that this thing, which had received such imperfect animation, would subside into dead matter; and he might sleep in the belief that the silence of the grave would quench for ever the transient existence of the hideous corpse which he had looked upon as the cradle of life. He sleeps; but he is awakened; he opens his eyes; behold, the horrid thing stands at his bedside, opening his curtains, and looking on him with yellow, watery, but speculative eyes.

Mary opened her own eyes in terror. The idea so possessed her mind, she said, that a thrill of fear ran through her. Shelley was asleep beside her, the bedroom was familiar and the solid reality of the white Alps stood beyond the windows, but she could not rid herself of the hideous phantom that had been born in her imagination. Then a new thought occurred to her: if she could only write a story that would frighten her readers as she had frightened herself!

In that instant she knew she had found the story she had so desperately been seeking. Unable to sleep, she slipped into a robe and hurried to her desk, where she scribbled the opening lines that would become famous: "It was a dreary night in November . . ." The creation of *Frankenstein* had started.

Mary was uniquely qualified to write this tale of the supernatural, a logical extension of the early Gothic novels that were just becoming popular in England. Her intellectual approach to life, combined with her chronic, offbeat sense of morbidity, were qualities that breathed life into what she regarded as a philosophical extension of the ghost stories that she, Shelley and Byron had been telling every evening.

Shelley was delighted when Mary told him at breakfast that she had found the essence of her story, but he disagreed when she said she intended to write it as a short piece. If she allowed herself to dwell on the various problems that the creation of her inhuman creature would raise, she would soon see that she could not do her subject justice in a short story. She would need to write a full-length novel that would explore every aspect of the matter.

Self-doubts again assailed Mary, but Shelley would not listen, and continued to encourage her until his unflagging enthusiasm for the project gave her the courage to make the attempt. Byron, who read the opening chapters, agreed so heartily with Shelley that Mary's self-confidence was restored, and she worked steadily during the rest of the summer in Switzerland, completing the book after returning to England.

Unlike Shelley, who constantly revised his work, Mary made few changes in her manuscript. She labored slowly but steadily, and once she had committed an idea to paper she was reluctant to tamper with it for fear that she would spoil the atmosphere and mood she was creating, both of them of paramount importance in a book of this sort.

From the outset her approach to her work was thoroughly professional. The daughter of a man who earned his living with his pen, the lifelong friend of many authors and the mistress of a highly disciplined poet, she fell naturally into her work routines. After breakfast every morning she played with little William for an hour, then retired to her study, remaining there from ten o'clock in the morning until two in the afternoon. She allowed no interruptions, and stopped writing only if William or Shelley truly needed her.

Claire was miffed, to be sure. At loose ends during the

morning, Claire liked nothing better than to sit down with Mary over the coffee to which both were becoming addicted and chat about the events of the previous evening. But Mary kept the door to her study locked, and Claire had to fend for herself.

The entries in Mary's *Journal* during the early stages of the preparation of *Frankenstein* indicate her certainty, virtually from the outset, that the book would be published. She appeared to entertain no doubts that it would be read, and she was confident that she would achieve her deceptively simple goal, that of frightening her readers as badly as she had frightened herself. This self-assurance was remarkable, as was the sure hand she displayed in her actual writing, particularly when it is remembered that she had just passed her nineteenth birthday.

It was inevitable that many people refused to believe that Mary wrote *Frankenstein* herself, and for years it was rumored that Shelley was the real author. Mary took notice of these stories in the introduction to the 1831 edition, when she freely admitted that Shelley wrote the preface, but quietly insisted that every other word in the book had been her own. Leigh Hunt, Trelawny and other friends who knew the Shelleys through the years did not doubt that Mary was the sole author of *Frankenstein*. She and Shelley were writers of such integrity that nothing would have induced them to fool the reading public.

Neither Mary nor Shelley could have guessed that *Frankenstein* would become the most popular novel published in the English-speaking world in the first three decades of the nineteenth century, that it would be hailed as a masterpiece within a decade of its original appearance after first winning only mild critical acclaim or that it would be regarded as a classic one hundred and fifty years after it first began to captivate—and frighten—delighted readers.

Mary put the final touches on her manuscript in the

spring of 1817, and in May of that year, after she had made a clean copy in her own hand, Shelley offered it to his own publishers. They showed no interest in it, so he showed it to several other publishers before the firm of Lackington, Hughes, Harding, Mayor and Jones, of Finsbury Square, agreed to take the book and paid the author a token advance royalty.

Published in March, 1818, *Frankenstein* won the partial approval of the reviewers for the four literary journals in England whose opinions made and broke reputations. But the public's response was less reserved, and the original edition of one thousand copies was sold out in six weeks. Lackington immediately brought out a new printing, and thereafter, for the next forty years, brought out at least two more printings each year in an attempt to satisfy the demand.

Ever since it was first published, *Frankenstein* has never been out of print; it has been done in at least twenty-nine languages, and has sold many millions of copies. Mary's story has been copied by innumerable other novelists; nine successful plays have used her theme, and *Frankenstein* has served as the basis of at least five major motion pictures. Rarely has any first novel enjoyed such lasting, continuing popularity. The book won Mary far greater renown than Shelley was accorded in their lifetimes, and created such respect for her that, for more than a quarter of a century, she was regarded as a major novelist married to a minor poet.

Frankenstein earned more for Mary in a month than Shelley's poetry brought him in a year, and was a major factor in her struggle for solvency after his death. Inadequate and sloppy records kept by publishers in many lands have made it impossible to estimate the total number of copies sold.

The unprecedented success placed Mary in the forefront

of women authors fighting to be recognized as the equals of men. Mary Wollstonecraft had blazed the trail, but her daughter was the true pioneer who broke precedent and proved that mass audiences would be willing to read the works of a woman. George Eliot, George Sand and the Brontë sisters, to mention only a few prominent members of her sex who were nineteenth-century authors, owed her a permanent debt of gratitude.

In her own day Mary was regarded as the first woman of letters in England, and on the Continent her reputation was surpassed only by that of Madame de Staël, who died a year before *Frankenstein* was published, and whose contemporary fame was based, in part, on the fact that the all-powerful Napoleon had been unable to silence her or suppress her works.

It should be noted, too, that although posterity has evaluated *Frankenstein* as no more and no less than a horror story, albeit the first and purest of its kind, the critics and reading public of nineteenth-century England considered it an intellectual and literary exercise of great merit. The novel embodied many of William Godwin's basic precepts, and accomplished more in the dissemination of his philosophical ideas than did all of his own works in his lifetime and thereafter. Viewed exclusively on an intellectual level, the book was to be seen as a negation of Godwin's theory that man can achieve perfection, since it argues that man, in his search for ultimate perfection, destroys himself.

The story, which Mary presented as something of a plot within a plot, told of a German nobleman named Frankenstein, a scientist of note, who decided to devote all of his energies to a search for the elixir of life. His efforts were successful, and he created a monster so terrible to behold that he fled from it. The monster killed Frankenstein's brother, and the scientist, after seeking and finding the creature he had created, had the opportunity to retaliate.

But the monster said to him, "All men hate the wretched." Lonely and miserable, the monster declared that he was deprived of love, and promised to leave mankind in peace if the scientist would make another monster and bring it to life to be his wife. Taking pity on the creature, Frankenstein traveled to the far northern end of the Orkney Islands, off the coast of Scotland, and there went to work.

He made another creature, overcoming his loathing, but before bringing it to life he was assailed by doubts. Suppose these monsters produced a new breed that would drive man from the globe and would themselves become the masters of the earth? The possibility was too frightful even to contemplate, the risk was too great.

So Frankenstein destroyed the female monster without bringing it to life, only to find the enraged male monster at the window, threatening him with the curse, "I will be with you on your wedding night." The creature kept his word, murdering Frankenstein's bride, Elizabeth, on their honeymoon at Lake Como. The scientist vowed to pursue the monster to the ends of the earth, and it was in the Arctic, near the end of the trail, that he found the Englishman, Walton, and told him his story before dying.

Did the monster kill Frankenstein? Walton was not sure, but found the creature weeping over his creator's body. Instead of obeying his instinct and killing the creature immediately, Walton made the mistake of listening to the loathsome beast's lament. He had caused enough suffering, the monster said, and could do penance only by doing away with himself. Leaping from Walton's ship onto an ice raft that lay close to the vessel, he was carried away into the Arctic night. Walton—and the reader—were left to wonder whether the monster's promise to kill himself was genuine, or whether he was still roaming the earth, waiting to strike down another innocent victim.

The prejudices against women were so strong that the first edition was published anonymously, and the reviewers were unanimous in believing that the author was a man. *Blackwood's* said the theme indicated the writer was a follower of Godwin, and the *Edinburgh,* which appeared about ten days later, made the ironic assertion that the book had been done by Shelley.

Not until the third printing, late in 1818, did the name Mary Wollstonecraft Shelley appear on the title page. The revelation created a sensation, and the critics who reviewed Mary's later works rarely failed to wonder, at length, that the tale of horror had been written by a woman.

Perhaps the strangest phenomenon connected with *Frankenstein* is that Mary inadvertently created a name that tens of millions have recognized, down to the present day. Although many may have heard of her novel, none of the misinformed have actually read it, since Frankenstein was the name of the scientist, not of the disgusting monster he made and brought to life.

The novel is regarded as a story to be enjoyed, perhaps as a curiosity. The scholar does not classify it as literature, in part because Mary told her story in the convoluted form popular in her day, and partly because her language was graceless and her characterizations lacked subtlety.

The superior gifts she showed in the fragments of her poetry that have survived have led a number of authorities to conclude that in *Frankenstein,* as well as in her later novels, Mary was presenting a dramatic story for its own sake and was not trying to produce a work of literary merit. Her own attitude, as seen in her *Journal* and correspondence, bears out this conclusion. In her time the novel was regarded as an art form much inferior to poetry, and any author who wanted enduring fame sought immortality in verse rather than in prose. That the works of Mary Shelley have survived in spite of their obvious faults is, however, a tribute to her genius.

She herself, sitting in her study overlooking Lake Geneva in the summer of 1816, would have been the last to believe —or even hope—that the book she was writing would win her a permanent niche in literary history.

VIII

THE HAPPY GROUP of self-exiles celebrated Shelley's twenty-fourth birthday with a sail on the lake, followed by a dinner party, and Shelley revealed his plans for an extended journey by boat on the major waterways of the Continent. But within the next week he and Mary received urgent reminders that their immediate presence was required in England. William Godwin's latest financial crisis was responsible; he needed two thousand pounds, and only Shelley could provide him with that large a sum.

Shelley had already written to his father to ask for money, intending to use a portion to pay off the last of his own debts. But Sir Timothy had been offended by his son's abrupt, unannounced departure, and replied through his attorney that not another farthing would be forthcoming until the wanderer returned to England.

Meanwhile Mary received a letter from Fanny Imlay in which her half-sister gently reproached her for her supposed neglect of the father who was still refusing to recognize her existence. First Fanny passed along the latest gossip. Coleridge's health was improved, and he was hard at work on *Christabel;* Lamb and his sister were enjoying a holiday in the country; Papa's good friend, Richard Brinsley Sheridan, the great dramatist, had died, hounded by bailiffs to the end of his days, and Papa paid frequent visits to his grave.

Then Fanny came to the heart of the matter. Papa's situation was far more serious than Mary and Shelley knew, and in their happiness they failed to appreciate the difficulties of a genius who was distracted by his worries. It was her duty to tell them the real nature of his situation, Fanny said, because "you often deceive yourself about things." Papa needed help that only they could provide, and Fanny knew that if he had the peace of mind to concentrate on the writing of his new book, it would be his best. The letter ended on a note that said a great deal about life in the Godwin household and about Fanny's own state of depression, her most obvious inheritance from her mother:

> Write small, for Mamma complains of the double postage of a double letter. I pay the full postage of all the letters I send, and you know I have not a sou of my own. Mamma is much better, though not without rheumatism. William is better than he ever was in his life. I am not well; my mind always keeps my body in a fever; but never mind me. Adieu, my dear sister. Let me entreat you to consider seriously all that I have said concerning your father.

Mary's concern for Godwin and Shelley's inability to obtain any money for himself caused them to postpone their tour of Europe's waterways, and they planned to leave Geneva in mid-September. But their departure was hastened by a crisis much closer to home. Claire revealed to them she was pregnant, and Byron, who was already cooling in his attitude toward her, received the news with indifference and a touch of petulant indignation. In spite of all the rumors that had been drifting back to England all summer, the Godwins did not know for certain of Claire's affair, so Mary and Shelley decided they would be forced to look after her and, if they could, conceal her baby from her mother and stepfather.

Mary was far more upset by the development than was Claire herself, and Shelley shared the moral indignation of his mistress. They admired Byron's mind and enjoyed his company, but they agreed that his moral standards were deplorable, and Mary indicated that she was not eager to renew the friendship with him at some future time. How differently she regarded his affair with Claire from her own relationship with Shelley, to which they so often referred as "a true marriage of true minds."

They left Geneva on August 29, and nine days later landed at Portsmouth. Mary, accompanied by her baby, the nursemaid and Claire, went straight to Bath, as they did not want to run the risk of exposing Claire to the gaze and questions of the family. Meanwhile Shelley traveled to London so he could look after his finances.

The sudden adjustment to life in England was not easy for Mary, who remembered countless details of the happy days in Switzerland. Now Claire was always at hand, complaining. The snubs Mary endured when she saw ladies and gentlemen she had known in the past were constant reminders that she had returned to the country where Shelley's wife and legitimate children lived. And the future was so unsettled that she didn't yet know where she, Shelley and little William would live. But one thing was all too certain: wherever they went, Claire would go with them.

Shelley completed his financial transactions, obtaining less than he had hoped to receive, yet generously giving the better part of the sum to Godwin, whose demands were endless. Then Mary and little William joined him, leaving Claire in Bath, and they spent two relaxed weeks at the country home of Shelley's good friend, Thomas Love Peacock, who was handling most of the poet's business affairs. It was during this period that Mary, who had always known very little of Shelley's finances, persuaded Peacock to tell her the truth of his situation, and she was shocked to learn that, as always, he was skirting the edge of ruin.

When they returned to Bath, Mary informed Shelley that she was taking the management of their money into her own hands, and that she intended to begin by practicing various economies. The very idea of a woman handling their finances amused Shelley, and perhaps he wanted to humor her, but Mary soon proved she was in earnest. She found a house that cost much less than the hotel in which they had quarters, she dismissed the nursemaid, and then informed the dismayed Claire, whose baby was due in January, that henceforth they would share the housework.

The autumn of 1816 soon became a tranquil time for Mary. She worked on *Frankenstein,* learned to cook and not only prepared meals but attended the chores that the lazy Claire neglected. She looked after William, who was becoming livelier each day, and she took drawing lessons. And in addition to all of her other activities she found the time to read even more books than Shelley. He, too, was happy and busy, his days filled with writing, reading and walking, and even Claire was fairly subdued, so she did not annoy him too much.

Suddenly, on October 9, Mary and Shelley received a note from Fanny, who had stopped at Bristol while supposedly making a journey to visit her aunts in Ireland. She wrote: "I depart immediately to the spot from which I hope never to remove." They sensed her desperation, and Shelley immediately went in search of her, following her from Bristol to Swansea, in Wales, where the trail ended abruptly. There Fanny had rented a room, and had been found the next morning, an empty bottle of laudanum still clutched in her dead hand. There he learned she had left a note to Godwin as brief as it was pathetic:

I have long determined that the best thing I could do was to put an end to the existence of a being whose birth was unfortunate, and whose life has been a series of pain to those persons who have hurt their health in endeavoring to promote her welfare. Perhaps to hear of my death will give you pain, but you will soon have the blessing of forgetting that such a creature ever existed as Fanny Imlay.

Mary was so shocked by her half-sister's suicide that she took to her bed, and Shelley gave vent to his own grief by writing a poem in memory of a departed friend. It was obvious to them, as it was to other members of the family, that Fanny long had felt unwanted. Her aunts in Dublin had not offered the teaching post she had sought, she had become little more than a servant in her stepfather's house, and her stepmother had given her no peace.

As soon as Mary recovered sufficiently to gather her wits, she wrote a letter of condolence to her father. Godwin had not been Fanny's blood relative, it was true, but he had acted as her father since she had been three, and had been his only link, other than Mary, with the departed Mary Wollstonecraft.

Godwin's reply was significant because it was the first communication of any kind that Mary had received from him since her elopement with Shelley. The letter's chill and Godwin's concern over the proprieties, apparently his only worry, speak for themselves:

> I did indeed expect it.
> I cannot but thank you for your strong expression of sympathy.
> I do not see, however, that that sympathy can be of any service to me; but it is best. My advice and earnest prayer is that you would avoid anything that leads to publicity.

Go not to Swansea; disturb not the silent dead; do nothing to destroy the obscurity she so much desired that now rests upon the event. It was, as I said, her last wish; it was the motive that led her from London to Bristol, and from Bristol to Swansea.

I said that your sympathy could be of no service to me, but I retract that assertion; by observing what I have just recommended to you, it may be of infinite service. Think what is the situation of my wife and myself, now deprived of all our children but the youngest; so do not expose us to those idle questions, which to a mind in anguish is the most severe of all trials. We are at this moment in doubt whether, during the first shock, we shall say she is gone to Ireland to her aunt, a thing that has been in contemplation. Do not take from us the power to exercise our own discretion. We shall hear again tomorrow.

What I have most of all in horror is the public papers, and I thank you for your caution, as it might act on this.

We have so conducted ourselves that not one person in our home has the smallest apprehension of the truth. Our feelings are less tumultuous than deep. God only knows what they may become . . .

The authorities in Swansea cooperated with Godwin by recording only that Fanny had been found dead; had they listed her as a suicide she would have been denied burial under English law. So Godwin's attempt to play down the tragedy was not as absurd as it appeared at first glance, and a few days later he acted in accordance with his own advice by writing to his friend Baxter that Fanny had been carried away by a fever she had contracted.

But as Godwin should have known, it was impossible to conceal the truth, and within a short time everyone who knew or had heard of the family learned that Fanny had done away with herself.

Mary and Shelley suffered in silence. Keeping their own

counsel and isolating themselves, they received few visitors, refrained from mentioning the tragedy in correspondence and said nothing outside the immediate family circle. Claire's reactions are unknown, but even if she wanted to talk, Mary and Shelley gave her no opportunity. She, too, stayed behind the closed doors of the house in Bath and communicated with no one.

Within a short time after Fanny's death a new, ugly rumor began to be heard. She had killed herself, it was said, because she had been in love with Shelley for years and had finally realized he had no intention of making her his mistress. No story could have been further from the truth. Fanny and Shelley had been acquainted since he had first visited the Godwin house, and had been friends who had corresponded from time to time in a desultory fashion, but they had never been intimate, and neither had ever displayed a strong personal interest in the other.

Common sense alone should have refuted the lie. If Fanny had truly been in love with Shelley, she well might have shown some reaction when he had eloped with her half-sister. But she had remained tranquil, and had been on the best of terms with them, although from a distance, when they had become settled in their domestic routines and were rearing their child together. But logic has rarely been a factor in the dissemination of malicious gossip, and those who considered Shelley depraved added another black mark after his name.

The dignity Mary and Shelley demonstrated in the face of the absurd charge was remarkable. A number of friends wrote, telling them the story, but they made no reply. Neither did they issue any statement or otherwise clarify the situation, and by treating the rumor with silence they apparently hoped to stifle it.

But the rumor did not die, and persisted for so long that some of Shelley's early biographers treated it with far greater seriousness than it deserved. There was a reason for the story's longevity, but Mary did not learn it until many years later, after the death of Shelley, her father and Mrs. Godwin. The startling truth of the matter was that the originator of the lie had been none other than Mary Jane Godwin.

Her motive had been self-protective rather than deliberately vicious. She had long known that a great many of her husband's literary friends were not fond of her, and were inclined to be critical of her harsh treatment of the children under the Godwin roof, particularly the daughters of Mary Wollstonecraft. It would seem she reasoned these prominent authors, reviewers and editors would blame her for Fanny's death, claiming that her nagging had driven the sensitive girl to her grave, and she hoped to ward off such an attack by striking first, creating a diversion that would direct attention elsewhere.

In spite of Mary's unhappiness, however, she allowed nothing to interfere with her work schedules or her other duties, and late in October she and Shelley began the study of chemistry together. It was at approximately this time that they began their lifelong friendship with Leigh Hunt, the editor of the liberal review, the *Examiner,* and his eminently practical wife, Marianne. Hunt had given Shelley's *Alastor* its most favorable review, and had the perspicacity to call Shelley and the even younger John Keats the two most promising poets in England. At the beginning of December Shelley met Keats at Hunt's house, and life seemed to be returning to normal.

For all practical purposes Harriet Westbrook Shelley no longer played an active role in the lives of Mary and Shelley, and there had been no mention of her in Mary's *Journal* for several months. They may or may not have known that in September she had sent her children to friends in the country, and leaving her father's house, had taken lodgings of her own. There has never been verification of Shelley's later claim that Harriet was forced to leave because of the jealousy of her sister Eliza. Shelley loathed Eliza, who despised him in return, and there can be little question that she was a cause of the failure of Shelley's first marriage.

It is unlikely that either Mary or Shelley had learned that Harriet had disappeared from her lodgings on the night of November 9 after writing a long letter to Eliza that made it clear she intended to commit suicide. In the letter she begged Eliza to take care of her children, saying she would be a better guardian for them than would her husband, to whom she referred as Bysshe. But the communication also made it abundantly clear that she still loved Shelley.

As far as is known, neither Mary nor Shelley ever saw this communication. They did not know, either, that Harriet's family and close friends instituted a search for her, but could find no trace of her.

On the morning of December 10 the body of a woman was seen floating in the Serpentine, in the heart of London, and a coroner's verdict, printed by the London newspapers of December 12, stated only that "a respectable woman far advanced in pregnancy" had been found dead in the Serpentine River. Care was taken to avoid any mention of suicide, but there were no marks of violence on the body of the deceased, and a valuable ring was found on one of her fingers, which made murder following robbery unlikely.

On December 15 Shelley received a letter from a friend in London telling him the shocking news that the drowned woman was Harriet. He and Mary immediately went out for a long walk to discuss the situation; both were primarily concerned about Harriet's children, and Shelley left at once for London to try to obtain custody of them.

Mary's reaction to the grave crisis revealed the depth of her love for Shelley, her courage and her firm desire to act in accordance with the principles she held dear. Her own emotions are evident in her correspondence with him during the trying days he spent in London. Her hand trembled, so she could not write the long letters he wanted, but she called him her "best love," and said, "To you do I owe every joy, every perfection that I may enjoy or boast of. Love me, sweet, for ever." She knew what others did not, that Shelley was badly shaken by the catastrophe, and that the calm facade he presented to his friends was only a pretense.

Repeatedly she urged him to bring Ianthe and Charles back to Bath with him. She already loved them tenderly, she declared, and William would be joined by an older brother and sister, so he would be served third at the table. "How very happy I shall be to possess those darling treasures that are yours," she told him, and in her eagerness to welcome the children she was already preparing appropriate quarters for them.

Nowhere in her correspondence did she let him see her own agitation, and she carefully refrained from telling him that, because of the tension, she could neither eat nor sleep. He needed her support, and she gave it to him unstintingly, without thought of her own situation. Apparently it did not occur to her, as it had not to Shelley, that the Westbrook family might try to prevent them from gaining custody of Harriet's children. Mary's indignation on Shelley's behalf was boundless when the situation was gradually revealed to them.

Shelley paid two calls on Harriet's father and sister, but they refused to see him, so he wrote a long letter to Eliza, which she did not answer. Although he did not yet know it, the Westbrooks were prepared to fight for Ianthe and Charles.

The way was now open for the marriage of Mary and Shelley, and both realized it from the time they learned of Harriet's death. They treated the subject in a completely matter-of-fact manner, each of them taking it for granted that they would marry in the immediate future. Shelley mentioned the matter briefly in his first letter to Mary from London, and in her reply she said only that she wanted the ceremony to take place in London, presumably so her father and stepmother could be present.

Out of the tragedy of Harriet's death a new chapter was about to begin in the life of Mary Wollstonecraft Godwin.

IX

SHELLEY RETURNED to Bath for Christmas, and three days later he and Mary traveled to London. Taking William with them, they went straight to the house on Skinner Street, where they explained their plans to the Godwins, whom Mary was seeing for the first time since her elopement. The family rift was healed without further ado, and Godwin accompanied Shelley on a quick trip to obtain a marriage license.

The wedding ceremony was performed on the following morning, December 29, 1816, at Saint Mildred's Church in Bread Street, with the Godwins acting as official witnesses. According to the letters Mary and Shelley wrote to Claire, whose advanced pregnancy, unknown even to her mother and stepfather, had forced her to remain behind in Bath, the change in Mary's status had a "magical" effect on their relations with her family. The close father-daughter relationship Mary had enjoyed with Godwin prior to her elopement was restored instantly, although William Godwin was no more effusive now than he had been in the past. Mrs. Godwin and Mary were civil in their approach to each other, but the young woman made no attempt to draw closer to the stepmother she had so long disliked. Godwin treated Shelley with a new courtesy and was almost jovial with him, making it clear that he regarded his son-in-law as an equal. Shelley said little to Mary Jane Godwin, however, finding it difficult to conceal his intense dislike for her. Both he and Mary were unable to relax in the house on Skinner Street because too many bitter memories made them uncomfortable.

The Godwins soon proved, however, that they could be as loyal in a time of stress as they had been implacable in their enmity, and they closed ranks behind Mary and Shelley in the battle that loomed over the custody of Shelley's older children. The fight began to take shape early in January, 1817, when Shelley, after escorting Mary and William back to Bath, returned to London.

Not waiting for Shelley to take action, the Westbrooks struck first, and on January 6 they filed a bill in the Chancery Court, asking that Eliza—or some other proper person —be named the legal guardian of Ianthe and Charles. They also requested that Shelley be restrained from taking custody of them at any time.

Their suit cited particulars to demonstrate Shelley's unworthiness as a father. He was an atheist and a radical revolutionist, the Westbrooks declared, and submitted a copy of *Queen Mab* to the court to prove it. They also outlined the details of Shelley's affair with Mary, claiming that he had deserted Harriet for her, and indicating, indirectly, that they held him responsible for his first wife's death.

Mary and Shelley were required to make an immediate decision. If they contested the Westbrooks' action the case would be noted in detail by the press, and the scandal of their affair would be revived. In his first letter to Mary after returning to London and learning of the action the Westbrooks had taken, Shelley said he wanted to fight, but indicated he would defer to Mary's wishes.

Her reply, which she sent the same day she received his letter, was uncompromising: "Nothing matters to me but those dear babes! The Westbrooks be damned, and damn the gossip that a fight will let loose. I cannot be hurt, save by a defeat that would take sweet Ianthe and Charles from us. I think of them as my own, and I long for them with a mother's tender passion."

Shelley tried to reassure her, saying he was answering the bill, but expressing confidence that the court would refuse to hear the Westbrooks' petition.

In the midst of the crisis, on January 13, Claire Clairmont gave birth to Lord Byron's child, a daughter. She named the baby Alba, after Byron's nickname Albè, but later changed her name to Allegra when he suggested it. The event was almost unnoticed, so great were the tensions over the Westbrooks' attempts to win custody of Ianthe and Charles.

Shelley filed his reply to his first wife's family on January 18. He had not abandoned Harriet, he asserted, but they had separated by mutual consent. Because of their children's tender years he had permitted them to remain with their mother, but now he wanted to rear and educate them, which was his prerogative as their father.

His confidence that the Westbrooks' petition would be dismissed without a hearing proved unjustified, and arguments for both sides were heard on January 24. The court reserved judgment, and Shelley, with Mary's assistance, began the preparation of a long defense of his political and religious beliefs. He also received considerable assistance from Godwin and Leigh Hunt in the writing and editing of this document.

The newspapers made the most of the case, further damaging the already soiled reputations of Mary and Shelley. Meanwhile the gossips went to work with a vengeance, and the members of the Godwin family, Claire included, contributed their fair share to the defense of Mary by attacking Harriet's good name. It was during this period that the rumors about Harriet's past began to circulate.

The most obvious weakness was her advanced pregnancy

at the time her body was found, and the paternity of her unborn child was attributed to a number of persons, Shelley himself among them, as well as to mysterious unknowns with whom she allegedly had consorted. It has also been claimed that she long had been mentally unbalanced, that she drank to excess and that she habitually used potent drugs. Literary detectives have worked for more than a century and a half without success to separate fact from fiction, but it is unlikely that the truth about Harriet's last months will ever be known.

Mary made no contributions to the rumors, but her attitude throughout the period of the crisis—and thereafter—remained unchanged. Harriet had lacked the stability of temperament necessary to insure Shelley's happiness, she wrote in a number of letters, and she resented the attempts being made by the ignorant and biased to represent the first Mrs. Percy Bysshe Shelley as an angel. Harriet had damaged Shelley enough, she said, and he deserved not only happiness but the right to gain custody of his children and bring them up in a way that would enable them to reap the benefits of his beliefs. Unyielding and firm in her resolve, Mary nevertheless refrained from climbing into the arena of combat and joining the mudslingers.

On March 27, 1817, after a wait of two months, the court announced its decision. It was clear, the court declared, that custody of Ianthe and Charles should not be given to their father, but it was stressed that his affair with Mary Godwin, which had since been altered by marriage, was not responsible. The judgment was made on the basis of his ideas, which the court deemed immoral. At the same time it was anything but clear that the Westbrooks should be given custody of the children. All concerned parties were invited to submit plans, and pending a final determination of the issue, Shelley was specifically forbidden to see the children. In order to expedite the matter, a master in chancery was directed to submit a specific plan that would deal with the maintenance and education of the children.

Mary was crushed by the court's adverse decision, and could take no pleasure in her new home at Marlow, Albion House, into which she and Claire had moved a month earlier with their children. In her later Notes to the *Poems* of 1817, she lived the bitter days again, and accurately reflected Shelley's feelings when she wrote:

> No words can express the anguish he felt when his older children were torn from him. In his first resentment against the Chancellor, on the passing of the decree, he had written a curse, in which there breathes, besides a haughty indignation, all the tenderness of a father's love, which could imagine and fondly dwell upon its loss and consequences. . . . [These poems] were not written to exhibit his pangs of distress to the public; they were the spontaneous outbursts of a man who brooded over his wrongs and woes, and was impelled to shed the grace of his genius over the uncontrollable emotions of his heart.

The question of the custody of Ianthe and Charles created problems for many years. The court rejected the guardians nominated by both Shelley and the Westbrooks, and they were placed in the care of a young clergyman and his wife who had children of their own. After Shelley's death the custody of Ianthe was awarded to Eliza Westbrook, who had married, and the girl appeared to enjoy a happy life with her aunt. As an adult she made a happy marriage of her own, and lived until 1876. Charles was given into the custody of Sir Timothy Shelley, who placed him, at the age of eight, in the same school where his father had been so unhappy. The child was physically delicate and emotionally sensitive, the rigors of boarding school life overwhelmed him, and he died at the age of eleven in 1826.

"Shelley never saw his two eldest children again," Mary wrote many years later. "His grief over their loss was never assuaged, nor was mine."

Work and an active social life were necessary to dull the sharp pain of the loss, and both Mary and Shelley were sensible enough to realize it. On their many visits to London they saw a great deal of Godwin's friends, among them the Hazlitts and Lamb, who made no attempt to hide his disapproval of Shelley. The friendship with Leigh Hunt ripened, and the Shelleys became the close friends of the entire Hunt family, including their large brood of children. They also established a solid relationship with Horace Smith, a sensible and wealthy banker who wrote light verse. But they were less successful in their attempts to find a rapport with John Keats, who was too shy to say more than a few words to Mary. Her brilliant conversational talents frightened him, and he was so overwhelmed by Shelley's intellect he was afraid he might lose his own identity if they pursued the relationship.

Life in England was marred by internal turmoil in 1816 and 1817. Prices were rising in an inflationary spiral, unemployment was widespread as veterans came home from the Napoleonic Wars, and the rapid spread of the Industrial Revolution added to the chaos. Riots erupted all over the country, and the government, becoming panicky, temporarily suspended the right of habeas corpus and tried to muzzle the press.

Mary and Shelley joined other liberals who challenged the government's actions, and although women usually stood apart from politics, Mary did not hesitate to express her views in pungent terms. Shelley went further and wrote a short pamphlet advocating government reforms. These activities won him the disapproval of Hazlitt, who admired his poems but thought him too radical. Hazlitt took care not to castigate Mary, however, and gallantly said he thought she was being influenced by her husband.

Albion House, the couple's new home at Marlow, also provided them with distractions. It was a large, rambling structure with many rooms, and the Shelleys worked hard to put it into shape. Servants were necessary to maintain it, so they rehired their Swiss nurse, then added a cook and manservant to the staff. Mary showed an unexpected talent for growing vegetables and flowers, and Shelley cut back the woods that were encroaching on one side of the house. A piano was purchased in London for Claire, and the secret of her baby's birth was so well kept that visitors believed the story she and the Shelleys told to the effect that Allegra was the daughter of a London friend who had been forced to make an emergency trip abroad.

Guests kept Mary busy as a hostess. The Godwins, who still didn't know that Claire was a mother, came for a stay of several weeks, and then the Leigh Hunts appeared with their four children, remaining for a month. On weekends other friends came from London, and the house was filled. Shelley had a new boat, often taking Mary and various guests for a sail, and each day the couple went out together for their regular walk.

But Mary managed to complete the manuscript of *Frankenstein* and copied it. Even her most severe critic, Mrs. Godwin, was compelled to admit she was attentive to little William and at no time neglected his health or welfare. And she continued to read extensively.

But the strain she had undergone as a result of the suicides of Fanny and Harriet had taken their toll. She was no longer the lively, exceptionally pretty girl she had been, and was not yet the serene beauty who would captivate everyone she met. She looked haggard, a number of friends and relatives noted in their correspondence, and for the first time in her life she was dressing carelessly, paying little or no attention to her appearance. She was often waspish, too, and the Hunts observed that she was highly critical of both Peacock and Hogg, calling the latter "a butterfly who has never had an original idea or philosophical notion, but who would like to pose, if he could, as a man of intellect."

Claire's presence frequently irritated her, too, but that was nothing new. They quibbled and quarreled as they had done for years, and since Byron did not want Claire to join him, it seemed likely that her problem would remain unresolved for a long time to come. Charles Clairmont paid a visit to Albion House, his mind filled with one of his many impractical money-making schemes, and tried to obtain a substantial loan from Shelley, who was in no position to offer him a penny. Charles was referred to his stepsister, and Mary became so annoyed that he accused her of resembling his mother.

The comparison with Mary Jane Godwin restored Mary's good humor, shocking her into the realization that she had been acting like a shrew, but she still had no interest in food and suffered from insomnia. Her relations with Shelley and their baby remained constant, however, no matter what her problems with others might be. She was depending on her husband as much as he was leaning on her, and sometimes asked him the plaintive question, "Ought we not to be happy?" On these occasions Shelley comforted her by listing their blessings, not the least of which was the legitimacy of their relationship. Although neither of them quite knew it, they were becoming increasingly orthodox in their personal views and actions, and no longer tried to live according to Godwin's precepts, although they continued to believe that mankind would benefit if those principles were adopted and utilized by society.

Early in the period that the family lived at Albion

House, Shelley developed a deep interest in the poor of the neighborhood, and on his walks began to carry a bag of coins so he could dispense money to those in need. He also formed the habit of giving away Mary's old clothes and his own, and sometimes made the mistake of getting rid of one of her infrequent recent purchases.

Mary remonstrated with him in vain, and could not convince him they were in no position to act like the lord and lady of the manor. She was finding it difficult to pay their own bills, and his largesse exasperated her, but she found it impossible to grow angry with him, and after an attempt to dissuade him failed, she usually burst into laughter, kissed him and called him the most generous of men.

The mistress of a large, busy household could not come and go as she pleased, so Mary usually remained at Albion House when Shelley went into London. They exchanged daily letters when he was absent, and he told her the details of his activities in town. Her own life was so full now that, she wrote, she envied him only his visits to the theater, which she had enjoyed since childhood. She had little to envy, however, since Shelley was bored by plays, and confessed to her that he preferred to read a drama than to watch it slowly unfold on a stage.

There was little doubt that the Shelleys enjoyed the benefits of life at Albion House. The poet wrote the longest of his works, *The Revolt of Islam,* while living there, and also completed the better portion of *Rosalind and Helen,* as well as turning out between twenty-five and thirty shorter poems. Mary began to cast about for the central theme of another novel, and in the meantime she tried her own hand at poetry, but thought so little of her efforts that none were published during her own lifetime. Her health improved, and early in the summer it became obvious that she was pregnant again.

The serenity of life at Marlow was threatened by the

appearance of familiar problems. Godwin was again in financial difficulties and came to his son-in-law for assistance, but Shelley, who had been advancing money to Hunt and had gone on several buying sprees in London, was himself in debt again. The continuing presence of Claire and her child under the Shelley roof was a source of embarrassment, and no relief was in sight.

Albion House, on which they had taken a twenty-year lease, began to lose some of its appeal, especially as the place cost more than the Shelleys could afford to pay for its operation and upkeep. "This house is very damp," Mary wrote to Mr. Baxter. "All the books in the library are mildewed, so I am afraid we must quit the place. But it will not be easy to terminate our lease, and we cannot afford to pay the entire sum. We have been thinking and talking of taking up permanent residence in Italy, where living is so inexpensive that we would pay only a small portion of our present expenditures. But there are so many obstacles to be overcome that I fear we may be indulging in an idle dream that may never be realized."

The troubles that were besetting the Shelleys undoubtedly contributed to their wanderlust, and Mary did not mention to Mr. Baxter that her husband was gripped by a new, totally unreasonable fear that made him think it might be necessary to flee to Italy. The victim of his own imagination, Shelley conceived the notion that the courts might try to take little William away from him and Mary. There was no basis in fact for this belief, and Mary tried in vain to persuade him that he was the victim of his own fears. Hunt, Peacock and Horace Smith were equally unsuccessful, and on occasion Shelley spoke of little else.

Then Mary was beset by troubles of her own. On September 9, 1817, she gave birth to a daughter, whom she and Shelley named Clara. Her delivery was easy, the baby was healthy and Mary quickly recovered her own strength, but she suffered the familiar symptoms of what a later generation would call a postpartum depression.

Mary realized her mental state was irrational, and tried to conquer it, but everything seemed to be going badly. London publishers were showing no interest in *Frankenstein*, William was suffering from a severe head cold, which his mother attributed to the dampness of the house, and Shelley, who was in London, wrote gloomy letters about his own financial situation. In spite of these obstacles, Mary recovered her spirits in ten days because she knew that she alone had the strength to hold her family together, as she later, in Italy, confessed to Maria Gisborne, her mother's close friend, who had taken care of Mary after Mary Wollstonecraft's death and had continued to look after her until Maria remarried several years later following the death of her own first husband.

X

Mary was opposed to Shelley's idea of moving to Italy on practical financial grounds, but by the end of September his health declined and she began to waver. In October he improved only sporadically, and seemed worse after each relapse. It is impossible, more than one hundred and fifty years later, to determine the extent to which his illness was imaginary, but the symptoms he displayed were acute, and caused Mary to become alarmed. He lost weight, he was lethargic, and when he tried to work he often fell asleep.

He visited several physicians in London, and they told him what he wanted to hear: the climate of rural England was too severe for him, and he would benefit immeasurably by a move to a warmer place. It is not surprising that, in November, his ailment became still worse.

Late in November, when Shelley went off for yet another visit to the physicians in London, Mary capitulated, writing to him: "When I see you, drooping and languid, in pain, and unable to enjoy life, then on your account I ardently wish for bright skies and Italian sun."

By the beginning of December they began to make their plans, and Shelley instructed his attorney to find some way to break the Albion House lease. Some of their difficulties were financial, and Mary spent long hours wrestling with figures. Godwin was demanding another loan, Hunt and Peacock were receiving regular payments, and it soon appeared unlikely that the Shelleys would receive more than a token refund of the twelve hundred pounds they had paid for Albion House. Shelley owed several hundred pounds to the Chancery Court for the expenses of the hearing, and would be sent to prison for contempt unless he paid in full before the end of the year. In addition the tradespeople of Marlow heard from the servants of the impending move, and began to clamor for the payment of bills that Shelley had allowed to accumulate.

Mary was reluctant to mention the move to her father, knowing he would make an unpleasant scene, so Shelley offered to tell him, but procrastinated when Godwin took umbrage, real or imagined, over a supposed slight to his wife. Mary dreaded the confrontation, and repeatedly urged her husband to end the suspense.

But Shelley had what he regarded as more important matters on his mind, and borrowed the sum of two hundred and fifty pounds from banker friend and literary admirer Horace Smith. The exasperated Mary told him, in a tart letter, that he was badly underestimating the extent of his debts. "You tell me the Italian sun will be the best physician. Be it so," she wrote. "But money, money, money!"

There was one bright note. Lackington agreed to publish *Frankenstein* and paid Mary an advance royalty of fifty pounds. She immediately added the money to the sum Smith had given Shelley, but it was not nearly enough to stem the tide. Mary spent an entire evening calculating, and estimated that they would require at least fifteen hundred pounds in cash to leave England.

Shelley, on one of his trips into London, was arrested by bailiffs at the instigation of an uncle, to whom he had long owed money, and spent two mortifying days in jail before Mary could send the thirty pounds necessary to obtain his release. By now Shelley was becoming desperate, but a lack of funds still tied his hands, and he wondered whether a move to the southern part of Kent might not serve as a substitute for a move to Italy.

A change in Claire's situation helped to bring matters to a head. She heard from Byron to the effect that he was willing to take custody of his daughter and provide for her support, and Claire, knowing there was no possibility of resuming her own relationship with him and realizing she was in no position to rear Allegra herself, was anxious to meet him in Italy and settle the details.

Mary, who well understood that she and Shelley would never be rid of Claire until provision was made for Allegra, decided that a move to Kent was out of the question. They would either go to Italy or they would stay at Albion House.

That settled the question, and Shelley went off to London again to raise fifteen hundred pounds in the only way he knew, by obtaining a loan from a post-obit broker, even though he had given his father his solemn promise he would never again sell a post-obit. Sir Timothy heard of the transactions his son was making, and a number of relatives and friends urged him to advance the money to Percy himself rather than cause complications for the entire estate at some future time.

The days passed, Christmas came and went, and both Mary and Shelley tried to pretend their problems did not exist. They followed their usual routines, reading and walking, and entertained more than usual. In January, Sir Timothy continued to temporize, so his son went to London, and completing his post-obit agreement, obtained the fifteen hundred pounds he so badly needed.

By this time Shelley finally realized that his so-called loans to William Godwin were the equivalent of throwing money into a bottomless pit. Even though his knowledge of financial matters was sadly lacking, the poet saw that his father-in-law knew even less, and that it was impossible for him to become solvent. Godwin's cold manner and insistence on finding slights where none had been intended were annoying, too, and Shelley decided to take a new approach.

Instead of giving Godwin the money he had promised, he handed him only half of that sum, and when the older man became insulting, Shelley made it clear to him that he was being helpful only for Mary's sake. If Godwin didn't like it, he could look elsewhere for funds. Mary was forced to agree with her husband's attitude, but continued to worry about her father, and even though she knew it was unfair to expect Shelley to accept the burden of responsibility for the Godwin family, she understood her father sufficiently well to know he would flounder if Shelley failed to offer him further assistance.

The proprietor of Albion House refused to refund any of the money that Shelley had paid for his long-term lease, but even Mary, who had been reluctant to leave without getting something in return, realized that she and her husband faced a clear choice. Either they would have to give up their move or write off the twelve hundred pounds they had paid for the house. Shelley was so anxious to go that she stifled her own misgivings and threw herself into the task of packing the belongings they had accumulated, including their furniture and several thousand books.

Early in February, 1818, they said farewell to rural England and went to London for the final month prior to their departure, taking lodgings on Great Russell Street. This period is noteworthy for two reasons: the Shelleys were so busy that, for the first time, they neglected their reading, and although they dined with many friends, they saw virtually nothing of the Godwins. Mary could never be indifferent to her father's welfare, but she was no longer emotionally dependent upon him, and she, even more than

Shelley, was responsible for the decision that it was better to avoid the Godwins than to spend a thoroughly unpleasant evening in their company.

The couple went regularly to the theater and the opera, they spent long hours in various libraries, and they twice went to the British Museum to view the Elgin Marbles. Then, on March 9, William and Clara were taken to church and christened, an act that surprised most of Shelley's friends, who knew he was fond of saying, "I do not believe in God Almighty and cannot accept the fact of His existence."

A number of scholars have felt that Shelley deliberately exaggerated his attitude toward religion because of the shocking effect his words produced in his listeners. Regardless of whether this notion is correct, he had little choice in the question of the children's baptism. Mary, who had paid her own lip service to her husband's brand of atheism, had no intention of taking William and Clara away from England for a prolonged stay until they were christened. She had not attended religious services since her stay with the Baxters in Scotland as a girl, and she belonged to no church, but when circumstances cornered her she was willing to admit her Christian convictions. Shelley knew she would pay little heed to his objections, so he made only a token protest, and then accompanied his wife to the christening.

Leigh and Marianne Hunt spent the better part of the afternoon of March 11 at Great Russell Street, and Mary Lamb, who was fond of Mary, sufficiently conquered her dislike of Shelley to pay a call. That night Godwin came to bid farewell to his daughter, son-in-law and grandchildren, but was not accompanied by his wife. Whether Mary Jane Godwin absented herself of her own volition or stayed away because Mary and Shelley had made it plain they did not want to see her is unknown.

Early on the morning of March 12 the party, which included Claire, her baby and two nursemaids, set out from London and traveled to Dover. There they caught a packet boat that picked up favorable winds, and the England that Shelley would never again see faded from view. That night they lodged at a hotel in Calais, and the next day resumed their journey, bypassing Paris in their eagerness to reach Italy as soon as possible.

After spending a week on the road, however, they were forced to halt for four days in Lyons because the children were unhappy and the adults, as a consequence, needed a rest. Claire had written a number of letters to Byron, but had received no reply from him, so at Mary's suggestion Shelley sent him a short letter to inform him they were coming to Milan.

The mountains of Savoy thrilled Shelley, but Mary wrote in her *Journal* that she felt there was something dreadful and ominous in the air when she traveled on the edge of an overhanging precipice that was sheathed from top to bottom in ice. The mammoth, perpendicular rocks at Chambéry fascinated Shelley, and five years later, when Mary was returning to England, she passed the same spot, which caused her to write in her *Journal* that "the dark high precipices towering above gave Shelley the idea of his Prometheus." So it is no exaggeration to say that this journey inspired the greatest of Shelley's poems, *Prometheus Unbound*.

On April 4 the party reached Milan, and there learned that Byron was in Venice, so Shelley wrote to him immediately to inform him of their arrival. The same day Mary, her husband and Claire went to see the cathedral, and that night they attended a performance of the opera. It was during this sojourn that the Shelleys formed the habit of engaging in intensive sightseeing whenever they came to a place they did not know.

They were in the vanguard of the English colony that settled in various parts of Italy during the nineteenth century, and their attitudes helped to set a precedent for those who followed them. When they were criticized for "taking a little corner of England with them wherever they went," Mary and Shelley admitted that the description was accurate. They were fascinated by ancient ruins and medieval buildings, they visited the graves of great literary figures of the past, and they sometimes dipped into the cultural life of a community, as they did when attending the opera in Milan. But they were indifferent to the local life around them, they showed no interest in the customs, food and clothing of Italians, and they developed a social life with fellow expatriates, rarely admitting Italians to their circle. It is said that, even after they had spent several years in Italy, Mary and Shelley were noticeable on their daily walks because their clothes and manners were completely English, and they made no concessions to local ways.

Certainly it did not occur to the nineteenth-century Englishman to adapt himself to the civilization of a foreign land in which he might be residing. He believed that everything English, the climate excepted, was superior to anything he found elsewhere.

Mary Shelley proved herself far more malleable than most of her compatriots of the period. She gained an appreciation of Italian cooking and not only bought native produce, but enjoyed eating it. Her long years of Latin study, combined with her talent for picking up foreign languages, enabled her to master Italian before setting out from England, and this proficiency soon proved to be of great value.

Two days after their arrival in Milan, Mary and Shelley went to Lake Como to look for a house they could rent for the summer, leaving Claire, the nursemaids and the children behind. They fell in love with the beauty of Como's scenery, as have the countless thousands of tourists who have followed them there, and after looking at several villas they found one they liked. They opened negotiations for it, and took lodgings at a small hotel.

The following morning, as they left for a walk after breakfast, Shelley was politely but firmly placed under arrest by the local constabulary. Not until he and Mary reached the court of the Como judge did they learn that he had broken a local law by carrying a pistol. Shelley insisted on representing himself at the hearing, in spite of his imperfect command of Italian, and managed to convey to the court his innocence of wrongdoing. It was obvious to the judge that the visitor knew nothing of local law, so he was released.

But the court refused to return his pistol, and Shelley became increasingly angry as he demanded his property. Mary, who had been amused by the incident, finally intervened when it became apparent that her husband might be charged with contempt of court if the altercation continued. She and the judge conversed easily in rapid-fire Italian, and Mary quickly understood the court's position.

Her husband, the judge said, did not look like a man who might commit a robbery, but it was possible he might want to put a bullet into his own head. Mary gravely assured the court she would not allow her husband to do away with himself, so the judge ordered the pistol given to this sensible young woman.

Thereafter the weapon was recognized within the family as Mary's property, although she never touched it, and Shelley, who was an excellent shot, always went through the motions of asking permission to use the pistol for the target practice he enjoyed. The elaborate joke remained a family ritual until the end of Shelley's life.

On April 12, with negotiations for the rental of the villa not yet concluded, Mary and Shelley returned to Milan, where they found Claire deeply disturbed. There had been no reply from Lord Byron to either of Shelley's letters, and Claire had been told by some English acquaintances who had just come from Venice that Byron was leading a profligate life there. Mary was shocked by the tales of sexual debauchery that Claire told, but agreed with Shelley that Byron should be invited to join them at Como. There seemed to be no other way to prod the somewhat older poet, so Shelley sent him a briefly worded but polite invitation.

Byron finally sent a reply that reached Milan ten days later, and his coldly hostile tone was a far cry from the friendship he had demonstrated for Mary and Shelley at Geneva. But it was his terms regarding the disposition of Allegra that shocked Mary. Byron agreed to take custody of his daughter and accept full responsibility, financial and otherwise, for rearing her, but only on condition that Claire would give up the child completely and would promise never to see Allegra again.

His terms, as harsh as they were unexpected, made Claire unhappy, but she indicated her willingness to accept them because, she believed, she had no choice.

Mary begged her to refuse, emphasizing that Claire would regret the abandonment of her child as long as she lived, and Shelley added his own arguments to his wife's. Some way would be found, the Shelleys said, to persuade Byron that he was being unnecessarily cruel, and in time he would soften his demands. Mary added that no power on earth could persuade or force her to part with her own children, and she begged Claire not to act too hastily.

Shelley sent a long letter to Byron, as dignified as it was cogent, that forcefully expressed his love of justice and his compassionate regard for humanity. He and Mary had formed a strong attachment to Allegra, and both were badly upset.

Everything seemed to go wrong at once, and negotiations for the Como villa collapsed, so the Shelleys changed their plans and decided to go to Pisa, where, they had been told, they could rent a villa for a small sum of money. They planned to leave Milan at once, and Claire, to whom suspense of any kind was intolerable, announced that she was accepting Byron's terms and would send Allegra to him before they set out for Pisa.

Mary fought the decision until she collapsed in hysteria, but Claire refused to change her mind, saying only that she hoped the passage of time would change Byron's attitude. One of the nursemaids departed for Venice with Allegra on the morning of April 28, and it was Mary rather than Claire who remained in bed all day, weeping.

XI

TORRENTS OF RAIN FELL on northern Italy in the spring of 1818, but Shelley seemed unaware of the sun's absence, and Mary noted in her *Journal* that his health was miraculously improved. She alone knew that his physical condition depended on his state of mind, but she was too wise to mention the obvious to him, and always rejoiced with him when he recovered his high spirits and energy.

The journey to Pisa required a week of travel, and at first glance did not appear to have been worth the effort. Pausing only for an overnight stay, the Shelleys and Claire pushed on to Leghorn, a bustling little seaport, which they also disliked. Mary called it "a stupid town," and Shelley wrote to Peacock that it was the "most unattractive of cities." All the same, they rented an apartment for four weeks, and after spending almost two months on the road, settled down to enjoy their respite.

Shelley, who refused to admit he was homesick, found Leghorn to his liking because English was spoken and understood there, thanks to the presence of a large number of British importing and exporting companies. Mary looked forward to the stay for a far more personal reason. The city was the home of Maria Gisborne.

Maria Gisborne was as lovely as Mary had imagined her, and, although reserved, had easy manners. For all practical purposes the older woman had been Mary's godmother, and within a very short time they established an intimate friendship. Mary had found a true mother-substitute who was happy to become her confidante.

John Gisborne, a retired merchant, was a quiet, unprepossessing man, and Mary was prepared from the outset to dislike him because, she reasoned, Maria had married him instead of Godwin. But he proved to be intelligent, sensitive and exceptionally good company, and both Mary and Shelley grew fond of him. His only apparent weakness was his tendency to spoil his stepson, Henry Reveley, a young engineer of about thirty. Mary found it impossible to converse with Henry, but Shelley became friendly with him because of their shared interest in science.

The Shelleys and the Gisbornes saw each other daily during the next month, and then, with Maria's help, they found a small villa in the Apennines at Bagni di Lucca, about fifty miles north of Leghorn, where they settled for the next nine weeks. That stay was one of the most pleasant and uneventful they had ever known, and they settled quickly into their routine of reading, studying and walking.

Claire became acquainted with several members of the English summer colony, and was underfoot far less of the time, which relieved the Shelleys. Mary complained in a letter to Maria that they had met no Italians and saw only other English couples, but she and Shelley made no attempt to break out of a familiar mold.

Mary's thoughts were turning to her work again, and after considerable thought she rejected the suggestion made by her father that she write a biography of Cromwell, the Lord Protector of England after the defeat and beheading of Charles I. She found Cromwell's personality cold and was irritated by his Puritanism, so she could not engender any enthusiasm for the subject, and instead started to prepare an outline for a play on the unfortunate Charles I, with whom she sympathized. Shelley, who had discovered, in Leghorn, a manuscript dealing with the life of a fascinating woman of the Italian Renaissance, Beatrice Cenci, urged Mary to write a play about her and the other members of the Cenci family.

Respecting her husband's judgment, Mary made the effort, and delved so deeply into her research that she became an expert on the story of the Cenci, but she was unable to share her husband's enthusiasm for the subject. Eventually she turned all of the material over to him, and he used this data as the basis for one of his most important and dramatic poems, *The Cenci.*

In mid-August Mary asked Mrs. Gisborne to visit her, writing that Shelley and Claire had gone to Venice on "important business." Lord Byron had already grown tired of keeping Allegra under his own roof, and had placed her in the home of the British consul, Belgrave Hoppner, and his warmhearted but scatterbrained Swiss-born wife. Claire believed the time had come even sooner than she had expected when Byron would be willing to soften his custody terms.

He proved himself surprisingly adamant, however, and capitulated only after a long meeting with a firm, persuasive Shelley. The first Mary learned of the matter was when she received an urgent letter from her husband, telling her that Byron had placed his villa at Este at their disposal, and was permitting Allegra to go there with Claire, provided the Shelleys were also present.

Even though John and Maria Gisborne had just arrived at Bagni di Lucca, Mary felt compelled to leave them there and set out at once, taking William and Clara with her. The baby was teething, and consequently was inclined to be fretful, but the Shelley children were accustomed to travel, and it did not occur to Mary to leave her daughter behind.

The heat on the road was suffocating, and as Mary was anxious to reach Este as soon as possible, she spent long hours on the road. By the time she reached Byron's villa, little Clara was suffering from a severe attack of dysentery. Mary immediately called in the local physician, and when he proved to be an incompetent bungler she sent for a more experienced doctor from Padua. By the time he finally arrived, Clara's condition was alarming. Mary, and Shelley, who had also arrived, sat up all night at their daughter's bedside, but by morning her condition appeared to be somewhat improved.

While the baby slept, Shelley worked on the first act of his ambitious *Prometheus Unbound,* and Mary labored on a translation of Monti's *Caio Gracco,* a project which she abandoned immediately thereafter and which subsequently was lost to posterity. Claire and Allegra arrived, and a few days later Shelley decided the time was ripe for a return to Venice. Byron, he thought, could be persuaded to change his harsh custody terms, and Mary agreed that she might be helpful if she joined the discussions.

Clara appeared to be completely recovered from her bout of dysentery, but Mary was reluctant to leave her behind with Claire, William and Allegra, so Shelley readily agreed that the baby should accompany them. After they passed the halfway point on their journey, Clara suddenly fell ill again, and declined rapidly. By late afternoon she was frothing at the mouth and suffering convulsions, and her parents were becoming frantic. Mary hurried with her to their hotel as soon as they reached Venice, while Shelley raced off to find a physician whom he had met on his previous visit there.

The hotel manager called in yet another doctor, but by the time Shelley and his physician arrived soon thereafter, the medical men agreed there was nothing they could do for the baby. Less than an hour later Clara Everina Shelley was dead at the age of one year and three weeks.

Consul Hoppner and his wife immediately took the dazed parents into their own home, a gesture for which Mary remained grateful for the rest of her life. The following day Clara was buried on the Lido, an island off the coast.

Noting the baby's death in her *Journal,* Mary could only comment, "This is the journal of misfortunes." She could not trust herself to write to anyone about the tragedy, leaving that difficult task to her husband. She suffered in silence, and did not commit her sorrow to paper until, shortly after Shelley's death, she included a stanza on Clara in a poem she called "The Choice":

> A happy Mother first I saw this sun,
> Beneath this sky my race of joy was run,
> First my sweet girl, whose face resembled his,
> Slept on bleak Lido, near Venetian seas.

A few days later the grieving couple returned to Este, and for the next few weeks they tried desperately to observe their normal routines. Mary kept even busier than usual by copying, for Byron, his *Mazeppa* and "Ode to Venice," which she had brought with her.

The spirits of the Shelleys could not have been improved by a letter of condolence Mary received from her father. Assuming his most remote, philosophical air, Godwin told her, "We seldom indulge long in depression and mourning, except when we think secretly that there is something very refined in it."

Mary's attempts to occupy herself did not help, and her sorrow became all-consuming. She withdrew so completely into an emotional shell that she rarely addressed Claire, communicated only infrequently with her husband and concealed her true feelings only when with little William. Shelley poured his own grief onto paper in a number of melancholy poems, but he needed, too, to reach out to Mary, and it disturbed him when she seemed unaware of his proximity and was cold to his touch. Apparently he did not realize her shock was so great that she was incapable of responding to anyone, even to him.

The months that followed the death of Clara produced the first and most serious rift in the marriage of Mary and Shelley. She was unable to rouse herself from her apathy, and the more frenzied he became, the more she withdrew. Each misunderstood and resented the other's self-protective gestures, but both were so overcome by their grief that they were powerless to alter their situation.

Some of Shelley's biographers have speculated that he had an affair with Claire at this time, and that the liaison was responsible for the rift. But the more authoritative scholars are agreed that this tale is totally lacking in substance. Their marital unhappiness in the autumn of 1818 was caused by their sorrow over Clara's death and their subsequent inability to communicate with each other.

Mary herself verified this analysis in the notes and comments that she appended to Shelley's poems in the years following his death. Her comments on this period reflect a sense of shame, and in a number of remarks she revealed to her readers that she had been unable to help Shelley at a time when he had needed her. Mary was the stronger partner in the marriage, and when her own emotions overwhelmed and numbed her, she could only think that she had failed her husband. Nothing in her words or in Shelley's poems and letters written after the tragedy even suggest that either of them thought it might be his duty to offer her emotional support at this critical time.

It was unfortunate that Mary insisted on returning to Venice in October to visit Clara's grave, and Shelley agreed to make the journey because their business with Byron regarding the custody arrangements for his daughter were not yet concluded. Mary's melancholy became even deeper after she had spent a day on the windswept sands of the

Lido, and talks with Byron proved unsatisfactory. He not only refused to change the custody agreement, but the Shelleys were so disgusted with the life he was leading that they blamed themselves for not having intervened more forcefully and prevented Claire from accepting the arrangement. Shelley expressed their mutual feelings about Byron freely in a letter to Peacock:

> He associates with wretches who seem almost to have lost the gait and physiognomy of man, and who do not scruple to avow practices which are not only not named, but I believe seldom even conceived in England. He says he disapproves, but he endures. He is heartily and deeply discontented with himself, and contemplating in the distorted mirror of his own thoughts the nature and the destiny of man, what can he behold but objects of contempt and despair? But that he is a great poet, I think the Address to Ocean proves. And he has a certain degree of candour while you talk to him, but unfortunately it does not outlast your departure.

Mary's nerves were so raw that she made something of a scene on the last night of their stay in Venice, when she cast aside discretion and good manners, and for the first time since Shelley had known her did not behave like a lady. The immediate cause of her wrath was Byron's current mistress, the blowsy wife of a baker who was known as "la Fornarina." Mary had seen her under Byron's Venetian roof a number of times, and presumably had addressed a few glacial words to her on occasion. But on this evening the woman's presence at Byron's table was too much for her.

She could think only that her baby daughter was lying in a grave a short distance away, while she was expected to dine with a creature who was the symbol, in her eyes, of all that was loathsome and degenerate in Lord Byron. Quietly at first, then with a rising voice, she refused to sit at the same table with la Fornarina, and an embarrassed Shelley was forced to take her back to their hotel. It might be noted in passing that Byron was not offended, but recognizing a virtuous woman, respected her all the more.

By early November Mary began to recover from her depression and Shelley became more stable. Perhaps they were inclined to forget their own miseries because Claire needed them. Byron insisted on Allegra's return, and Claire, whose guilts over her own daughter undoubtedly had been intensified by little Clara's death, was crushed. Mary and Shelley rallied to her support, and suggested new travels, which they were coming to regard as a cure-all, at least for the troubles of others. Besides, northern Italy was growing chilly, and they had decided to go south to Naples for the winter.

Mary and Shelley were becoming closer again, but their first moves were tentative, and as both of them were proud, sensitive people, they did not end their estrangement overnight. By December, certainly, they reestablished their emotional and spiritual intimacy, but subtle changes had taken place in their relationship. The suffering they had endured separately gave them a more mature appreciation of each other, and there was a sobriety in their mutual esteem and regard that was evident for the first time. It might not be too much to suggest that they were no longer infatuated with each other, and they themselves recognized that they were finding new depths in their relationship.

Gradually, as they regained their spirits and equilibrium, they resumed their correspondence with friends and relatives, and as they traveled south they gradually regained their enthusiasm and zest for life. Whether Claire benefited from the journey is more difficult to determine, and the notes she made in her diary were prosaic.

The party spent two days in Bologna visiting palaces and churches, and Shelley was so impressed by the paintings he saw that he could speak of little else. Mary thought the Velino Falls at Terni were beautiful beyond description, but their initial reaction to Rome was sour. A heavy rain was falling when they reached the city, an innkeeper tried to cheat them and it was late before they found satisfactory quarters.

The next morning the sun came out, and thereafter they spent a breathless week sightseeing, but did little else, as they planned to return to Rome for several months around the end of February. Then they continued their journey to Naples, and their first reaction to it was one of shock. People were forced to live under conditions that degraded humanity, Shelley wrote, and he and Mary were sickened by the poverty of the brawling, filthy city. But the scenery, he told Peacock in a letter, was "more delightful than any within the immediate reach of civilized man." They bought a carriage and a team of horses, and sightseeing became their principal diversion.

It may have been their only pleasure during January and February, 1819, which was one of the bleakest periods of their married life. Shelley's health was not good, and for once his complaint appears to have been legitimate. An English physician who was living in Naples treated him for internal disorders, and although his condition improved somewhat, he and Mary were forced to live quietly. They met literally no one during their Neapolitan sojourn, and when they were not venturing out on sightseeing expeditions they spent most of their time in the lodgings they had rented in one of the city's better neighborhoods.

They read incessantly, of course, and with time hanging heavily on their hands they wrote more letters than usual. Claire, who was beginning to realize that Lord Byron would never consent to a change in their custody agreement, was unusually subdued, and the frictions of living under the same roof with her were reduced to a minimum.

The quiet was disturbed only by a minor incident, to which neither Mary nor Shelley paid much attention at the time, but which was destined to create viciously unpleasant repercussions.

Two of the servants on their household staff at this time were a lady's maid named Elise, who had spent the better part of her time as a nursemaid, and a coachman, Paolo, who doubled as a man of all work. Elise came to Mary one day to say that she was pregnant and that Paolo was responsible. Mary, true to her own basic convictions rather than the theories to which she had paid lip service, insisted they marry and then discharged them. She and Shelley promptly forgot the couple, but would learn that Paolo carried a grudge and was determined to obtain revenge in his own way.

On February 27, 1819, Shelley performed an act that not even the most authoritative of his biographers have been able to understand, and the matter has remained something of a mystery down to the present. On that date he went to a Neapolitan magistrate, accompanied by two local citizens of stature, and signed a certificate stating that a baby daughter had been born to him and Mary on the preceding December 27. Later that day an infant was baptized in the parish of Saint Joseph under the name of Elena Adelaide Shelley.

The correspondence of both Mary and Shelley over a period of months proves beyond all reasonable doubt that Mary did not give birth to a child at that time. She made no mention of the baby in her *Journal,* and both she and Shelley were silent on the subject in their correspondence —except in their dealings with Maria and John Gisborne, in whom they confided. Compounding the mystery, the key letters on the subject that the Shelleys wrote to the Gisbornes vanished, although the rest of their correspondence was preserved.

From the remaining bits and pieces of the puzzle, principally in brief references to Elena Adelaide found in other letters that Shelley wrote to the Gisbornes, literary detectives have found a solution they regard as probable. According to this theory, Mary and Shelley were so upset by the poverty they saw around them in Naples that they wanted to make a personal gesture to alleviate the situation to the best of their limited ability.

Therefore they adopted a baby girl whose parents—and their connection with the Shelleys—are still unknown. It has been argued that the Shelleys were planning to return to England at some future time which they had not yet determined, and intended to bring their adopted child with them. It must be remembered that Shelley was bitter because of the loss of his two children by Harriet to the Westbrook family. Some of his biographers claim that little William and Clara were baptized before the family's departure from England in order to make it more difficult for the Lord Chancellor to take these youngsters from them, an act that Shelley feared. By claiming that an adopted baby was their own child, Mary and Shelley presumably believed they were making their legal position more secure.

Later events must be mentioned here, at least in passing. In the summer of 1820 Elise and Paolo went to Mrs Hoppner, the wife of the British consul in Venice, and told her a story to the effect that Claire Clairmont had given birth to Shelley's child in Naples, *without Mary's knowledge*. According to this highly improbable tale, the baby was then smuggled into an orphanage, and Shelley promptly adopted her, claiming that he and Mary were the parents.

Inasmuch as Claire was living with the Shelleys, credulity is strained to the breaking point if this story is taken at face value. Had Claire been pregnant, Mary would have known it. Other facts also indicate that the fanciful tale was the product of a disgruntled couple's vengeful imagination. Claire, who had already lost her daughter Allegra to Lord Byron, would not have ignored a second child, but she showed no interest in Elena Adelaide, and may never even have seen the child.

Mary and Shelley were still grieving over the tragic death of little Clara, and well may have wanted to adopt a new baby daughter in order to compensate, at least in part, for their loss. This would have been in keeping with their characters, and would have been a natural act for them to have performed.

Various theories have also been advanced for the next move in the mysterious drama. The Shelleys left Naples on February 28, a scant twenty-four hours after Shelley had gone to court and had the baby baptized. Elena did not accompany them, but was left behind with a family of substance living at 45 Vico Canale, and thereafter Shelley provided the funds for the infant's care. It is difficult to read sinister implications into the fact that they did not take Elena with them. On the contrary, they had learned to their everlasting sorrow that it was dangerous to travel with a very small child in a land where sanitary conditions were not up to English standards. So it makes good sense to assume that Mary and Shelley left Elena with people competent to look after her, and intended to return for her some months later, when she would be better able to tolerate the rigors of the Italian roads.

The precise plans the Shelleys had in mind have never been known, and probably will never be discovered. Baby Elena Adelaide Shelley died a few months after her birth during one of the epidemics that raged through Naples periodically during the early nineteenth century, as they had for so many hundreds of years. So Mary and Shelley never saw her again after their departure from the city at the end of February, 1819, and the secret of her story, along with that of the intentions and hopes of her foster parents, died with her.

The silence of Mary and Shelley after Elena's death cannot be regarded as significant, either, if it is remembered that no one outside the immediate family, with the exception of Maria and John Gisborne, had ever learned of her existence. Too long and complicated an explanation would have been required had Mary and Shelley written to others about the infant's passing.

The significance of Elena's brief role in the lives of Mary and Shelley is difficult to determine. Certainly the breach that had separated them after the loss of little Clara was completely healed by the time they left Naples. And, as will be seen, posterity owes a debt of gratitude to Elise and Paolo for their lie to Mrs. Hoppner, because the crisis caused by that incident demonstrated, beyond all doubt, the depth of Mary's love for Shelley and of his for her.

XII

ROME WAS FAR MORE to the liking of Mary and Shelley than Naples, and after settling into lodgings there on March 5, 1819, the tempo of their lives increased. They went sightseeing with the energy and determination of the American tourists who would follow them to Italy a century later, and they saw a great deal of various members of the English colony, among them Sir William Drummond, a distinguished archaeologist and diplomat. They also became friendly with a patrician Roman lady, Signora Marianna Candida Dionigi, at whose weekly salon they enlarged their circle of acquaintances. Mary demonstrated that she had recovered her spirits by writing to Mrs. Gisborne that the Roman lady was "very old, very miserly and very mean, but a center of intellectual culture in Rome, and able to gather many strangers to her conversazioni."

Shelley's health improved, and he began writing poetry again, but Mary discovered she was too restless to concentrate on her writing, even though the success of *Frankenstein* was bringing her an unexpected income that would taper off somewhat but would continue for the better part of her life. She sought another outlet for her energies, and Shelley encouraged her to develop her natural talent for painting, about which she knew nothing. So they engaged a drawing master, and she spent two hours each day at lessons, then set up her easel and worked for several hours more.

One afternoon in late April, when Mary and Claire were driving through the Borghese Gardens, they saw a woman whom Mary recognized. She was Amelia Curran, a talented amateur painter, whose father, John Philpot Curran, the Irish patriot and philosopher, was one of William Godwin's close friends. The acquaintance with Miss Curran was renewed, and soon ripened into a close friendship. In the weeks that followed, Amelia Curran not only encouraged Mary's painting, but herself did portraits of the Shelley family. That of Mary is the only known painting of her during this period, and the family treasured her portrait of little William. That of Shelley proved less successful and was abandoned, but Miss Curran completed it after the poet's death, and it is the only painting of him made during his last years that has survived.

The Shelleys planned to return to Naples in May for Elena, whose untimely death caused them to think in terms of moving to the north of Italy for the summer. Mary was pregnant again, and placed herself under the care of a Dr. Bell, an English physician living in Rome. Then, on May 25, little William fell ill, but he was a robust child who had always enjoyed good health, and the following day he appeared better. On May 27 his fever subsided, and Dr. Bell allowed him to leave his bed; but on June 2 his fever returned, and the physician was forced to make repeated visits to him that day.

For the next seventy-two hours Mary was too busy to record entries in her *Journal*. A brief note she sent to Mrs. Gisborne on June 5 speaks for itself:

> William is in the greatest danger. We do not quite despair, yet we have the least possible reason to hope. Yesterday he was in the convulsions of death and he was saved from them—yet we dare not, must not hope.
> I will write as soon as any change takes place. The

misery of these hours is beyond calculating. The hopes of my life are bound up in him.

William died on June 7 under the gaze of his helpless, exhausted parents, who had spent more than sixty hours at his bedside without sleep or rest.

Three days later the childless Shelleys, accompanied by Claire, left Rome for Leghorn, and Mary made an entry in her *Journal:* "Begun July 21, 1816. Ended with my happiness June 7, 1819."

The double blow of her daughter's death, followed by that of her son, left her dazed. Shelley sent a brief letter to Hogg, telling him of the tragedy, and after remarking vaguely that his own health had deteriorated again under the strain, added, "Mary bears it, as you may naturally imagine, worse than I do."

Mary found herself scarcely able to function. When she tried to read her eyes filled with tears and she could not concentrate on the printed page. When she tried to paint her hand trembled so violently that she could not hold the brush in her fingers. Late in June she tried to express her feelings in a letter to Amelia Curran:

> I no sooner take up my pen than my thoughts run away with me, and I cannot guide it except on *one* subject, and that I must avoid. . . . I never shall recover that blow; I feel it more now than at Rome, the thought never leaves me for a single moment; everything on earth has lost its interest for me.

Forty eight hours later she wrote to Marianne Hunt in a similar vein:

> We went from England comparatively prosperous and happy; I shall return broken hearted and miserable. I never know one moment's ease from the wretchedness and despair that possess me. May you, my dear Marianne, never know what it is to lose two only and lovely

children in one year—to watch their dying moments, and then at last to be left childless and for ever miserable. It is useless complaining and I shall therefore write only a short letter, for as all my thoughts are nothing but misery it is not kind to transmit them to you.

Shelley's grief was almost as great as his wife's. He had learned from the rift that had followed the death of Clara, and tried to reach out to her, but she seemed unaware of his touch. He expressed his despair in a poem that was not published until many years after his own death:

> My dearest Mary, wherefore hast thou gone,
> And left me in this dreary world alone?
> Thy form is here indeed—a lovely one—
> But thou art fled, gone down the dreary road,
> That leads to Sorrow's most obscure abode;
> Thou sittest on the hearth of pale despair,
> Where
> For thine own sake I cannot follow thee.

William Godwin, too inhibited to reveal his own inner feelings, wrote to his daughter in a philosophical vein:

> Remember . . . though at first your nearest connections may pity you in this state, yet that when they see you fixed in selfishness and ill humor, and regardless of the happiness of everyone else, they will finally cease to love you, and scarcely learn to endure you.

Shelley didn't know whether she grasped the meaning of her father's words, but he refused to allow himself to sink into despondency. He devoted himself to the completion of *The Cenci,* on which he had been working without interruption since March, and at his request Mrs. Gisborne began to teach him Spanish. He planted a garden, although the season was advanced, and tried to coax

Mary into helping him grow cabbages, celery and Indian corn.

The efforts of Shelley, Godwin and the warmly sympathetic Maria Gisborne had no effect, or so it seemed, but Mary had also learned from the earlier death of little Clara that her marriage and sanity were at issue. Literally nothing is known of the hard battle she waged within herself to conquer the feeling of despair that overwhelmed her, but she knew that for her husband's sake, her own and that of the new baby she was carrying, she had to fight.

On August 4 she took an unused, bound notebook from a supply shelf, and demonstrating a courage whose cost no one else would ever know, she made her initial entry in a new *Journal:*

> I begin my Journal on Shelley's birthday. We have now lived five years together; and if all the events of the five years were blotted out, I might be happy; but to have won, and then cruelly to have lost, the associations of four years is not an accident to which the human mind can bend without much suffering.

Immediately thereafter she and Shelley resumed an active life together, but their routines were somewhat changed. Neither was capable, as yet, of sustaining long hours of solitary reading, so they read Dante's works aloud to each other. Their reserves of stamina were depleted, they discovered; they temporarily abandoned their habit of taking long, daily walks, and contented themselves with brief strolls around the garden of their rented house. Their social life was more active than ever before, although restricted to a few friends, and they spent almost every evening with the Gisbornes. Shelley required less outside companionship than Mary, but he recognized her need and unselfishly saw the Gisbornes nightly. Mary, in return, was aware of all he was doing for her, and went out of her way to make certain that nothing interfered with the last stages of his work on *The Cenci.*

The greatest difference between the relations of the couple after the death of Clara and that of William is that the former caused severe, although temporary, damage to their marriage, while the latter brought them closer together. This process was speeded, inadvertently, by a blundering letter, completely lacking in diplomacy, that William Godwin wrote to his daughter.

Shelley had written privately to Godwin, telling him of Mary's despair and asking for any advice the older man could give that might be of specific, practical help to her. Godwin elected to send his reply direct to Mary, and complained bitterly about her husband, who, he claimed, still owed him financial assistance. A wildly indignant Shelley explained the situation in a letter to Leigh Hunt:

> The *very* next letter, received yesterday, and addressed to her, called her husband (me) "a disgraceful and flagrant person," tried to persuade that I was under great engagements to give him *more* money (after having given him £4700), and urged her if she ever wished a connection to continue between him and her to force me to get money for him.
>
> He cannot persuade her that I am what I am not, nor place a shade of enmity between her and me, but he heaps on her misery, still misery. I have not yet shown her the letter—but I must. I doubt whether I ought not to expose this solemn lie; for such, and not a man, is Godwin. But I shall, as is our custom (I mean yours and mine), err on the side of patience and endurance.

Shelley found still more ways ot show his consideration for his suffering wife, and distracted her from her misery by consulting her on every step in his writing of *The Cenci.* It was her research that had made it possible for him to write the play, and he not only sought her expert help but deferred to her opinions. The play was finished in the latter part of August, and soon thereafter Mary's thoughts were turning from the tragic past to hopes for a brighter future. In September, with her new baby due in about two months, she wrote to Marianne Hunt asking for a long list of infant's clothing unavailable in Italy.

Charles Clairmont came to Leghorn in September, and his visit also helped Mary to forget her troubles. Her step-brother always had financial problems, but he was an exceptionally cheerful young man, and was endowed with a quick wit similar to Claire's, but lacking the cynical bitterness she usually displayed.

Charles was on hand when the Shelleys decided to move to Florence for the winter, the new change dictated by the fact that Dr. Bell, "the only physician in Italy we trust," as Mary wrote, was going to be there for the next six months. Shelley and Charles went ahead to Florence to obtain accommodations, then returned to Leghorn for Mary and Claire.

The party stayed overnight in Pisa on their two-day journey, and the stop was important because it enabled Mary to form a new, close friendship with a woman much nearer her own age than Mrs. Gisborne. Mary's mother had been the tutor and idol of a young aristocrat, the daughter of Lord and Lady Kingsborough, who had become Lady Mountcashell after her marriage. Long separated from her husband, she had for many years been living with George William Tighe, the son of an Irish Member of Parliament. Calling themselves "Mr. and Mrs. Mason," they had two daughters, were established in Pisa and were almost universally accepted by members of the English community in Italy.

Mrs. Mason was a tall, exceptionally handsome woman, and was known for her blunt speech, hatred of sham and practical outlook on life. Her commonlaw husband was a man with a penetrating mind, who regarded the world through calm, sane eyes. Some of their acquaintances thought of them as mildly eccentric because, in spite of their wealth, they thought so little of clothes that they dressed carelessly, and on occasion had been mistaken for peasants when taking a constitutional on country roads.

Maria Gisborne, who was more of a substitute mother than a friend, had been Mary's only confidante in Italy, and she needed another, someone whose views were closer to her own. She and Mrs. Mason established an immediate rapport, and Shelley, who was almost always reserved with strangers, struck up a friendship with Mr. Mason.

The Masons soon proved their value to their new friends. They sent Shelley to a Florentine physician whose treatment restored him to the best health he had known in years. They convinced Claire it was urgently important for her and for the Shelleys that she develop a life of her own, apart from theirs. And Mrs. Mason, writing a letter that minced no words, told Mary that unless she overcame her melancholy before the birth of her new baby, she would jeopardize the infant's health if she tried to nurse it. The advice stunned Mary, which had been Mrs. Mason's intent, and she successfully redoubled her efforts to improve her state of mind.

Shelley wrote the bulk of his greatest work, *Prometheus Unbound,* in this year, 1819, and although Mary made no active contribution of her own intellect to it, her husband shared his concepts with her from day to day as he wrote it. Consequently she was in a position to make a unique contribution of her own to posterity, which she did in the notes she wrote to the edition published after his death. She provided clues of enormous value to later generations when she revealed that his imagery, which had been criticized as abstruse, was based on the works of Sophocles. The imagery of Shelley's masterpiece was not vague, she declared, but subtle, and required a mind as subtle and penetrating as his own to grasp his many meanings.

If Mary erred in her notes, it was on the side of conservatism. Critics have admitted that she understood the work better than any of her husband's other contemporaries, but they have charged her with a failure to comprehend the enormous scope of his achievement. It can only be argued, in rebuttal, that as Shelley's wife, endowed with an independent mind of her own, she was guilty of no literary crime other than that of presenting her husband's work with modesty. It has been said that, like Shelley himself, she preferred to let the reader of *Prometheus Unbound* explore the breadth and depth of its author's philosophical and metaphysical vision.

Mary erred only in her belief that *The Cenci* was her husband's finest work and therefore was superior to *Prometheus Unbound,* an opinion posterity has not shared. Her evaluation was not owing to a critical weakness on her part, however, but to other factors. Her own mind had long been suffused with the philosophical doctrines of Godwin, which Shelley used as the base for his own thinking, so it was natural for her to think that *The Cenci,* with its scrutiny of evil in the human soul, was the more original. And, having engaged in the historical research that had made it possible for him to write *The Cenci,* she had developed an absorbing and abiding interest in the subject matter.

Seen from the perspective of Mary's own story, the importance of her fascination with her husband's writing in 1819 cannot be overemphasized. During the long months in Leghorn after William's death, followed by a stay of several months prior to the birth of her new baby in Florence, where they knew no one, she read only Shelley's poems. Unable to concentrate on other reading, she was able to regain her perspective and her emotional health by inundating her mind with the work of the man whose intellect she respected above all others.

Aware of her debt to him, she spent the rest of her life repaying it.

XIII

"I HAVE not kept my journal all this time," Mary wrote on December 31, 1819, "but I have little to say all this time except that in the morning of Friday, November 13th little Percy Florence was born. . . . I now begin a new year—may it be a happier one than the last unhappy one."

Mary, who had not been able to shed her superstitions, believed that the omens were favorable. She gave birth to her new son after a labor of less than two hours, and the baby was robust, perfectly formed and cheerful. She even insisted her son had been born on November twelfth rather than Friday the thirteenth, a date which Shelley wrote on the baptismal certificate when Percy Florence was christened by an Anglican clergyman late in January, 1820.

For the first time since little Clara's death Mary was truly happy, and when the baby was awake she spent most of her time with him. She even luxuriated in a lazy way of life completely alien to her, and somewhat to Shelley's surprise she neither read extensively nor allowed herself to feel guilty because she could take no interest in books. She had not lost her ability to look at herself with humor, however, and a few weeks after Percy Florence came into the world she wrote to Mrs. Gisborne:

> Study I cannot, for I have no books, and I may not call simple reading study, for Papa is continually saying and writing that to read one book without others beside

you to which you may refer is mere child's work. But still I hope now to get on with Latin and Spanish.

Mary's idea of what she called simple reading was not like that of people who lacked her intellect and training, of course. Her *Journal* indicates that she was reading the works of Livy, Byron's *Don Juan*, the Books of Proverbs and Ecclesiastes, Bernard de Mandeville's *Fable of the Bees,* a history of Mexico and, with Shelley, a number of Shakespeare's plays. In addition, strictly for the pleasure of the mental exercise it afforded her, she translated into English those metaphysical works of Spinoza which had been written in Dutch.

Claire, who was following Mrs. Mason's advice, was absorbed in singing lessons and was creating a somewhat separate social life of her own in the English colony of Florence, so she was causing less friction with Mary than formerly. The atmosphere in the Shelley household was so improved that Mary sent an invitation to Leigh and Marianne Hunt, asking them to come to Italy for a visit. She also conquered her dislike of Peacock and Hogg sufficiently to make no protest when Shelley sent them similar invitations.

But she drew at least a temporary line when her husband suggested that William and Mary Jane Godwin come to Florence for a visit. Shelley, who was still annoyed with his father-in-law, nevertheless knew Mary was worried because of Godwin's continuing financial difficulties, and was particularly concerned because it appeared that he could no longer afford his Skinner Street office and home. So a trip to Italy might provide a respite from his unending financial problems.

Mary not only despised her stepmother, a feeling that had not abated through the years, but was afraid that Godwin's presence in Florence might create new troubles. She asked the advice of Mrs. Mason, who had become well acquainted with Godwin before moving to Italy, and received a typically blunt reply. Her father, Mary was told, was a man whose feelings of inferiority were so marked that a trip abroad would aggravate them. In order to restore his inner balance he would behave like a tyrant and would create new unhappiness not only for himself but for the Shelley family, too. So, for her own sake as well as her father's, Mary was urged to extend no invitation to the Godwins, whose dissatisfaction with their lot would be less intense in England than it would be in Italy as the guests of a daughter who had outgrown them and a son-in-law whose relations with them were badly strained. Mary showed the letter to Shelley, and the question of extending an invitation to the Godwins did not arise again.

As it happened, Shelley was in no position to give any additional financial help to his father-in-law unless he returned to England and increased his own indebtedness. The young boating enthusiast had no cash to spare, thanks to a venture that, he was convinced, would earn him a fortune. Steamboats were responsible for a revolution in water transportation in England and America, and in Italy, too, there was a growing excitement, even though there was little industry in the country. So Shelley invested two hundred pounds, perhaps a larger sum, in a steam engine invented by Mrs. Gisborne's son, Henry Reveley. Shelley could ill afford the gesture, which forced Mary to curtail her household expenses, but he was an incurable optimist who dreamed of profits, and was convinced they would earn vast sums of money within a few months.

But the steam engine proved to be a severe drain, and Shelley was compelled to make further investments in it to protect what he had already advanced. Mary's careful stewardship of their resources, combined with the *Frankenstein* royalties she had earned, had kept the family out of serious financial difficulties during their entire Italian sojourn, but Shelley's sponsorship of Reveley created problems too serious to ignore.

So Mary tightened the purse strings. Shelley could no longer pour money into the steam engine, and at her instigation he requested a return of some sort on what he had already put into the enterprise. But Reveley was encountering troubles of his own. His engine needed modifications that required infusions of additional capital, and it became evident to Mary, if not to Shelley, that he would fail.

Wanting to salvage something from the collapse of the dream, Mary hoped the equipment could be sold. But Reveley refused to dismantle his engine, and when his mother supported his decision, a new coolness crept into the relationship of the Shelleys and the Gisbornes. They remained friends, and eventually they patched their differences, but the intimacy the two families had enjoyed until this time was not restored.

In spite of their concern about money, however, Mary and Shelley gradually drifted into the routines to which they had been accustomed. The poet wrote his "Ode to the West Wind" and a number of short works, and Mary began to think about the germ of an idea for a new novel. She often accompanied him on his rambling walks, but returned early to their lodgings. The loss of her two elder children made her determined to protect Percy Florence at all costs, and she refused to leave the baby in the care of a nursemaid for more than an hour or two at a time.

Claire spent most of her evenings and many afternoons with her new friends in the English colony, but the social life of the Shelleys was far more restricted. They had a number of acquaintances in Florence with whom they occasionally exchanged visits, but they had no real friends in the community. This suited Shelley, whose self-sufficiency would have enabled him to lead a hermit's existence, but Mary, whose need for outside diversions was greater than his, felt a real sense of deprivation.

She made no attempts to enlarge their circle, however, or to involve them in a more active social life. With the possible exception of Leigh Hunt, she alone recognized her husband's stature as a poet, and she shielded him as fiercely as she protected her baby. The weather was the coldest Florence had known in years, and Shelley, who hated raw winds and low temperatures, became nervous and irritable. But Mary continued to soothe him, refused to be drawn into quarrels and showed no jealousy when young girls who regarded Shelley as a romantic, almost mysterious figure made a fuss over him.

One of these young ladies was Miss Sophia Stacey, the ward of one of Shelley's uncles, who came to Florence for the winter. She was so enamored of the poet that she and her traveling companion took rooms directly above the Shelleys' lodgings, and whenever Mary declined to accompany her husband on his walks, Miss Stacey went with him. She was an attractive young woman who had studied singing and had a well-trained voice, but her obvious adoration of Shelley and his equally apparent interest in her did not bother Mary. The girl's education had been typical of the upper reaches of the middle class, and although she appeared well informed on many subjects, Mary knew that her intellect was feeble and that, as a consequence, Shelley soon would be bored by her company.

Shelley addressed a number of lyric poems to Miss Stacey, just as he later wrote others hailing two other young women who would play even larger roles in his life. The beauty of his lines caused a number of his early biographers to question his fidelity to Mary, and, after his death, one of the objects of his inspiration deliberately misinterpreted his ardor and let it be known that he had been in love with her. But Mary was under no misapprehensions regarding the real state of his affections.

As her *Journal* and her correspondence with several friends after Shelley's death make abundantly clear, she recognized the difference between a genuine emotional involvement on Shelley's part and the intellectually idealized worship of pure beauty for its own sake that appeared in his poems. Sophia Stacey meant nothing to him as a person, and he actually found her a rather dull companion, but at the same time, in his own mind and writing, he could hail the feminine qualities she theoretically represented. Shelley, the man, knew that Miss Stacey was anything but perfect; Shelley, the poet, chose to ignore her imperfections, and for the sake of his poetry elected to pretend that she was endowed with great beauty and grace.

Nowhere did Mary Shelley better demonstrate her own extraordinary virtues than in her complete comprehension of her husband's attitude and approach to other women. Aware of the depth of his need for her alone, she realized what many of Shelley's contemporaries and subsequent biographers failed to grasp: the young women he idealized in rhapsodic verse were not Mary's rivals for his affections. Like the west wind and the skylark, they were impersonal objects, beings or forces to be glorified for their own sake. In brief, they were no more and no less than grist for a poet's mill.

Claire, who lacked Mary's insight into the personality of Shelley, warned her stepsister to beware of his seeming interest in Sophia Stacey, and pointed to his poems as proof of her contention that he was becoming involved with her. But Mary paid no attention to the supposed threat, and years later, in her correspondence with Edward John Trelawny, who liked to be called the "discoverer" of Shelley and Byron, she clearly expressed her thoughts on the subject:

Jane well knows that Shelley had no romantic interest in her, and seeks to increase her own fame through his growing fame. He was no more in love with her than he was with Sophia and Emilia before her. All three, together with several others, were but *symbols* to him, and the essence of their being was admired, extolled, worshipped, but always from a distance. I only regret that Jane cannot comprehend the meaning of Shelley's lines to her, for in them she will win immortality far greater than she will achieve in her own mean lifetime.

This understanding made it possible for Mary to send Shelley off for a long walk with Sophia Stacey, and to greet him with equanimity on his return. She happily accepted Sophia's invitation to Christmas dinner, and may have been privately amused when the girl complained to her, later that day, that Shelley had been silent and withdrawn during the festive meal. Mary could have told the younger girl that he often pulled into a shell when he was bored by the company of those who were not his intellectual peers.

In the main, however, Shelley's behavior was gracious toward the young women who admired him. When Sophia and her companion left for Rome at the end of the year, he gave her a warm letter of introduction to Signora Dionigi. Mary was equally pleasant, and sent letters to several other members of the English colony in Rome, asking them to extend their kindness to the young visitor.

Elise, the domestic servant who had been dismissed, came to Florence in January, 1820, with her husband Paolo and paid a call on the Shelleys. Mary treated her with every courtesy, and although her sense of principle would not permit her to rehire the couple, she nevertheless wrote a strong recommendation for them to Henry Reveley, who was looking for a pair of servants. It was only a few months after this visit that Elise caused so much trouble for the Shelleys, telling the story that, although a fabrication, has survived for more than a century and a half.

By January Mary went to work in earnest on a new book. It was to be called *Castruccio,* and she planned it as a novel "illustrative of the manners of the Middle Ages in Italy." She concentrated on her research, and studied more than fifty books in preparation for her own writing, which she began that spring. She was dissatisfied with her efforts, however, and by the following summer she abandoned the project. No copies of her original manuscript are extant, but her research did not go to waste, and in later years she used much of the material in the second of her published novels, *Valperga.*

The weather grew still colder, and by mid-January Shelley began to complain of new ailments. Mary knew he would not recover until they moved to a warmer place, and when Mrs. Mason wrote that she knew of a physician who could give Shelley immediate relief, the decision was made to leave Florence as soon as possible. Mary packed their belongings in a few days, and at the end of January the family left Florence for Pisa, which would become their principal home for the rest of Shelley's life.

Mrs. Mason helped Mary find new lodgings and sent Shelley to the noted physician, Dr. Vaccà Berlinghieri, who performed near-miracles in his treatment of his new patient. Shelley placed great trust in him, in part because they held similar political views, and thereafter his health was greatly improved.

The presence of the Masons made Pisa attractive, but there appeared to be little else to commend the city. Once a flourishing mercantile and political center, it had fallen on lean days, and in less than a century its population had fallen from almost one hundred and fifty thousand to approximately fifteen thousand. The Shelleys were inveterate sightseers, but there were no palaces, art galleries or churches of note for them to visit, and the architecture was Gothic, which they considered ugly.

The English colony there was small and lacked distinction. Mrs. Mason told the Shelleys that most of their compatriots were dullards, which they soon learned for themselves, and as a consequence they saw few people other than the Masons. Walter Savage Landor, the distinguished author, was living in the environs of Pisa, but his path and Shelley's did not cross, possibly because Landor was even more of a recluse than the poet. According to some authorities, Landor's avoidance of his fellow writer was a direct outgrowth of his correspondence with Southey, who had been Harriet Westbrook Shelley's firm champion. So it is possible that Landor acquired, sight unseen, Southey's prejudices against a man still regarded by many Englishmen as totally lacking in morality.

In spite of Pisa's many drawbacks, Mary and Shelley liked the place better than any other in Italy. The weather was mild, and Shelley accepted without question Dr. Berlinghieri's contention that the Arno River was filled with minerals that had healing properties. Undoubtedly the greatest attraction was the scenery, and Mary enjoyed the walks through the wooded hill country surrounding Pisa, as did Shelley.

Correspondence with various friends fell off after the family moved to Pisa, so the Shelleys were even more isolated than they had been. They professed to be content with their own company and that of the Masons, but Claire, who had enjoyed her life in Florence, was bored by the smaller, more provincial town. She expressed her thoughts freely, not only in her diary but in conversation, and Mrs. Mason launched into a campaign to persuade her to seek her own livelihood elsewhere. She had been supported by the Shelleys ever since they had come to Italy, and although Mary accepted her continuing presence with remarkable patience, it was the outsider who saw that Claire was the never-ending cause of minor irritations and frictions.

Renewed invitations were sent to various friends in England, and Shelley also wrote to John Keats, urging him to come to Italy for a visit. Keats, who was still afraid the stronger personality of his colleague might overwhelm him, was suffering from the consumption that soon would kill him, and was forced to decline.

Shelley also sent an invitation to his cousin, Tom Medwin, who shared his enthusiasm for sailing, and received a favorable response. Others, however, proved indifferent. Peacock had married, and his own life was too full and busy; Leigh Hunt could not afford to make the journey; Hogg appeared to have lost interest in his old friend, and wrote a single, casual note in which he said, without explanation, that it would not be possible for him to make the journey.

Mary had allowed her own correspondence with Amelia Curran to drop, and the chill in her friendship with the Gisbornes was responsible for a lessened correspondence with Maria, even though Leghorn was less than a morning's journey from Pisa. In the spring the Gisbornes left Italy for a visit to England, and exchanged several brief, polite visits with the Shelleys prior to their departure, but it was becoming plain to all concerned that the bonds of friendship were loosened.

Mrs. Mason was Mary's only confidante now, but no others were needed. The death of William and Clara, followed by the birth of Percy Florence, had completed the process of Mary's maturation. Her husband was still an emotional adolescent, in spite of his brilliance, frequently took refuge in psychosomatic illness and used imagined incidents as an excuse for his erratic behavior. But Mary achieved lifelong stability by the time she reached her twenty-third birthday. She had learned to curb the melancholia she had inherited from her mother, she had gleaned a remarkable understanding of human nature, and she had gained enough self-control to permit reason to guide her feelings.

Her teachers were her father and her husband, neither of whom was able to practice what he taught. Godwin stifled his emotions until they took command and forced him to behave irrationally, even stupidly, while Shelley, who was so complex that he almost defied analysis, released his feelings through regressions that denied the validity of the rule of reason he preached. Mary gave in to neither of these impulses.

She had coped with her father since infancy and with her husband since adolescence. For their sakes she had accepted their prejudices, catered to their whims and allowed their desires to take precedence over her own. Loving them, she had done everything in her power to advance their careers, to enhance their reputations at the expense of her own. Sensitive to their genius, she had catered to them, allowing their whims to stand in the way of her own progress.

She knew that Godwin's ambitions for her were unrealistic, and consequently he never praised her. Shelley, on the other hand, always encouraged her, but treated her like a tutor dealing with a pupil. Neither man, no matter how loudly he preached the doctrine of equality, was willing to admit she was his peer.

Knowing the limitations of her husband and her father, Mary did not expect the impossible from them. By the time she was twenty-three, she had achieved an understanding that not only enabled her to admire their strengths and pity their weaknesses, but that demanded, from society if not from them, what she so freely gave to them.

She would be forced to overcome a series of crises, including the tragic, premature death of her husband, before she would attain the freedom and recognition she deserved, yet she seemed content to advance one small step at a time. Not the least of her attributes was the patience, born of love, that endowed her with a worldly wisdom superior to that of the men around whom her life revolved.

XIV

PERCY BYSSHE AND MARY SHELLEY lived such full lives together, achieving and suffering so much, that it is sometimes difficult to remember that Shelley lived only until he was twenty-nine and that Mary was five years his junior. Trelawny was indulging in no mere figure of speech when, after his first meeting with them, he wrote that they were the reincarnation of Renaissance spirits who "set the world afire" before a single gray hair appeared on their heads.

By the late spring of 1820 the Shelleys were compelled to deal with so many emergencies and unpleasant situations that had arisen since their move to Pisa that it is small wonder they did not grow old before their time. Shelley, as usual, wanted to flee from the problems, and using illness as his crutch, proposed they move to the south of Italy for the summer. Mary knew they could not afford to make another move, however, and under no circumstances was she willing to subject Percy Florence to unnecessary risks by taking him on a long journey, so she vetoed the idea. She was already trying to cope with so many troubles that she had lost her appetite and slept poorly.

Worries about her father caused her the greatest concern. Godwin's chronic financial difficulties had finally threatened him with imprisonment for debt, and although he still hoped his son-in-law and daughter could save him again, the nasty letters he wrote to Shelley produced no positive, beneficial results. The truth of the matter was that Shelley's past financial sins had risen up to plague him, and he was in no position to be of help. Two money-lenders from whom he had borrowed were demanding payments that were past due, and he still owed a substantial sum to his Marlow landlord, who refused to release him from his obligation.

Every mail brought reminders of other debts. A final payment was due on the piano Shelley had bought for Mary a few months before their departure from England. The printers of *Alastor* and of *A Six Weeks' Tour* were threatening court action if they did not receive what was due them. A London tailor and his wife, a dressmaker, were harassing them. Leigh Hunt was on the verge of bankruptcy, and could be saved only if Shelley honored a promise to take care of the most pressing of his debts.

Once again Mary curtailed expenses, discharging all her servants except the cook, cancelling orders for new books and telling her husband that, until they could afford the luxury of buying their own, they would borrow books from the well-stocked library owned by Mr. and Mrs. Mason.

Life under the Shelley roof was further complicated by new difficulties Claire was encountering with Lord Byron, who refused to let her take Allegra to Pisa for a short visit. In the recent past Byron had become respectable, at least by his own standards, because he was now living with just one woman, the Countess Guiccioli. Writing an unnecessarily vicious letter, he told Claire he had no intention of subjecting Allegra to the heathen influences of the atheists with whom she was living. He hinted, too, that he was thinking of boarding Allegra at a convent school, which convinced Claire that her daughter would become virtually an orphan. In her desperation she enlisted Shelley's aid, and he opened a new correspondence with Byron on her behalf.

Mary and Claire were living under their separate tensions, but the former was wise enough to know they would take out their frustrations on each other, and therefore avoided her stepsister. Claire lacked the intelligence to follow her example, and interfering in domestic squabbles over money, took Shelley's part. She also criticized their meals, their social life and Mary's treatment of her son. When Mary retreated into a dignified silence, Claire goaded her unmercifully, and sooner or later Mary lost her temper.

It was no wonder that, early in July, Claire made a flippant entry in her diary that read:

> Heighho, the Claire and the Maie
> Find something to fight about every day.

In spite of their many distractions, the Shelleys observed their normal routines. Mary read incessantly, but abandoned her books to take care of her son when he contracted a mild case of the measles. She continued to work on her new novel, but abandoned it for a time after reading Machiavelli's *Life of Castruccio;* she was careful, however, to preserve her notes for future use. She also continued her translations of the works of Spinoza, a project in which her husband joined her. Shelley did not neglect his own work, and wrote "The Sensitive Plant," "A Vision of the Sea" and "Ode to Liberty," among other poems.

They exchanged daily visits with the Masons, and the two couples sometimes dined together, while Claire, demonstrating her growing independence, took daily walks with the Masons' teen-aged daughters and occasionally ate her meals with them. It was not easy for Mary to engage in so many activities at the same time, and an entry in her *Journal* late in the spring of 1820 reveals that she was not superhuman. "Read today," she wrote. "I am sure I forget what."

[*151*]

She and Shelley still had faith in their joint future, and as a symbol of their hope she spent a portion of a bank draft for *Frankenstein* royalties on a gold ring that she gave him on his birthday. It bore the inscription, *"Il buon tempo verra,"* or, the good time will come, and Shelley wore the ring from the day she presented it to him until his death.

His own vocational situation was unsatisfactory. No London theatrical manager had been willing to produce *The Cenci,* so it had been published, and most of the reviewers, although grudgingly forced to recognize the poet's talent, nevertheless attacked him on the grounds that he was a moral degenerate and an atheist. He knew they had prejudged him, but still hoped the tide of critical opinion would turn in his favor, and sent *Prometheus Unbound* to his publishers.

The *Literary Gazette* and the *London Monthly* went out of their way to attack Shelley personally, and their assaults were so unkind that an indignant Mary wrote sharp replies that she dared the magazines to publish. In this instance Shelley showed a greater common sense, realizing her response would cause the editors and reviewers to become even more venomous. So, instead of mailing Mary's letters, as she had requested, he burned them, thereby depriving posterity of her arguments, and diplomatically waited until she became calmer before he told her what he had done.

In mid-June a personal problem occupied the attention of the Shelleys for several days. Paolo, their discharged servant, wrote to them from Leghorn to the effect that he intended to make certain facts regarding their past known to the world unless they paid him a substantial sum of money. Mary and Shelley went to Leghorn without delay, taking Percy Florence with them, and moved into the empty house of the Gisbornes.

Seventy-two hours later Mary wrote to Maria Gisborne,

who was still in London, saying they were taking advantage of her unknowing hospitality, and explaining that their visit to the city was caused by "the most superlative scoundrel, Paolo, who is directing an infamous conspiracy against us."

The nature of the conspiracy was never in doubt, Paolo having made it clear he planned to spread the rumor that Claire had given birth to Shelley's child. Neither Mary nor Shelley had any intention of submitting to the blackmailer's demands, and knowing that the charge was false, they hired an attorney and instructed him to take action against their former servant.

There are no records of the events that transpired during the next two weeks, but the Shelleys were satisfied that they had silenced the blackmailer. Just before returning to Pisa, Shelley wrote to the Gisbornes again to report that "we have had a most infernal business with Paolo, whom, however, we have succeeded in crushing." It did not occur to them apparently, that although they had found some way to prevent Paolo from spreading lies, they had in no way limited his wife's freedom of action.

The relationship with William Godwin continued to deteriorate, and Mary became upset every time they received a letter from him, telling them in detail about his plight and demanding that they save him. On August 6 they received a communication in which he gave them a lurid description of the poverty and disgrace to which he would be subjected if they refused to assist him, and Mary, to whom Shelley read only a paragraph or two, unable to curb her feelings any longer, ran weeping from the room.

That was the last straw. Shelley's patience and courtesy were exhausted, and on August 7 he wrote an explicit, firm and long overdue letter to his mentor and father-in-law. Citing the particulars of their financial relationship, he made it clear that he would not and could not render

Godwin additional assistance. His own financial affairs were in a muddle, he said, and were even worse than Mary realized. He owed approximately two thousand pounds to various creditors, several of whom were expected to file suit against him in the immediate future.

He emphasized, too, that he had more than discharged his obligations, real and imagined, to Godwin. In all, he wrote, he had advanced his father-in-law the sum of almost five thousand pounds, for which moneylenders were charging him twenty thousand pounds. His own credit had vanished, and he was afraid he would leave virtually no fortune to his son—Godwin's grandson. He also reminded the older man that Godwin had promised to repay the various sums loaned to him, but had not sent his son-in-law a single ha'penny.

At last Shelley came to the heart of his argument, the sentiments and welfare of his wife. After the frightful events of the previous two years, he declared, Mary's life was bound up in that of her infant. Then, demonstrating dignity as well as courage, he added:

> Your letters, from their style and spirit (such is your erroneous notion of taste) never fail to produce an appalling effect on her frame. On one occasion agitation of mind produced through her a disorder in the child, similar to that which destroyed our little girl two years ago.
>
> On that occasion Mary, at my request, authorized me to intercept such letters or information as I might judge likely to disturb her mind. That discretion I have exercised with [the better part of] the letter to which this is a reply.

Shelley concluded on an uncompromising note. In the future, he said, he would show Mary no letters from her father demanding money or mentioning his financial situation, nor would he himself reply to any such communications. He hoped they would be able to enjoy amicable, loving relations with Mary's father, but the choice was Godwin's. He sympathized with his father-in-law's unfortunate financial condition, and would be of assistance if he could, but he was in no position to send four hundred pounds, and had no intention of going deeper into debt in order to satisfy Godwin's insatiable demands. In the future, if they were to have intercourse, Godwin would be obliged to refrain from mentioning in his correspondence all matters pertaining to money.

That letter marked the real turning point in the relations of the Shelleys with William Godwin. At first the old philosopher could not believe his son-in-law literally meant what he said, and wrote several more letters requesting money. But Shelley neither showed these communications to Mary nor replied to them. Then Godwin retreated into a sulking silence, and although he suffered a number of vicissitudes, including the loss of his home and office, he found another place to live and work, and was victimized by none of the calamitous indignities he had feared. Ultimately, when relations with his daughter were restored, he took care not to offend her, and Mary was spared the torment to which he had subjected her for years.

Mary and Shelley stayed on for several weeks at the Gisborne house, and knowing no one in Leghorn, they enjoyed a complete privacy that enabled them to concentrate on their work. It was during this period, after returning from an evening walk, that Shelley wrote the most famous of his poems, "To a Skylark," and the sadness that burdened the afflicted couple at this time is reflected in its lines.

The weather in Leghorn became unbearably hot, and Pisa was little better, so the Shelleys rented lodgings at the Baths of San Giuliano de Pisa, high in the hills a few miles from the latter city. Their quarters were so spacious and the climate so pleasant that they renewed their invitations to Tom Medwin and to John Keats, who was now seriously ill.

Claire moved with the Shelleys, but the total isolation of life in the remote resort made her so unhappy that she decided to leave, and neither Mary nor Shelley made any effort to stop her. She went to Leghorn for a protracted stay, writing to several friends that a physician, whom she did not name, had urged her to take daily sea baths for the sake of her health.

Percy Florence grew fat and tanned, and his father's health improved, too. Mary, who rarely interfered or made suggestions regarding her husband's work, took it upon herself to urge him to write more poems that could be understood by people of ordinary intelligence. Under no circumstances should he abandon his more cerebral work, she said, but he would attain greater popularity and increase his renown if he sometimes directed his poems to those whose grasp was limited. Her motive, which she did not spell out to him, was a desire to assuage the hurt he felt when reviewers dealt savagely with his serious efforts.

Shelley responded to his wife's pleas by writing *The Witch of Atlas,* which appears on the surface to be a light, almost playful work. On closer examination, however, it is seen as a study in praise of the only goddess Shelley ever worshiped, Intellectual Beauty. Mary, who never again tried to influence her husband, realized that even when he wrote with a light touch, he found it impossible to stray from the principles that were important to him.

A revolt in the two principal sections of the Kingdom of the Two Sicilies, Naples and Sicily, won the people of that realm constitutional guarantees of greater personal and political freedom, and Shelley saluted that victory in his "Ode to Naples." Mary cheered with him, but it was another political situation that absorbed her interest in the summer of 1820, although her approach was strictly that of a feminist rather than an amateur follower of politics.

King George III of England, who had been declared mad in 1810, finally died in January, 1820, and his son, the profligate prince regent, ascended the throne as George IV. He had acquired a reputation for treating his many mistresses with contempt, and had been even more cavalier in his attitudes toward his consort, Princess Caroline, who had been living in Italy for the past two years. The new monarch, supported by his Tory ministers, decided to give Caroline no place in the coronation ceremonies, which meant she could not be crowned queen. His reason, King George declared, was that she had been guilty of adultery.

In all probability the charge was true, Caroline having abandoned the role of a chaste wife after her husband had not only humiliated her by living openly with various mistresses, but also having subjected her to unwarranted personal abuse. Regardless of the validity of the king's claim, Caroline was lacking in neither courage nor initiative, and in the summer of 1820 returned to England to claim her rights. The Tory Party, which preferred to forget the matter, was forced to support the king, and the cabinet formally brought Caroline to trial on charges of adultery.

The Whig Party seized the opportunity to offer Caroline its full support, and the issue, which was but a surface manifestation of the differences between the conservative and liberal parties, brought England to the brink of civil war. Scores of books, pamphlets and songs were written, and the most popular of them sold hundreds of thousands of copies. New cartoons, many of them scurrilous, appeared daily. Supporters of both factions organized parades, and there were serious riots when they met in the streets.

Cabinet members were threatened, and required personal bodyguards to protect them; their houses were stoned, and their families were afraid to venture out in public. And when the Italian witnesses who were scheduled to testify against Princess Caroline arrived by ship and attempted to debark in London, they were attacked by a huge, infuriated mob. The witnesses retreated to their ship, troops were called out to protect them, and hundreds of citizens were wounded in the ensuing battle.

Princess Caroline had no more passionate supporter anywhere than Mary Shelley, who was not only convinced of her innocence, but insisted that even if she were guilty, a man of George IV's low character had no right to deprive her of her crown. One afternoon in August, when Mrs. Mason came to the house in the hills for a visit, Mary talked of nothing else, and could not be diverted from the subject.

The daughter of Mary Wollstonecraft had found a fight worthy of every woman's dedication, and she threw herself into the struggle with a zeal that surprised even Shelley. She sent letters to everyone she knew in England, and urged friends, relatives and even acquaintances to join in the struggle on Caroline's behalf. She even tried to write an essay on the subject, subsequently lost to posterity, but her indignation rendered her inarticulate.

Shelley's natural inclination was to take Princess Caroline's side, and his wife's single-minded devotion to the matter whipped up his own interest. So he entered the lists by writing a satiric poem, *Oedipus Tyrannus, or Swellfoot the Tyrant,* which he sent off to Horace Smith for publication in pamphlet form. Although it was one of his least majestic efforts, it succeeded brilliantly in making George IV look ridiculous. Two thousand copies were printed, but only a handful of them were sold because the king's partisans persuaded a private organization, the Society for the Prevention of Vice, to threaten prosecution. Shelley already having been condemned in the eyes of the society's members, they eagerly swallowed the bait, and the publisher, who wanted to avert a costly court fight, burned all remaining copies of the pamphlet.

Mary and Shelley were outraged, but saw their cause triumph later in the year. Although the evidence against Princess Caroline was strong, it was not conclusive, and the charges against her were dropped. The matter had been carried further than either political party had wanted, so a compromise was worked out: Caroline became queen, and was granted a private pension that would enable her to live apart from King George IV.

The more vocal of her partisans, Mary among them, were not willing to let the matter drop, however, and continued to support her by maintaining a steady critical barrage that attacked the king's lack of morality. Mary's interest in the issue and her personal involvement in the campaign are significant because they mark the first time in her life that she acted independently, on her own initiative in any public matter of concern to the English people.

She remained active, even writing letters to the London newspapers, until Caroline's death in 1821 abruptly terminated the unsavory matter. It is noteworthy that Mary had always signed herself Mary Godwin Shelley until she became one of Caroline's defenders. Then, deliberately recalling her mother's efforts in the movement to obtain equality for women, she signed her name as Mary Wollstonecraft Shelley, and used that version until the end of her days.

The struggle kept her mind so occupied that she was scarcely aware of the importance of events in her own life early in the autumn of 1820, when a burden was lifted from her, only to be replaced by another that was equally onerous.

XV

Mrs. Mason worked quietly, and in mid-October, 1820, obtained a permanent position for Claire Clairmont as an English tutor for the children of a Dr. Bojti, the court physician of the Grand Duke of Florence. It was a perfect situation for Claire because her duties were light, she would live in the Bojti house and would have ample opportunity to renew the social life she enjoyed with members of the English colony in Florence.

For the first time since Mary and Shelley had eloped, they were free of Claire, and Mary was at last able to call her home her own. Claire felt great relief, too, and neither young woman wept when they parted company on the morning of October 22, when Shelley escorted Claire to Florence. For the next three days Mary reveled in the luxury of being the undisputed mistress of her own domain, and looked forward to a period alone with her husband and baby.

On October 23 Shelley returned, bringing with him his cousin and Eton schoolmate, Tom Medwin, who planned to spend the winter with them. While Mary was trying to assimilate this situation, severe autumn rainstorms caused heavy flooding, and they were almost washed out of their lodgings. They had to move without delay, and while Mary engaged in the familiar, frantic process of packing, Shelley went ahead into Pisa and found a large apartment for them.

They moved before the end of October, and the Shelleys

became acquainted with Medwin, who liked to think of himself as a poet, and who had spent several years as an army officer in India. Mary discovered immediately that the visitor was a compulsive talker who had a need to dominate every conversation; unfortunately he was endowed with a shallow mind and could discuss little except trivia, laced with reminiscences of his life in India. His poetry was so inferior that Shelley was forced to use unaccustomed diplomacy in criticizing his work, and found that he had little in common with his relative except a love for sailing.

Very much abashed, Shelley confessed to Mary he had forgotten that, while still attending Eton, Medwin had shown every sign of being completely nonintellectual. He had been invited for a protracted stay, however, and little could be done to alter the situation. Shelley planned to start the study of Arabic with Medwin, but found conversations with him so painful that he soon abandoned his efforts to talk, and instead played chess in the evenings with the guest. He also found another use for Medwin: avoiding the calls on acquaintances and other social functions that Mary enjoyed, Shelley stayed home and gallantly permitted his cousin to act as his wife's escort on these occasions.

During the day, when Shelley was working, he locked himself behind the closed door of his study, and Medwin entertained enough respect for a poet in the throes of composition not to interrupt him. With little interest in reading and nothing else to occupy his time in a strange, foreign city, Medwin began to follow Mary around the house as she attended Percy Florence and looked after her household chores. It was almost impossible for her to avoid the voluble guest, and as Medwin had never before known a woman who read extensively, much less tried to engage in serious writing of her own, he gave her no peace.

Mary found him boring beyond description, and almost wished Claire had not gone. In order to obtain an occasional hour of precious privacy she was forced to retreat to her bedchamber, but Medwin followed her even there, tapping at the door and regaling her with stories of his experiences in India that she had heard many times.

Adding to her woes was a complete break with the Gisbornes. Henry Reveley came to Shelley with a novel proposition: he intended to use his steam engine to produce power in an iron foundry, but if Shelley insisted it be used in a ship, he would have to invest an additional four hundred pounds. This Shelley refused to do, and realizing that he had thrown away every penny he had given Reveley, he completely lost his temper.

Loyal to her husband, even though she had doubted the wisdom of his investment from the start, Mary told Mrs. Mason that the Gisbornes were "base, greedy and foolish people." Her affection for Maria Gisborne had been genuine, however, and she was vastly relieved when the breach was healed several months later, thanks to her own efforts and those of Mrs. Mason, who acted as a mediator.

Late in November Medwin fell ill, suffering a recurrence of a severe fever he had contracted in India, and for a month and a half he was confined to his bed. Nursing him was a burden Mary could not carry alone, when added to her other responsibilities, so Shelley neglected his own work to help her. He was so conscientious in the discharge of his duties that Medwin was not only astonished, but managed to improve the habits that had been driving his hostess and host to distraction.

During his convalescence he read almost all of the poetry Shelley had written, and with ample time to contemplate, ponder and analyze, he began to acquire at least some measure of qualities in which he had been lacking. Certainly it dawned on him that his relative and friend was no ordinary

[*165*]

mortal, but a poet whose talents could not be categorized.

Awed into unaccustomed silence, Medwin allowed himself to be maneuvered into an observance of the Shelley family's routines. He discovered hitherto unsuspected pleasures in reading a book, then listening to the explanations of Mary and Shelley that opened the doors of his mind to greater depths of understanding. He became so malleable that, by the time he recovered from his illness, he readily accepted the habits of Mary and Shelley. When they read or wrote, he buried himself in a book. He was not only overwhelmed by Shelley's writing, but after listening to Mary read aloud from her prose and poetry, he realized he would be wasting his time if he pursued his own literary ambitions.

Thereafter Medwin became a model guest. He had a flair for languages, and not only studied Arabic with Shelley, but often conversed with him in Spanish. And when Mary became restless he taught her the rudiments of Hindi. Having been reared in a semiaristocratic household that was unconsciously antiintellectual in its bias, he marveled at the Shelleys' unquenchable, ever-present thirst for knowledge.

Medwin was half-aware of his host's genius before he ever came to Pisa, but it astonished him to learn that his hostess was her husband's intellectual equal. Their urgent desire to be well-informed, coupled with a genuine indifference to worldly matters, sometimes caused amusing complications. It was a common practice for Shelley, an hour or two after dinner, to look up from his reading with a puzzled frown and ask, "Mary, have we dined?" And the guest found it difficult to refrain from laughing when Mary replied, "I think so, but I'm not certain." The comforts and conveniences so earnestly sought by most people meant nothing to the Shelleys. According to Medwin, the needs of their child were the only reality they knew, and they spent most of their nights as well as all of their days in reading, writing and discussing literature.

So Medwin not only fitted into a comfortable niche in the Shelley household, but eventually became Mary's ally in her never-ending struggle to preserve Shelley's health. Like so many others, he believed that the poet's physical well-being depended on his state of mind, and with Mary's active encouragement he experimented with hypnosis, which he had learned in India. Shelley responded to hypnotic treatment, readily accepting the suggestion that his ailments were imaginary and that he was enjoying robust health. So Medwin performed a valuable service that compensated in full for any inconvenience he might have caused the Shelleys.

If Mary thought she was truly rid of Claire Clairmont, however, she was mistaken. She was so relieved to be free of her stepsister that she refused to accept the task of corresponding with her, and Shelley, who felt sorry for Claire, took the responsibility. Mary was not spared, however, and within two weeks of her stepsister's departure she made the first of many entries in her *Journal* to the effect that Claire was bored and complained that life in Florence was dull.

To Mary's despair, Claire suddenly reappeared in Pisa a little more than a month after she had left, saying she could no longer tolerate her existence in Florence. And within twenty-four hours the lazy young woman had reassumed her accustomed place in the household, sleeping until noon, criticizing Mary's methods of bringing up her son and taking Shelley's part in marital discussions that were none of her concern.

Mary had no intention of reverting to a situation she had found intolerable, however, and immediately reminded Claire that she had undertaken an obligation in Florence, and could not shirk it. When her words had no effect, Mary appealed to her husband for help, but Shelley was too tenderhearted. Claire did not look well, he said, and he saw no reason why she should be compelled to act contrary to her own desires.

In her desperation Mary turned to the sensible Mrs. Mason, and that lady, as usual, was competent to deal with the situation. She held several private talks with Claire, who decided, on her own initiative, to return to the house of the Bojtis in Florence before Christmas. Her voluntary departure spared Mary the necessity of making an unpleasant scene that might have placed an unbearable strain on a lifelong relationship. The basic fact remains that Mary, having become the sole mistress of her own house, had no intention of sharing that position with Claire in the future.

It was during this period that the Shelleys widened their circle of friendships and became engaged in the most active social life they had known in Italy. The first to call regularly was a middle-aged Italian whose way of life and background were as unorthodox as his personality. Francesco Pacchiani was a professor of chemistry at the University of Pisa, and a poet and a part-time priest who acted as the confessor to the household of Pisa's governor. He was also an eccentric, and spent much of his time in the company of Pisa's courtesans.

He was, nevertheless, a man of considerable intellect and a brilliant conversationalist. The Shelleys were enchanted by him; Mary wrote in her *Journal* that he was the only Italian she knew who had a heart and soul, and Shelley paid the professor the highest of compliments by saying he was the equal of Coleridge as speaker. By the latter part of the following February, however, their ardor for him cooled.

The turning point in the relationship was an incident

that Mary noted in her *Journal*. Shelley, who was still regarded by so many of his fellow Englishmen both at home
and abroad as dissolute, perhaps degenerate, was disgusted
when the professor told an off-color story. Mary, who had
heard worse under her father's roof, was not shocked, but
sympathized with her husband's reaction and agreed with
him that they should discourage Pacchiani's visits.

Thereafter they saw little of him, but it was through him
they met Tommaso Sgricci, a man in his early thirties who
was one of Italy's leading entertainers. Calling himself an
improviser, he was the master of a theatrical art known
only in Italy. In response to suggestions from his audience
he made up dramatic scenes on the spur of the moment,
playing all roles, and on occasion he also improvised poems,
concentrating on verse of a patriotic nature in which he
urged the people of the various Italian states to form a
single nation.

Shelley called him an incomparable artist and praised
his poetry unstintingly, while Mary, after seeing his performance, wrote in her *Journal* that he "poured forth a
torrent of poetry clothed in the most beautiful language."
Sgricci became a regular member of the Shelley circle.

Mary's favorite was a dashing Greek prince, an exile
from his homeland who was playing an active role in the
underground movement that would wrest Greece from her
Turkish masters. Prince Alexander Movrocordato, only a
year older than Shelley, was a short, dark-skinned and intense young man who was destined to become one of his
nation's leaders. In 1822 he would serve as the president
of the first National Assembly of an independent Greece,
and after the establishment of a monarchy a decade later
he became his country's leading diplomat, serving with
great distinction as ambassador to several of Europe's leading nations.

[*169*]

He was known as "a devil with the ladies," as Claire wrote from Florence after learning he was paying daily visits to the Shelley apartment, and the young women of the various English colonies, not to mention those of the Italian aristocracy, regarded him as the epitome of all handsome, romantic figures. But the prince formed a relationship with Mary that was anything but romantic, and she ignored, as did Shelley, the inevitable rumors that she had become his mistress.

Anyone who had heard of the prince and those who knew Mary only by reputation found it difficult to believe that their friendship was innocent. But the truth of the matter was that they had struck a bargain as mutually beneficial as it was extraordinary. Prince Mavrocordato, impressed by Mary's intellect and desire to learn, came to the Shelley lodgings every morning and, sitting across from Mary in the drawing room, spent an hour and a half teaching her modern Greek. Then, supposedly for another hour and a half, Mary taught him English, but he was a better teacher than he was a pupil, and often cut short this portion of the lesson.

Mary dismissed the rumors about her and the prince because she was secure in her own innocence. A naive, rhetorical question that she wrote in a letter to Maria Gisborne reflects her almost girlish attitude: "Do you not envy my luck that, having begun Greek, an amiable, young, agreeable, and learned Greek Prince comes every morning to give me a lesson of an hour and a half?"

Shelley, who dedicated his *Hellas* to Mavrocordato, also formed a close friendship with him. They read the tragedies of Sophocles and Euripides in Greek together, as well as Milton's *Paradise Lost,* Shelley's favorite poetic work, in English. They saw each other regularly, often daily, until the prince departed for Greece in June, 1821, to take part in the uprising there. But both were men who held firmly rooted opinions, so it was inevitable there should be a clash of intellects.

They quarreled frequently over some of the more esoteric of Sophocles' meanings, and although Shelley continued to admire and respect the prince, he was often irritated by him. When Mavrocordato finally left Pisa, Shelley expressed himself candidly in a letter to Claire: "He is a great loss to Mary, and *therefore* to me . . . but not otherwise."

Yet another of the Shelleys' new friends was the Irish-born Count Taafe, who was an acquaintance of Byron's and liked to call himself the poet laureate of Pisa. An amiable man who spoke ill of no one, he was such good company that Mary and Shelley forgave him for the wretched poetry that he wrote and insisted on reading to them. He was proud of his translation of Dante's *Divine Comedy* into English, but both Mary and Shelley secretly thought he had made a hopeless mess of the task. His prose was of a far higher order, however, and he wrote a "Commentary" on Dante that impressed Shelley so much he sent it to friends in England, who published it.

Tom Medwin was the only member of the household who did not appreciate the enlargement of the Shelleys' social circle. He was devoting much of his own time to the writing of poetry, thinking of Shelley as his teacher and of Mary as an assistant tutor, so he resented the time they devoted to others. He began to make a nuisance of himself by falling madly in love with his own work, and Mary complained accordingly in a letter to Claire, whom she could treat as something of a confidante now that they no longer were living together. "He sits with us," she wrote, "and be one reading or writing, he insists upon interrupting one every moment to read aloud all the fine things he writes or reads."

Mary's annoyance with Medwin was a minor matter,

however, and she paid little attention to him. Much of her energy and thought late in 1820 and early in 1821 were directed toward something far more serious, the most famous of Shelley's intellectual romances, which would have destroyed their marriage had Mary been a less understanding, patient and wise woman.

XVI

LATE IN NOVEMBER, 1820, Professor Pacchiani took Mary Shelley and Claire Clairmont with him on a visit to the Convent of Saint Anna on the outskirts of Pisa to meet a young woman whose confessor he had been and who had been his student when he had served on the faculty of the convent's school. Neither he nor Mary could have imagined the consequences of that innocent visit.

Teresa Emilia Viviani was a tall, slender and exceptionally beautiful girl of nineteen, the elder daughter of the elderly Niccolò Viviani, the governor of Pisa and viceroy of one of the principal districts in the Grand Duchy of Tuscany. He was one of the most important and powerful men in the country, which made his daughter a person of consequence, too. Married to a wife more than thirty years his junior, he was easily swayed by her, and when she discovered that her daughters were detracting from her own beauty, he readily agreed with her suggestion that they be sent to different convent schools. Emilia had been incarcerated at the Convent of Saint Anna since the age of sixteen, paying visits to her father's palace only on special occasions, and would remain behind the convent's high walls until her parents arranged a suitable marriage for her.

Mary and Claire were horrified by Emilia's plight, failing to realize that the girl saw nothing out of the ordinary in her situation, or that she was waiting with patience and equanimity until the day a proper marriage would set her free. Returning home from the visit, Mary described the girl to Shelley as "a helpless prisoner." Her beauty was dazzling, but she would be wasted on an old man not of her own choice, and meanwhile she was permanently confined behind the high, barred windows and thick walls of the cheerless, cold convent.

Mary's description of the place chilled her husband's blood. There were no curtains or other bright touches anywhere. The heavy, wooden furniture was as ugly as it was functional. Every waking moment of the "inmates'" lives was regulated, and Emilia's cell was meaner than that found in any English prison. How Mary knew this particular claim was true is difficult to determine, since she had never seen the inside of an English prison.

Mary's story, even more highly colored by Claire's additions, so excited and angered Shelley that he accompanied his wife on a visit to the convent a few days later. The situation, as he saw it, was even worse than Mary had described it. Emilia was slightly older than most of the other girls attending the convent school, and was the only aristocrat enrolled there, the others coming from the small but prosperous middle class. Bored by her lot, indifferent to her companions, hating the dull food and having learned all the faculty had tried to teach her, Emilia had found an outlet for her emotions common to literate young girls through the ages. She had been writing large quantities of dramatically intense, romantic verse.

If all of these factors had not been enough to arouse Shelley's sympathy, Emilia's beauty stunned him. Although her hair and eye color were different from Mary's, she was the same physical type, and the helplessness of her position, as the Shelleys saw it, compounded her appeal. Many of Shelley's biographers have agreed that not since he had met and fallen in love with Mary Wollstonecraft Godwin had he encountered a young woman who had made such a sharp, deep impression on him.

He read some of Emilia's verses at their first meeting, and flattered her beyond measure by telling her that she wrote superb poetry. The girl was overwhelmed by the sympathy he and Mary displayed, and she would have been other than human had she not begun to feel sorry for herself. Languishing in unrelieved boredom behind the convent walls, uncertain of her future, she listened avidly as the impassioned Mary spoke to her of the equality with men that all women deserved. And she was forced to agree, in spite of her background and training, when Shelley declared that it was her right to love and marry a man of her own choice.

Herself warmly sympathetic as well as impressionable, Emilia was quick to take an interest in her would-be saviors. She learned of the death of Mary's older children, and was solicitous in her regard for the welfare of Percy Florence. She was sensitive to Shelley's claims of ill health, and in her correspondence unfailingly inquired about his headaches and other ailments. This regard alone was almost enough to turn Shelley's head.

Claire returned to Florence soon after her initial meeting with Emilia, but maintained a lively interest in her, and corresponded with her more or less regularly. The principal burden of maintaining the relationship fell on Mary, however, and it is obvious that she had no idea she was sowing the seeds of a whirlwind. For a period of four months, that is, from December of 1820 through March of 1821 she paid regular weekly visits to Emilia at the convent, and thereafter, for the next two months, she continued to call frequently, although not on a scheduled basis.

Treating the girl as though she were truly a prisoner, Mary brought her books to read, some of which were too liberal in content and tone for the convent authorities, and had to be smuggled into Emilia's cell at the bottom of picnic hampers filled with various delicacies that helped to overcome the monotony of unimaginative institutional meals. Mary thoughtfully brought other gifts, too, including such forbidden treasures as perfumes, cosmetics and silk scarves.

No woman could have been more attentive. In the hope of relieving the girl's boredom, Mary taught her Greek and Spanish, which won the hearty approval of the mother superior, who gave orders that Mrs. Shelley was to be admitted at any time. Claire had hoped to teach Emilia English, but as she was absent, Mary added that language to the curriculum.

It so happened that Mrs. Shelley was accompanied on her visits, more often than not, by Mr. Shelley, and neither Mary nor the convent authorities became aware of the dangerous situation that was developing. It must be noted that at no time prior to May, 1821, did Shelley visit the convent unless Mary was also present.

Emilia, to be sure, was as innocent and naive as was Mary. The girl was grateful for the attention and loving friendship of the generous young English couple, and always thought of them jointly, referring to them, when corresponding with one or another, as "your family." A letter she sent to Shelley a scant two weeks after their first meeting reveals not only her highly charged emotional state but clearly indicates she was not thinking in terms of intimacy with Shelley in a man-woman relationship:

> My dear Brother,—Your courteous attentions overwhelm me, for I know that in no wise do I deserve them. Beside the trouble that Claire takes to teach me your native tongue, you give me books! Oh, my good, my dear friend! how can I prove to you my gratitude and make a return for your favors? My situation prevents me from doing this, notwithstanding my will, my duty, and the affection which I bear you. Pity me, therefore,

and be assured of my eternal gratitude. Call me always, if you like, your Sister, for so sweet a name is very dear to me; and I too will always call you my dear Brother, and will consider you as though you were such indeed. You have already seen that I had anticipated you in this, which means that our hearts understand each other, that they have the same sentiments, and were created to be bound by a strong and constant friendship. I embrace my very beloved and beautiful sister, Mary, whose company is so agreeable to me. Adieu, wise Percy; take every care of your health, and do not forget your most affectionate sister and friend, Teresa Emilia.

Emilia wrote many letters to the Shelleys, most of which have been preserved, and directed the majority of them to Mary, whom she regarded with even greater affection than she did her other new friends. In one of her brief communications she indicated her admiration by writing, "You have much talent, my Mary, which, together with your virtue and your excellent heart, makes you one of the loveliest of God's or Nature's creatures."

The girl was somewhat in awe of Shelley, as another of her letters to Mary reveals: "His many misfortunes, his unjust persecutions, and his firm and innate virtue in the midst of these terrible and unmerited sorrows filled my heart with admiration and affection and made me think, and perhaps not untruly, that he is not a human creature; he has only a human exterior, but the interior is all divine."

Not satisfied with their attempts to make Emilia's lot more bearable, Mary and Shelley explored the possibilities of winning the girl her freedom. It was obvious to them from the outset that an appeal to her father would fail, so they decided to go over his head to the ultimate authority, the Grand Duke. Shelley wrote a petition, subsequently lost to posterity, and Mary called it "eloquent and filled with compassion."

They sent the document to Claire in the hope that she

would be able to use her ties with Dr. Bojti and his family to insure that it reached the Grand Duke himself. Presumably the petition was duly delivered, but that was the end of the matter, since the Grand Duke did not agree with the meddling, romantic foreigner that the plight of his immediate subordinate's daughter was desperate.

Shelley wrote to Claire that Emilia enchanted him, but took care to assure her that his personal feelings were not involved. "I am deeply interested in her destiny, and that interest can in no manner influence it," he declared, adding a line that emphatically clarifies his own emotional state: "There is no reason that you should fear any mixture of that which you call love."

Mary completely understood her husband's attitude and approach to Emilia, as her correspondence with Leigh Hunt and others proves. Under no circumstances did she believe literally in his longing for a spiritual union with Emilia that he expressed in *Epipsychidion,* which has often been called one of the purest of love poems ever written.

Mary also knew that Shelley was not literally suggesting in *Epipsychidion* that he wanted Emilia to elope with him to an isolated Greek island. He was engaging in a poetic flight of fancy, and Emilia herself, who was not in love with him, could not have taken the suggestion seriously.

The poem, written in the heat of inspiration during a period of about two weeks in February, 1821, was Shelley's ultimate expression of his intellectual concept of love, and Mary recognized it as such. He was like an artist who, having found a model to illustrate his spiritual ideas, painted a portrait that presented his subject as perfect.

Mary's summary of the poem demonstrates that she had no doubts regarding the true state of her husband's affections, and she is known to have admired *Epipsychidion,* so she was not being cynical when she called it "Shelley's Italian Platonics."

After completing the poem, which ran a total of six hundred and four lines, Shelley sent it to England, with instructions that it was not to bear his name because too many people would draw the wrong conclusions. Only a few hundred copies were printed, but the poet's expectation that the work would receive scant critical and public attention was mistaken. *Epipsychidion* was the first of his works to receive almost universal critical praise, and the edition sold so quickly that another had to be printed. Some of the reviewers guessed that Lord Byron was the author, but many attributed the work to Shelley, and, inevitably, a rumor spread quickly throughout England to the effect that he was about to leave Mary for an Italian woman.

Shelley's marked attentions to Emilia did not pass unnoticed in Pisa, either. Governor Viviani was no ordinary man, and the citizens of the little city maintained a lively interest in him and his family. The Shelleys could no longer walk unnoticed through the streets of Pisa, but were conscious of stares, whispers and nudges.

The situation was difficult for Mary to bear, but she did not lose her dignity, and refused to permit either local gossip or the talk in England to influence her relationship with Emilia, whom she continued to visit. Her situation was made no easier by Claire, who teased her in several letters about Shelley's "new love."

But Mary refused to be goaded, and continuing to express her sympathy for Emilia, nevertheless remarked candidly in a letter she wrote to Claire in May, 1821, that she could not help regarding the entire friendship as something of a "misfortune" because the Shelley family had already been the object of too much malicious gossip.

Mary would have been less than human had she not shown her natural reserve in her dealings with Emilia, and the sensitive girl asked Shelley if his wife was miffed with her. He reassured her, saying that Mary's manner concealed an affectionate heart.

On another occasion, in the late spring of 1821, Emilia wrote to Shelley, "Mary does not write to me. Is it possible that she loves me less than the others do? I should be very much pained by that. I wish to flatter myself that it is only her son and her occupations which cause this. Is not this the case?"

Shelley told Emilia that Mary's regard for her had not changed, and he emphasized that he, too, felt as he had the previous winter. But this was not the case. An artist loses interest in his model after he has painted his portrait, and Shelley's passion was spent after he wrote *Epipsychidion*.

Mary expressed Shelley's feelings as well as her own in a sensible, realistic letter to Leigh Hunt:

> It is grievous to see this beautiful girl wearing out the best years of her life in an odious convent, where both mind and body are sick for want of appropriate exercise for each. I think she has great talent, if not genius— or if not an internal fountain, how could she have acquired the mastery she has of her own language, which she writes so beautifully, or those ideas which lift her so far above the rest of the Italians? She has not studied much, and now, hopeless from a five years' confinement, everything disgusts her, and she looks with hatred and distaste even on the alleviations of her situation. Her only hope is in a marriage which her parents tell her is concluded, although she has never seen the person intended for her.

The extent to which Emilia's friendship with Shelley was responsible for her marriage arrangements is not known, but her parents could not have been unaware of the gossip, and they moved quickly before her reputation was harmed. In September, 1821, she was married to a nobleman named Biondi who was many years her senior. The wedding reception was held on the grounds of her father's official palace, and was well attended, as befitted Governor Viviani's exalted rank. But Mary and Percy Bysshe Shelley were not among the invited guests.

They wrote separate letters to Emilia, wishing her happiness, but she did not reply to either. Some months later Shelley received an unexpected communication from her, and was stunned when he read that she wanted to borrow money from him. This sorry ending to the spiritual union he had envisaged in *Epipsychidion* so enraged him that he refused to reply.

Mary expressed her final thoughts on the subject in a letter to Maria Gisborne:

> Emilia has married Biondi; we hear that she leads him and his mother (to use a vulgarism) a devil of a life. The conclusion of our friendship (*à la Italiana*) puts me in mind of a nursery rhyme which runs thus—
>
> "As I was going down Cranbourne Lane,
>   Cranbourne Lane was dirty,
>   And there I met a pretty maid
>   Who dropt to me a curtsey.
>
> "I gave her cakes, I gave her wine,
>   I gave her sugar-candy;
>   But oh! the naughty little girl
>   She asked me for some brandy."
>
> Now turn Cranbourne Lane into Pisan acquaintances, which, I am sure, are dirty enough, and "brandy" into that wherewithal to buy brandy (and that no small sum *però*), and you have the whole story of Shelley's Italian Platonics.

Mary could laugh at herself and her husband, showing only slight bitterness, but Shelley's sense of humor was less generous. He knew, however, that Emilia had inspired one of his finest poems, and that realization consoled him.

The significance of the Emilia Viviani episode, seen in exclusively personal terms, is that Mary sensibly did not allow her husband's sympathy for the girl or the writing of *Epipsychidion* to influence their marital relationship. It is true that both of the Shelleys sometimes suffered from a sense of inadequacy, Shelley apparently feeling that his intellect might be inferior to his wife's, while Mary occasionally believed she was too undemonstrative for his needs. In the main, however, each felt secure in the other's love.

Mary was annoyed, now and again, by the reactions of outsiders to her husband's relationship with Emilia, but her ire did not include him. And it did not occur to Shelley, who was far less sensible than his wife, that Mary might feel even a twinge of jealousy over the feelings he expressed in the poem that made Emilia Viviani immortal. He and Mary loved each other in real life, and her understanding gave him the poetic license to indulge in his imaginative fancy in his work. He found it difficult to believe Hunt, Horace Smith and other friends who wrote to him that *Epipsychidion* had placed Mary in an exceptionally uncomfortable position.

XVII

THE FRIENDSHIP with Emilia Viviani occupied only a small portion of the Shelleys' time, and they followed their customary routines of writing, reading and walking, now enhanced by the increase in their social circle. In mid-January, 1821, another couple, destined to play important roles in the lives of the Shelleys, arrived in Pisa.

Lieutenant Edward Ellerker Williams, an officer a year younger than Shelley, who had retired on half-pay, was Tom Medwin's good friend and had served with him in India. Williams had a mania for boating as intense as Shelley's, was a hearty, practical man fond of all outdoor sports, and in a later era would have been known as a man's man. He was also surprisingly sensitive, had written quantities of crude poetry that nevertheless showed promise, and was a talented painter who liked to work in watercolors.

Jane Williams, his common-law wife, who was Mary's age, was the young sister of the general commanding the British army in India. Unhappily married early in life, she had left her domineering husband, and since she was unable to obtain a divorce, she had been living with Williams for several years. They had a son, Edward, who was a year old, and in mid-March, two months after their arrival in Pisa, Jane gave birth to a daughter, Rosalind.

An exceptionally pretty girl, Jane made no pretense of being intellectual, but was warm, sympathetic to those who were in trouble and engaged in friendships that were open and uncomplicated. She was devoted to her husband and children, and her interests revolved around her household. She loved to cook, and was shocked when Mary knew no recipes to exchange with her.

Shelley and Williams took to each other from the start, and soon developed a close friendship, with the former soldier openly in awe of the poet's genius, which he called "astonishing." He also established a rapport with Mary, and found it easy to converse with her, an experience not shared by many who lacked her mind.

Jane was overwhelmed by the Shelleys, however, and for months after meeting them was so shy she fell silent in their company. They neither liked nor disliked her, and for a time, until they came to know her better, they merely tolerated her company, sometimes forgetting she was present at the dinner table or during an evening's discussion. It was during this time that Mary called her "a violet by a mossy bank." Eventually, however, she learned to appreciate Jane's virtues, and they drew closer, but it is unlikely they would have found much in common had their husbands not become good friends.

Shelley, Williams and Medwin began to make plans for boating expeditions on the Arno, and when Tom Medwin was forced to end his visit, the others continued to search for an appropriate craft. They were aided in their project by Henry Reveley, with whom Shelley had now made his peace, and who reported that he could purchase a frail boat of wood and canvas, about ten feet in length. It had been used for duck hunting in marshes, but whether it would be safe on a swift-moving river was questionable. The enthusiasm of Shelley and Williams was undiminished, but Mary, who felt misgivings, wrote to Maria Gisborne that she was concerned.

She had few other worries in the winter and spring of

1821, however, and her life was more tranquil than it had been in a long time. During this period she received two letters from her father, who had taken Shelley's warnings to heart. Godwin did not mention his own financial problems, which had not improved, and he took care not to criticize his son-in-law. Claire wrote from Florence that Allegra was much on her mind, but that Byron was not answering her letters, and she wanted to know if Shelley would intervene again on her behalf. Mary knew Byron was adamant, and wanting to spare her husband, urged Claire to be patient a little longer.

The most important of Mary's activities in the spring of 1821 was her return to her own writing. Although she had discarded the opening chapters of her new book, she decided to make a fresh start, using the same material. Her subject was Castruccio, an Italian soldier and political leader who had lived in the late thirteenth and early fourteenth centuries, and had been idealized by Machiavelli as a perfect prince. She called her book *Valperga*.

Her attempt to focus on the manners of the Middle Ages having failed, Mary decided to write a romantic historical novel. She was indebted to Sir Walter Scott, whose meticulously accurate studies of the past had not only made him the most popular of living authors, but had won a new respectability for the novel. Mary had too much integrity to imitate Scott's style or copy his ideas, but she did not hesitate to utilize his basic concept, that of weaving her story around real people and real events, which took place in real, accurately portrayed settings.

Valperga was an ambitious undertaking, but Mary had accumulated vast stores of background material, and had even visited the ruins of Castruccio's castle. So she felt no qualms regarding her competence to deal with her subject. *Valperga* was not related to *Frankenstein* in subject matter or approach, and would require the establishment of a far different mood, as well as the use of dissimilar storytelling techniques. But Mary regarded the problems of handling *Valperga* with the quiet self-confidence of a professional writer, even though *Frankenstein* had been her only published effort to date. And if she suffered any qualms, she revealed them to no one.

The writing of her first book had been relatively easy, but the new project required the expenditure of far more time and energy. Mary was traveling across unfamiliar ground, so she had to experiment and test, and she completely revised her opening chapters three or four times before they satisfied her. This kind of writing was painfully slow, which gained her an even greater appreciation of Shelley's work habits, and by midyear she had written only a few opening chapters strong enough to withstand her own critical gaze.

Her own hard work, combined with Shelley's needs, caused her to place firm restrictions on their social life. Knowing that their various new friends might be inclined to call at any hour, she made it a rule to receive no one until teatime in the late afternoon, but took care to make an exception of Prince Mavrocordato, who arrived soon after breakfast each day for their exchange of language lessons.

Correspondence with various friends in England languished. Horace Smith had planned to spend a year or two in Italy, presumably near the Shelleys, but his business affairs kept him in London. Peacock's infrequent letters were hurried, and contained less gossip than usual. Only Leigh and Marianne Hunt wrote at length, and their news was depressing. Hunt was now the only publisher as well as the printer of the *Examiner,* his brother having been sent to prison for a year because of a series of attacks on the House of Commons he had launched in the columns of the magazine. Two of the Hunt children were ill, and the family desperately needed financial help.

Shelley was in no position to give it. Mary was restricting his use of their funds, and they appeared to be winning their slow struggle to attain solvency, so he did not even ask her for her permission to send something to the Hunts. But Mary relented on her own initiative, and unable to tolerate the continued suffering of good friends who were in dire need, she urged Shelley to send Marianne and Leigh Hunt a substantial sum.

In mid-April of 1821 Shelley and Williams went to Leghorn to launch their boat, and conceived the mad idea of sailing it by moonlight upstream to Pisa. Mary was alarmed, Shelley never having learned to swim, and sent an urgent letter to Maria Gisborne that produced desired results. Mrs. Gisborne, reacting as though she were dealing with children, announced that she would neither permit Henry to sell his friends the boat nor would she sanction the voyage from Leghorn to Pisa unless her son, who was an expert swimmer, was a member of the party.

It was fortunate that she set these conditions. Within an hour of the time the trio cast off from Leghorn, the boat capsized in midstream. Edward Williams, who was a fair swimmer, managed to reach shore unaided, but Shelley would have drowned if Henry Reveley had not come to his help. Henry was astonished by the poet's cheerful calm; showing no signs of fear, he followed instructions to the letter and appeared completely unperturbed. When they reached the bank, however, he stood erect, took a few steps on dry land and then fainted.

The boat was repaired, and the voyage was continued without further mishap. Soon thereafter Shelley and Williams did what little they could to make the craft more reliable, and their enthusiasm undiminished, they went out onto the water for a daily sail, no matter what the weather. Shelley ordered a larger boat made to his specifications in Leghorn, and looked forward to its use during the coming summer months.

By May there were new complications in the life of Claire, who had gone to Leghorn for the sea bathing there. She wrote that Byron had placed Allegra in a convent school, refusing to allow her to visit the child there, but she consoled herself with the thought that Byron would be nearby and would see her regularly. The Shelleys knew this was not the case, however, having just learned in a letter from Byron that he was planning to resume his travels.

Mary insisted that nothing be said to Claire about the situation for the present, as she was unable to influence Byron. It was possible, however, that the older poet would listen to his colleague, so Shelley made plans to visit him and present a new idea for his consideration. Mary was suggesting that Allegra be placed in the custody of the Shelleys, who were very fond of her, and that they bring her up with Percy Florence. Even as unpredictable a man as Lord Byron, she and Shelley believed, would prefer to see his child reared in an artistic English household than in a foreign convent. But Byron disliked the idea.

The Shelleys returned for the summer to the Baths of Pisa above the city, and every day the master of the house sailed his new boat on the canal that took him to the Williams house. The summer was tranquil, Shelley having recovered from the depressed state into which he had fallen after learning in April of the death of John Keats. He wrote one of his most famous poems, *Adonais,* in praise of Keats, and Mary was relieved when he made a swift recovery after sending the work to be printed in London.

Claire came from Leghorn for a visit, and within hours of her arrival quarreled with Mary. Shelley persuaded both to apologize, and for his sake they observed the ritual, but it was apparent to Mary that she and her stepsister could never again dwell under the same roof. Both Mary and Shelley prized the independence they had been enjoying since Claire had moved to Florence, and neither was willing to make the sacrifices that would be necessary if they lived together. Claire had planned to stay for a month, but returned to Leghorn at the end of a week.

In June the circle of the Shelleys' friends began to diminish. Prince Mavrocordato sailed for Greece, telling Mary he would write to her when he could. A few days later Tommaso Sgricci left for Milan, where he intended to make a number of theatrical appearances.

At the end of July the Gisbornes came to the Shelley house for a brief farewell visit. They were departing for England, and having sold their household furnishings and other belongings, thought it unlikely that they would return to Italy. For a month prior to their departure Mary worked feverishly on the manuscript of *Valperga,* hoping to finish it in time for them to take it to London on her behalf. But she set an impossible task for herself, and realizing it about a week before the Gisbornes arrived, she slowed her writing to her normal pace. No matter how great her anxiety to see the work in print, she wrote, she could not allow haste to spoil a book on which she had labored so hard.

At the beginning of August, Shelley received a letter from Lord Byron, telling him that the father and brother of the Countess Guiccioli had been expelled from Ravenna for engaging in revolutionary activities and that Teresa Guiccioli had taken temporary refuge in Florence. It was apparent that Byron would not linger for any length of time in Ravenna himself, so Shelley left without delay to visit him for the purpose of making new arrangements for Allegra.

On August 4, 1821, Shelley's twenty-ninth birthday, Mary read, wrote and had her last sitting for the miniature that Edward Williams was painting. That night she noted in her *Journal* that it was Shelley's birthday, and her mood reflective, added:

> Seven years are now gone; what changes! What a life! We now appear tranquil; yet who knows what wind— but I will not prognosticate evil; we have had enough of it. When Shelley (and I) came to Italy, I said all is well if it were permanent; it was more passing than an Italian twilight. I now say the same. May it be a Polar day; yet that day, too, has an end.

On August 6 Shelley reached Ravenna, and Byron entertained him in the home of Countess Guiccioli's husband. They spent the night talking politics and literature, Shelley wrote to his wife, reporting that Byron was observing a careful diet of food and drink, and that his health was much improved. At the end of his letter Shelley dropped his bombshell.

Although he hated to cause Mary pain, Byron had shown him a letter from the Hoppners, who expressed shock after having been told by Elise Foggi, the former servant of the Shelleys, that Claire had given birth to Shelley's baby in Naples.

Shelley suggested that Mary write at once to the Hoppners in order to stifle the lie before it spread any further. He did not know the address of the Hoppners, and Lord Byron was asleep, he said, but he promised to forward the letter if Mary sent it to him by return post.

Mary's reply to her husband speaks for itself:

> My dear Shelley,
>
> Shocked beyond all measure as I was, I instantly wrote the enclosed. If the task be not too dreadful, pray copy it for me; I cannot.

Read that part of your letter that contains the accusation. I tried, but I could not write it. I think I could as soon have died. I send also Elise's last letter; enclose it or not, as you think best.

I wrote to you with far different feelings last night, beloved friend. Our barque is indeed "tempest-tost," but love me as you have ever done, and God preserve my child to me, and our enemies shall not be too much for us. Consider well if Florence be a fit residence for us. I love, I own, to face danger, but I would not be imprudent.

Pray get my letter to Mrs. Hoppner copied for a thousand reasons. Adieu, dearest! Take care of yourself—all is yet well. The shock for me is over, and I now despise the slander; but it must not pass uncontradicted. I sincerely thank Lord Byron for his kind unbelief.

Affectionately yours,
M.W.S.

Do not think me imprudent in mentioning Claire's illness at Naples. It is well to meet facts. They are as cunning as wicked. I have read over my letter, it is written in haste, but it were as well that the first burst of feeling should be expressed.

No letters.

The lucidity of the letter that Mary wrote to Mrs. Hoppner when in a state of shock and anger is remarkable. The communication filled many pages, and every line reflects the sincerity and integrity of Mary's faith in her husband; every paragraph was a testimonial to the depth of their mutual love. Although it was not written as a love letter, certainly, it has become a monument that honors the memory of the seven years that Mary and Shelley had spent together. Mary could not have been more forthright or convincing had she worked many days at her writing desk, composing the letter.

She began by expressing her sorrow over the need to write such a painful letter, and outlined, in detail, the employment by the Shelleys of both Elise and Paolo. Then, after dealing candidly with Paolo's blackmail attempt, she launched into an even longer discussion of Claire. Casting aside her pride, she described the lodgings they had occupied in Naples, and bluntly stated that the physical arrangement of the apartment was such that she would have been aware of any improper liaison.

After describing in detail the recurrence of a minor ailment that had forced Claire to spend two days in bed, Mary uncompromisingly asserted that neither at Naples nor at any other place had Claire ever been Shelley's mistress. Claire had no child, she declared, and the rest of the story was equally false. Then, after solemnly affirming that every word she wrote was the complete truth, Mary closed the letter with three blazing paragraphs:

> Shelley is as incapable of cruelty as the softest woman. To those who know him his humanity is almost as a proverb. He has been unfortunate as a father, the laws of his country and death have cut him off from his dearest hopes. But his enemies have done him incredible mischief—but that you should believe such a tale coming from such a hand, is beyond all belief, a blow quite unexpected, and the very idea of it beyond words shocking.
>
> But I have said enough to convince you, and are you not convinced? Are not my words the words of truth? Repair, I conjure you, the evil you have done by retracting your confidence in one so vile as Elise, and by writing to me that you now reject as false every circumstance of her infamous tale.
>
> You were kind to us, and I shall never forget it; now I require justice; you must believe me, I solemnly entreat you, the justice to confess that you do so.

The next act in the drama has been shrouded in mystery for a century and a half, and the biographers of both Shelley and Byron have dealt with it at length, but have discovered no factual answers to the questions that disturbed Mary Shelley and have puzzled posterity. The known facts are few and simple.

Shelley, who was still in Ravenna, received his wife's letter, which was unsealed, and copied it, as she had requested. He showed the unsealed communication to Lord Byron, who read it, and then Shelley sealed it with his own seal. Byron promised to send it on to the Hoppners that day, together with a brief covering letter of his own. Shelley departed almost immediately for Pisa, and had to be content with that promise. Hoppner was still the British consul in Venice, and Byron, who corresponded with him from time to time, undoubtedly knew his address.

Did Byron send Mary Shelley's letter to Mrs. Hoppner, with or without a covering letter of his own? That is the principal question that has never been satisfactorily answered.

Mary received no reply whatever from Mrs. Hoppner, and for the rest of her life never heard from the lady or her husband. Were the Hoppners too abashed and ashamed to write? No one has ever known.

The original letter was found among Byron's papers in 1824, after his death, by the executors of his will. Shelley's seal had been crushed, as though pressed by the seal placed on a covering letter. Why was the letter in Byron's possession? Had the Hoppners returned it to him for some reason? Those questions, too, have never been answered.

Lord Byron could have had no reason to refrain from forwarding Mary's letter, and having already read it himself, he could not have been motivated by a desire to read it after Shelley's departure from Ravenna. The worst charge that could be made against him is that he was careless and forgot to send the communication to the Hoppners, but that explanation lacks plausibility, too, since he was aware of the importance of the letter in the eyes of the Shelleys.

Even if the mystery is never solved, Mary Shelley's letter served its purpose. Regardless of what the Hoppners may have thought, Mary made it clear to posterity that Shelley and Claire were innocent of the malicious charges made by a disgruntled servant.

XVIII

THERE WAS one positive result of Shelley's mission to Ravenna, or so he thought: Byron said he had no intention of leaving Allegra at a convent near the town while he went off to some other country. Proving that he intended to keep his word, he also asked Shelley to rent a large house for him in Pisa. Before his departure Shelley visited Allegra, and was able to write to Claire that the child was in good health and high spirits.

Something that held promise of literary substance emerged from the Ravenna talks, too. The two poets made plans to found a new magazine, to which both would contribute, and they agreed to bring Leigh Hunt to Italy as their editor and partner, with Byron pledging himself to pay a portion of the traveling expenses of Hunt and his family.

The relatively good news about Allegra cheered Mary, who was still upset about Elise's lie to the Hoppners, and the prospect of seeing Marianne and Leigh Hunt again pleased her. But she showed far less enthusiasm for the prospect of greeting Byron as a neighbor, and thought Shelley might be exaggerating when he told her that Byron had changed for the better. She could not forget their last meeting in Venice, and made it plain to her husband that she would neither welcome Byron under her roof nor visit his house if he continued to dissipate.

In spite of her doubts about their friend, however, she

was making plans to establish permanent roots in Pisa. Tired of moving so frequently from one place to another, weary of living with the belongings of others, she began to buy furniture, linens and chinaware as soon as the family returned to Pisa in October. She wanted Percy Florence to be reared in one place, and it disturbed her when she was forced to give up her association with the friends she had made in one community and begin anew the process of becoming acquainted with others elsewhere.

It is possible that Mary's desire to establish a permanent home was spurred by signs of familiar restlessness she saw in Shelley. He had written to Peacock, who worked for the East India Company, to suggest that a place might be found for him on the concern's staff in India, and Mary had been relieved when Peacock replied that he did not qualify for the type of positions that were open. He also spoke of moving to Greece after that country won her independence, but Mary knew him well enough to realize this was just a passing phase. He was working on his *Hellas* in the autumn of 1821, and consequently was enthusiastic about all things Greek, but she felt certain he would become calmer and more sensible after he completed the poem.

Paying as little attention as she could to her husband's vague ideas, Mary went about the task of setting her own house in order. She found a magnificent villa for Byron, the Casa Lanfranchi, and took a large apartment for her own family in a building directly across the street. Edward and Jane Williams rented the apartment on the first floor of the same place, and continued to see the Shelleys daily.

On the first day of November, Lord Byron arrived to take possession of his villa. He was accompanied by Teresa Guiccioli and her brother, Count Gamba, and his coach was followed by a long procession of carts containing various household goods, the hundreds of books that accompanied him everywhere and a menagerie of a dozen or more pets.

Mary greeted him with reserve, but was pleasantly surprised to discover that Countess Guiccioli was "a nice, pretty girl without pretensions, good-hearted and amiable." She also appeared to be sensible, and Byron listened to her, often accommodating himself to her likes and dislikes, which was more than he did for any other woman. It was possible, Mary told Mrs. Mason, that Byron had indeed reformed, as Shelley had indicated.

The proximity of Byron altered Shelley's routines somewhat. In midafternoon, after dinner, he frequently joined Byron for a ride into the hills or a game of billiards. Sometimes they practiced their marksmanship with pistols, and always they engaged in lively conversation on the many topics they found of mutual interest. On occasion Shelley stayed at the villa for a light supper, and on these evenings Teresa Guiccioli crossed the street and dined with Mary, because Byron in his present mood seldom entertained ladies at his table.

Mary became friendly with the Countess, whose company she enjoyed, and felt sorry for her, too, knowing that Byron would grow tired of her. Still maintaining a wary distance, Mary herself saw very little of Lord Byron. When there were no guests filling the villa, he and the Countess sometimes came to the Shelley apartment for tea, but Mary crossed the street only to visit the Countess in her private quarters. After a time she was willing to concede that Byron's habits had changed for the better, but she was not fond of him and saw no reason to seek his company, although she granted Shelley the right to his own friendship.

Most of the poets' contemporaries assumed that Shelley more or less joined Byron's entourage during the autumn and winter of 1821–22, but this was not the case. If either man was the leader in the relationship, it was Shelley, who maintained his objectivity as well as his intellectual integrity. He thoroughly understood Byron, viewed him from a distance and did not always like what he saw, as much as he enjoyed their discussions. His private comments on Teresa Guiccioli are indicative of his ability to pass clear-eyed judgments on Byron: "She is a very pretty, sentimental, innocent, superficial Italian, who has sacrificed an immense fortune to live with Lord Byron, and who, if I know anything of my friend, of her, and of human nature will hereafter have plenty of leisure and opportunity to repent her rashness."

Many years later, long after the death of both poets, a remark was made in Mary Shelley's hearing to the effect that her husband had been Byron's follower. She shook her head, smiled and gently rebuked the speaker: "Shelley followed no man, and Byron was independent, too; but if either accepted the other's ideas, it was Lord Byron who listened to Shelley. My husband admired Byron only for his poetry, but disapproved of him in all else."

The association was beneficial to Shelley in an unexpected way. His health was improved, and Mary attributed his robust condition to the exercise he took riding horseback with Byron each day. When Tom Medwin returned to Pisa late in the autumn of 1821, he was agreeably surprised by Shelley's turn for the better.

The presence of Byron in Pisa did not detract from the normal social life that Mary and Shelley enjoyed, and they made and received so many calls that Shelley wrote, but without rancor, that their evening reading was curtailed by what he called "light entertainment." The one major disappointment of the autumn was the failure of the Hunts to arrive in Italy. Shelley fretted, and Mary worried, too, but they finally received word from Hunt that Marianne had been ill and that their departure would be delayed until early in the new year.

By the end of November, Mary finished writing the last chapter of *Valperga,* and began the onerous task of copying the book; it was so long that, when published, it would fill four volumes, so the copying chore required many months of painstaking labor, which became even worse than Mary anticipated because, she discovered, she was constantly making new changes.

Shelley, who was the first to read her manuscript, was deeply impressed, and predicted that *Valperga* would prove to be an even bigger success than *Frankenstein.* At his instigation Byron also read the book, and he, too, said it would enhance her reputation. Byron was struck by the extent and depth of Mary's research, and if she noted that an aura of warmth was lacking in his praise, it was only because she assumed, correctly, that he found it difficult to regard any woman writer as his peer. To an extent, it is true, he had been responsible for *Frankenstein,* but Mary was probably right when she told Mrs. Mason and wrote to Maria Gisborne that Byron often seemed uncomfortable and at a loss for words in her presence. The primary function of women, in his world, was not cerebral.

Mary's opinion of Lord Byron demonstrates her own maturation:

> There was something enchanting in his manner, his voice, his smile—a fascination in them; but on leaving him, I have often marveled that I gained so little from him worth carrying away; whilst every word of Shelley's was almost oracular; his reasoning subtle and profound; his opinions, whatever they were, sincere and undisguised; whilst with Byron, such was his love of mystification, it was impossible to know when he was in earnest.

Shelley made no secret of his own opinion of his colleague, and often complained openly that Byron jumped too quickly from subject to subject in a conversation, never carrying any theme to completion. Byron was sometimes inclined to indulge in bawdy humor, and on these occasions Shelley, who loathed vulgarity, clamped his hat on his head and walked, stiff-backed, across the street to his own lodgings. Had anyone else displayed such sensitivity, Byron would have teased him without mercy, but his respect for Shelley was so great that he refrained from comment when his friend departed.

Shelley drew Edward Williams, Count Taafe and Tom Medwin into Byron's circle with him, and Mary frequently expressed her pity for Medwin. Most of the talk at the villa soared over his head, but it did not occur to him that he might be missing the better part of what was said. Mary stopped being concerned when she finally realized he was happy in his ignorance.

Early in 1822 a man who was a good friend of Edward Williams arrived in Pisa, and from that time down to the present his name has been closely associated with those of Percy Bysshe Shelley and Lord Byron, as well as with Mary Wollstonecraft Shelley. Judged by any standard, not excluding his own inflated opinion of himself, Edward John Trelawny was a remarkable man, and no one whose path crossed his ever forgot him.

He was twenty-nine, a few months younger than Shelley, when he arrived in Pisa, his worldwide renown still ahead of him, but although he was still unknown, he created a stir. He was six feet tall, which caused his contemporaries to regard him as a giant, and was one of the most handsome men of the century, with broad shoulders, a tapering, athletic physique and the dark hair, swarthy skin and pale eyes that marked him as a Cornishman. He was a member of a distinguished family that had included high government officials, noted bishops and soldiers, and was following in their footsteps. Entering the Royal Navy as a midshipman at the age of thirteen, he had served with distinction in the war with Napoleon. He had lived in

India, where he had come to know Edward Williams, and among his numerous exploits had been the capture of a privateer he had later commanded.

The swashbuckling Trelawny, who was a superb swordsman, exuded an aura of romantic glamour, but he was also an intellectual, a liberal and, above all, a "hater of wrong," as Swinburne wrote many years later. He became the close friend of Shelley and Byron in 1822, accompanied the latter on his expedition to the Greek War of Independence the following year, and was the first important biographer of both poets, writing two books about them that were regarded as classics until scholars began to question his veracity.

He became a member of Shelley's and Byron's circle as soon as he arrived in Pisa, and his judgment of them confirmed the opinions of others. Byron, he said, was quick-witted but superficial, and was inclined to shift his ground in an argument because he lacked deep convictions. But Shelley, whom he admired more than all other men and considered the greatest genius of the age, was profound and steady. He "neither fled nor stood at bay, nor altered his course, but calmly went on with heart and mind intent on elevating his species. His words were, 'I always go on until I am stopped, and I never am stopped.'"

Mary Shelley also made a deep impression on Trelawny, and his description of her in his *Last Days of Shelley and Byron*, published a quarter of a century later, was regarded as the best word portrait of her ever drawn, even though it was inaccurate. He wrote:

> Such a rare pedigree of genius was enough to interest me in her, irrespective of her own merits as an authoress. The most striking feature in her face was her calm, grey eyes; she was rather under the English standard of woman's height, very fair and light-haired, witty, social, and animated in the society of friends, though mourn-

ful in solitude; like Shelley, though in a minor degree, she had the power of expressing her thoughts in varied and appropriate words, derived from familiarity with the works of our vigorous old writers.

Others portrayed Mary as tall, but Trelawny towered above everyone he knew, and therefore miscalculated. In any event, Mary was fascinated by him, and he immediately became her good friend as well as her husband's. His charm captivated her, and she found herself conversing with him by the hour, often neglecting her reading for the sake of yet another chat. She knew she was drawn to him and realized that the attraction was that of someone whose personality was the opposite of her own. She was contemplative, Trelawny was a man of action; she placed integrity above all else as a mark of character, while he carelessly refused to let truth stand in his way, and did not hesitate to lie or cheat if he could attain his desired ends.

Apparently unable to decide whether his influence was good or bad, merely pleasant or actively harmful, Mary wrote about him in a letter to Maria Gisborne that revealed her dilemma:

> He is a kind of half-Arab Englishman whose life has been as changeful as that of Anastasius, and who recounts his adventures as eloquently and as well as the imagined Greek. He is clever (a shade too clever, I sometimes think); for his moral qualities I am yet in the dark; he is a strange web which I am endeavoring to unravel. I would fain learn if generosity is united to impetuousness, probity of spirit to his assumption of singularity and independence. He is 6 feet high, raven black hair, which curls thickly and shortly, like a Moor's, dark gray expressive eyes, overhanging brows, upturned lips and a smile which expresses good nature and kindheartedness.

Trelawny had an immediate influence on Shelley after accepting an invitation to sail in the frail little craft from

Leghorn. The former sailor suggested that the poet and Edward Williams design a new, sturdier craft for themselves, including any features they particularly wanted. He would study their design with them and would make practical suggestions based on his own experience, and then he would see to it that the boat was built by a shipwright who was one of his good friends. Shelley, the inveterate boating enthusiast, needed nothing more than the offer to seal a friendship, and thereafter he and Trelawny became intimates who basked in a glow of mutual admiration.

Mary's relationship with Trelawny was far more complicated, and at the time of Shelley's death she had not yet made up her mind about him. His own feelings toward her became increasingly complex after she became the widow of the man he most admired. That involvement will be seen in detail in a later chapter. What mattered in the winter and spring of 1822 was that Shelley extended a hearty welcome to the newcomer, who accompanied him on most of his outings and became the most frequent of visitors to his house, and that Mary, who was trying to make her own estimate of Trelawny, gladly suffered his presence.

The coming of winter temporarily depressed the Shelleys, however, and Mary believed that the colder weather was responsible for what she called "rheumatism of the head," a condition that a later age would know as migraine headaches. What may have caused her condition, however, was tension; she had finished copying *Valperga* and had given it to Shelley to read. He sent it along to his own publisher with a letter far more glowing than Mary had dared to hope:

> The character of Beatrice, the prophetess, can only be done justice to in the very language of the author. I know nothing in Walter Scott's novels which at all approaches to the beauty and sublimity of this—creation, I may almost say, for it is perfectly original; and,

although founded upon the ideas and manners of the age which is represented, is wholly without a similitude in any fiction I ever read.

In spite of Shelley's enthusiasm his publisher decided not to do the book, and Mary's headaches returned. Then, after having pondered for a long time, she found what she hoped would be a solution to a problem that had plagued her for years. Her father's continuing financial problems still concerned her, but it upset her too much when Shelley was forced to extend aid to Godwin that he could ill afford. So she wrote to her father, proposing that he arrange for the publication of *Valperga;* in return for his efforts, she said, finding a way to permit him to keep his pride, he would be entitled to keep whatever sum the first printing earned. In this way, she estimated, she would be making a contribution of about four hundred pounds to her father while sparing her husband further financial distress.

She might have been afraid that Shelley would veto the idea, because she did not tell him what she had done until she had posted the letter to Godwin. If Shelley disapproved, it was too late for him to protest, so he gallantly told her the idea was sound. Her headaches disappeared, and Godwin, who succeeded in selling the book to a publisher for an advance payment of one hundred pounds, eventually received a total of more than four hundred and fifty pounds. Mary had no way of knowing that, when the time came, she herself would be in desperate need of additional funds.

Meanwhile a change was taking place in Shelley's attitude toward Jane Williams. For a time he had tolerated her presence, but now he began to find her pretty, although he still felt contempt for her domesticity. He enjoyed hearing her play the piano and sing, which she did one or two evenings a week, and he sent to England for a guitar so she could accompany herself on picnics and other outings.

By the spring of 1822 he was writing poems to Jane that were reminiscent of *Epipsychidion,* but Mary was not concerned. Her husband had merely found another model, and she understood his real-world opinion of Jane sufficiently well to know that he was neither infatuated with her nor becoming involved.

One significant change was taking place in the private lives of the Shelleys. They were seeing Edward and Jane Williams regularly, Trelawny was a visitor after dinner most evenings and Shelley spent at least a portion of every afternoon at Byron's villa. So there was less time for reading, which Mary's *Journal* reflects. It is possible, of course, that both were still reading more than she was recording, as she had other matters on her mind.

One of them was her husband's new boat, about which she felt misgivings that Jane Williams shared. Trelawny drew sketches of an American schooner of thirty feet, and proposed that a boat be built according to his design by his friend, a Captain Roberts of Genoa. Edward Williams had made a design of his own, with Shelley's help, and both were insistent that they preferred it to any other, so Trelawny sent the sketches to Captain Roberts.

Lord Byron listened to the many discussions of boats for a time, and then decided he wanted one built for himself. At his request Trelawny designed one for him, Byron's only stipulation being that it must be larger than that which Shelley and Williams had ordered. Meanwhile, as soon as the weather grew warmer, Shelley and Williams, accompanied by Trelawny, went sailing daily on the Arno, and there was constant talk of spending the summer on the Bay of Lerici, where they could sail in deep, salt waters in their new boat.

Mary Shelley and Jane Williams suffered these discussions in silence, and only when the men were not present did they admit to each other that the enthusiasms of amateur sailors left them cold, even apprehensive. Eventually Trelawny learned of their fears, and tried to soothe them, but he realized, when Mary told him Shelley could not swim, that she was not merely giving in to a wild and morbid imagination. He promised her that, when summer came, he would teach her husband to swim.

One afternoon in the spring of 1822 Trelawny performed a more immediate service. Shelley had gone off that morning for a walk in the woods near Pisa, and when he failed to return home for dinner, Mary became concerned. Trelawny accompanied her on a search, and when they reached an area so overgrown with brambles that a woman in skirts could not proceed, Mary waited while Trelawny went on alone.

After a time he found the poet, sitting at the edge of a small pool and staring at the water in deep concentration, a notebook on his knee. He was so completely lost in thought that he failed to notice his friend's approach until Trelawny announced in a loud voice that a "forsaken lady" was waiting for him.

Shelley leaped to his feet. "Poor Mary," he said, "hers is a sad fate. Come along; she can't bear solitude, nor I society —the quick coupled with the dead."

Mary was so relieved when she saw her husband that she called him a "wild goose" who was completely lacking in a sense of social obligation. Her release was so great that her behavior became silly, and the trio made a spectacle of themselves as they walked back to the Shelley house in Pisa, laughing with such abandon that people they passed on the road halted to stare at them in wonder.

That interlude was one of the last carefree hours that Mary Shelley and her husband would spend together.

XIX

Some of Shelley's early biographers, perhaps influenced by Jane Williams' claim that he had been in love with her, tried to read depth and significance that did not exist into the poems he wrote to her. He needed an object for his spiritual salutes to what he called Intellectual Beauty, and his relationship with Mary having progressed to a far more mature level of love, he used Jane as his symbol. Certainly Mary understood that he was indulging in a milder, less intense version of his imagined spiritual union with Emilia Viviani, and she knew, better than anyone else, that the real-life Shelley was frequently irritated by the inability of the real-life Jane to think in terms beyond the demands of her kitchen and the neatness of her house.

The real-life Shelley was fussing because crates of his books and Mary's desk, which had been stored in England, had not yet been shipped to them. Now that they were furnishing a home of their own they wanted these belongings, and the desk was particularly important to them, as it had been Mary Wollstonecraft's and was one of her few possessions that her daughter had inherited.

The real-life Shelley—and his wife—were disturbed by the complexities of their relationship with Lord Byron. Leigh Hunt and his family were ready to leave for Italy by the spring of 1822, and needed additional funds for the purpose, but Shelley could not provide the entire sum, and although he and Mary hated to go, hat in hand, to Byron for the money, they had no choice. He may have surprised them by accepting the entire burden with good grace.

Mary and Shelley were even more deeply involved in Claire Clairmont's efforts to obtain custody of her daughter from Byron, and whether Shelley would have remained friendly with Byron if the future of Allegra had not been at stake is questionable. His correspondence with Claire indicates that he and Mary might have seen much less of Byron had they not felt they could persuade him, in time, to deal more leniently with Claire. This concern flared into active anxiety, in the spring of 1822, when Claire confided in the Shelleys that she was thinking of abducting her child and running away with her. Mary knew that Claire was capable of destroying what was left of her reputation by such rash conduct, and Shelley was forced to write sternly in order to prevent Claire from carrying out her threat.

The debts Shelley had accumulated at the expense of his future inheritance were still on Mary's mind, and she convinced her husband that it was necessary to put his financial affairs in order. She did not care for herself, but wanted to protect their son, and her attitude inspired Shelley to take positive action. Horace Smith was no longer living in London and Peacock was busy looking after his own affairs, so Shelley corresponded more frequently with John and Maria Gisborne, using them, in effect, as his business advisers and agents.

A new tragedy occupied the minds and sapped the energies of the Shelleys late in April, when they, together with Edward and Jane Williams, were trying to find suitable summer quarters at the seashore. The day before they and Trelawny were intending to make a journey to Spezia to look at houses, they were shocked to learn from Lord Byron that Allegra had died at the convent school of a fever at the age of five years and three months. Neither they nor Claire had even known that the child was ill, and they were further numbed by the knowledge that Claire was scheduled to meet them at the shore.

They waited until she joined them before Mary and Shelley broke the news to her. They were not surprised by Claire's hysterical reaction: she not only sent Byron a wild letter in which she accused him of being their daughter's murderer, but called Mary and Shelley accomplices in the killing. Mary was forced to bear the brunt of her unreasoning hostility, and could be of little assistance to her husband, who managed to persuade Claire not to visit the convent to look at her child's body.

Mary was afraid Claire would go to Pisa to confront Byron, and thereafter might try to take her own life. But Claire demonstrated self-control as well as courage, and as soon as she grew calmer she returned to her position in Florence, almost completely concealing her grief and guilts. Mary offered her a place under the Shelley roof, but Claire refused, saying she did not want to inflict her burden on others; she preferred to be alone in a time of suffering, but agreed to visit them for a month during the summer.

Mary and Shelley hurriedly completed their plans for the summer, renting an unfurnished house called Casa Magni, which was located on the lonely little Bay of San Terenzo, which in turn opened onto the Gulf of Spezia. The setting was wild and sufficiently romantic to suit their purposes, and they were pleased because they could see the blue-green waters of the Mediterranean Sea from their second-floor bedchamber. There was one major drawback: Casa Magni was the only suitable dwelling that was available in the entire area, which meant the Shelleys would have to share it with Edward and Jane Williams. But Mary and Shelley took the place without hesitation, and all of

[*209*]

their friends, including Edward and Jane, assumed that Allegra's unexpected death was the cause of their haste.

That was only a part of their reason. There was another, even more compelling, that they revealed to no one at this time: Mary was pregnant again, and her physician had ordered her to obtain ample rest so she would not suffer from the sense of depression that had afflicted her after the birth of the still thriving Percy Florence. That made it necessary to move immediately, before her condition became more advanced, and Shelley felt that her grief over Allegra's death would make delays dangerous. Mary described her own feelings in graphic terms later in the summer, when she wrote to Maria Gisborne:

> I was not well in body or mind. My nerves were wound up to the utmost irritation, and the sense of misfortune hung over my spirits. I hated our house and the country about it. Shelley reproached me for this— his health was good, and the place was quite after his own heart. What could I answer? That the people were wild and hateful, that though the country was beautiful yet I liked a more countrified place, that there was great difficulty in living, that all our Tuscans would leave us, and that the very jargon of these Genovesi was disgusting. This was all I had to say, but no words could describe my feelings; the beauty of the woods made me weep and shudder; so vehement was my feeling of dislike that I used to rejoice when the winds and waves permitted me to go out in the boat, so that I was not obliged to take my usual walk down the shaded paths, alleys of vine-festooned trees—all that before I doted on, and that now weighed on me.

The charge made by some of Shelley's early biographers to the effect that he was insensitive to his wife's state of mind and devoted himself to Jane is untrue. He was ever conscious of his wife's moods, and the proximity to Jane, who spent most of her waking hours worrying about the next meal, was an annoyance he did not bear lightly. But there can be no doubt that he and Edward Williams enjoyed their boat.

Trelawny had agreed to become the master of Byron's much larger boat, the *Bolivar,* and therefore could not act as the third member of the schooner's crew, so Shelley and Williams hired Charles Vivian, the young boy who had sailed the boat to Spezia from Genoa. Trelawny told the proud owners their craft, the *Don Juan,* carried too much sail and was top-heavy, but they refused to listen to him. They went for a sail daily, and boasted that they were the proprietors of the fastest small craft in the Mediterranean.

Mary had little interest in boating. Little else made her happy. Her pregnancy was difficult, the servants complained of their separate quarters, and the house itself proved to be woefully inadequate for four adults and three small, active children. In fact, the place was badly in need of basic repairs. The walls were splotchy and cracked, plaster fell from the ceilings and floorboards were broken. The kitchen, a separate outbuilding of the type used since the Middle Ages, which Shelley considered quaint and romantic, was a nightmare. The wood stove not only smoked, but often could not be controlled, and as the dining room was located on the opposite side of the house, food cooled before it could be served.

"Only because Jane and I had been reared as English gentlewomen," Mary later remarked, "was it possible for us to observe the civilized amenities."

Mary and Shelley sometimes quarreled, and for the first time in the years they had been together, Mary occasionally indulged in open sarcasm when she addressed her husband. She wrote to Mrs. Mason, in whom she confided, that she was dreading Claire's visit later in the summer, and couldn't help wishing that Edward and Jane Williams lived elsewhere.

William Godwin's financial affairs had taken a severe turn for the worse, but still mindful of Shelley's firm instructions, he wrote to Mrs. Mason and asked her to forward his letter on the subject to Mary. Instead the loyal Mrs. Mason sent it to Shelley, who protected his wife by refraining from mentioning the contents to her. He sent a courteous reply to Godwin, saying he would be of assistance whenever his own situation improved.

But the old philosopher solved his immediate problems without the help of his daughter and son-in-law. The first Mary learned of the situation was contained in a letter from her half-brother, William, who wrote that the house on Skinner Street had been abandoned, and that, thanks to the cooperation of printers and suppliers, Godwin had established new living and working quarters in the Strand.

Claire arrived at Casa Magni early in June, but Mrs. Mason's fears were not realized. Her own suffering, together with the independent life she had been leading in Florence, had made a changed woman of Claire. Realizing that Mary was irritable because of her pregnancy and the crowded living conditions, her stepsister was diplomatic, cheerful and always ready to help. She looked after the children, joked with the men and, when Jane also sulked, supervised the preparation of the meals. She took charge of the purchases of food and other supplies, and when Mary and Jane were in despair because of a leaking roof, it was Claire who found a carpenter, then bullied him into coming to Casa Magni at once to repair the roof.

It was fortunate that Claire was present on June 16, when Mary unexpectedly suffered a miscarriage. While Edward Williams raced off to find the nearest doctor, who lived many miles away, Claire took command and her sensible care may have saved Mary's life. Meanwhile Shelley was hastily scanning every medical book in his library, and packed Mary's body from the waist down in ice, which halted her hemorrhage. The crisis had already ended by the time Edward returned with the physician.

Mary's convalescence was slow, and Claire prolonged her stay in order to take care of her. Gradually, as Mary regained her physical strength and her mental condition improved, she gleaned a new appreciation of her stepsister. By the time Claire finally returned to Florence in early July, the two young women had drawn closer together than they had been in years.

But a strange, inexplicable tension was beginning to pervade the house. On a number of occasions Shelley either dreamed or had waking visions of a catastrophe involving the sea. A few nights after Mary's miscarriage she was awakened from a deep sleep by the sound of Shelley's screams from the adjoining bed. Unable to rouse him, she went for help from the other adult members of the household. Eventually they managed to awaken Shelley, who had been terrified by a nightmare about the sea, but insisted he had not actually been sleeping.

Mary described the incident in detail in her *Journal* and correspondence, and soon thereafter she, too, began to dream of impending disaster. Even the prosaic, earth-bound Jane was affected, and one evening was certain she had seen Shelley followed on a walk across the terrace by his ghost. Before Claire returned to Florence she experienced several dreams that also seemed to warn of impending danger for Shelley, and only Edward Williams was free of psychic phenomena that could not be explained.

In spite of these forebodings and his wife's illness, Shelley thoroughly enjoyed the stay at Casa Magni. The sailing was a never-ending delight, he eagerly awaited the momentary arrival of Leigh Hunt, and was so lost in the composition of the last of his long poems, *The Triumph of Life,* that he was scarcely aware of the crowded living conditions and other inconveniences. In the last letter he wrote, he declared, "My only regret is that the summer must ever pass, or that Mary has not the same predilection for this place that I have, which would induce me never to shift my quarters."

Late in June the Hunts landed at Genoa, and an exuberant Shelley made plans to sail there for the long-awaited reunion. Mary was too weak to accompany him, and wept, inexplicably, when her husband sailed away with Edward Williams. Shelley met the Hunts, escorted them to Pisa and helped them settle into the quarters that had been rented for them there. A crisis loomed because the Countess Guiccioli's male relatives had just been sentenced to exile for life, and Byron was announcing his intention of leaving Pisa immediately.

Such a move would have made it impossible to publish the *Liberal,* the project that brought Leigh Hunt to Italy, and Shelley had to use all of his tact and powers of persuasion to right the situation. Byron finally agreed to stay, the crisis was resolved, and on the night of July 7 Shelley visited the Masons. The following morning Mrs. Mason wrote Mary to the effect that living conditions at Casa Magni might be primitive, but that she had never seen Shelley in such good health and spirits. He was enthusiastic about the publication of the new magazine, and said that never had his future been so bright.

On the morning of July 8, 1822, in Leghorn, Shelley and Williams bought food supplies and several items of clothing for their families, and then Shelley, who was accompanied by Trelawny, paid a brief visit to his bank. They parted after agreeing to dine together the following day at Casa Magni, and went to their separate boats. Shelley and Williams were the first to sail, and Captain Roberts, who was on board the *Bolivar,* remarked that a squall was coming up and that, in his opinion, the other vessel, the *Don Juan,* was carrying too much sail.

The departure of the *Bolivar* was delayed, and Captain Roberts went up to the port watchtower to observe the progress of the schooner. He caught his last glimpse of her at about three o'clock that afternoon, when she stood about ten miles offshore, and was disappearing into a thick fog bank.

When Trelawny reached Casa Magni the following day, he was surprised to learn that Shelley and Williams had not yet arrived, but he pretended that nothing was amiss as he didn't want to further upset their already disturbed wives. On July 10, when they still failed to appear, he rode hastily to Pisa to find out if Byron had received a message from them. Learning there had been no word, he sent orders to the *Bolivar* to begin a search, and arranged to meet his vessel at Viareggio. Reaching the town after a hard ride, he made inquiries, and was directed to the beach, where a water keg and several other articles had been washed ashore. He recognized the gear as the property of the *Don Juan,* and was afraid the consequences might be grave.

Mary remained in remarkably good spirits during the harrowing period of waiting. Jane gave in to uncontrolled fits of weeping, and Claire, who had come back from Florence, was almost as nervous, but Mary insisted there was no cause for concern.

On July 11 a note for Shelley from Leigh Hunt arrived by post, and Mary opened it. For the first time her nerves betrayed her, and her hands shook so badly she dropped the letter to the floor. Jane picked it up and read aloud: "Pray write to tell us how you got home, for they say that you had bad weather after you sailed on Monday, and we are anxious."

Jane was certain her husband and Shelley had been drowned, and Claire was stunned too, but Mary refused to admit that a tragedy had occurred. The women planned to hire a fishing boat and sail to Leghorn themselves on Friday to investigate the situation, but high seas kept them at home.

Even though Mary had not yet recovered her full strength she insisted on setting out by an overland route early on the morning of the thirteenth, and Jane accompanied her in the carriage. At Lerici they heard there was no news, and Mary declared their fears were groundless. After sixteen hours of travel they reached Pisa. Leigh Hunt was asleep, but Byron and Teresa Guiccioli saw them, and were forced to admit they had heard nothing.

Mary and Jane refused Byron's offer of a meal and a bedchamber, and set out without delay for Leghorn, where they arrived at three o'clock in the morning. At six they located Captain Roberts at a waterfront inn, and over breakfast, the first meal they had eaten since their departure, they learned what little he could tell them.

Mary had not slept in more than twenty-four hours, and her health was so fragile that Jane was afraid she would collapse. But she refused to rest, and calling on her remarkable inner resources, she insisted they return to Casa Magni in the hope their husbands had arrived during their absence. They traveled by way of Viareggio, and there saw the water cask and other gear. Trelawny, who was in the little town making inquiries, was unable to join them before they had been shown the equipment that had been washed ashore.

He accompanied them back to Casa Magni, and it was his courage and strength that sustained them for the next five days and nights. By now Mary's state of mind was as bad as Jane's, and she moved, pendulumlike, from hope to desolation to hope. She shed no tears, however, and told

Trelawny, "I shall not weep until I know for certain I have good cause."

On July 18 Trelawny left for Leghorn in search of information, and gave instructions that any letters arriving for him could be opened. A few hours after his departure a letter from Captain Roberts did arrive, and Claire intercepted it without the knowledge of the others. The message it contained was brief: the bodies of two men had been washed ashore near Viareggio.

Claire knew that Shelley and Williams were dead, but felt herself incapable of passing along the word to Mary and Jane, so she sent a brief letter to Leigh Hunt, asking him to come to Casa Magni at once and break the news.

Meanwhile Trelawny had picked up the word about the finding of two bodies several miles apart, and hastened to investigate. The features of the two men were no longer recognizable, but he instantly identified Shelley, who had been carrying a book of Sophocles' plays in one jacket pocket and a volume of poetry in another. He also positively identified Williams by his clothing.

Trelawny went straight to Casa Magni, arriving a short time after Claire had sent her appeal for help to Leigh Hunt. His expressive face revealed more than he intended, and a serving maid burst into tears. He found Mary, Jane and Claire on the terrace, and all three looked at him as he approached.

He discovered he could not speak, and Mary finally broke the long silence by asking, "Is there no hope?"

Trelawny shook his head, turned on his heel and went into the house, where he located the nursemaid, and sent her to the terrace with Shelley's son and the Williams children. By the time he saw Mary again, several hours later, she had regained some shreds of composure, and Trelawny won her lifelong gratitude by offering no condolences. Instead he spoke quietly and at length about Shelley's talent,

[*217*]

expressing the conviction that the day would come when the entire world would recognize the poet's genius.

On July 19 Trelawny escorted the women and children to Pisa, and protracted negotiations were instituted with the governments of Tuscany and Rome before permission was granted for the necessary funeral and burial arrangements. On August 13 the body of Edward Williams was cremated in the presence of Trelawny, Lord Byron and Hunt, and the ashes were presented to Jane, who was planning to leave at once for England.

On the following day Shelley's body was cremated. Trelawny was the only one of his friends who had the courage to attend the ceremony, and at one point, when the commander of the Tuscan troops who was in charge happened to be looking in another direction, he snatched the heart from the funeral pyre, burning his hand. Later, after the heart had been encased in a lead-lined, metal box, he presented it to Mary, who kept it for the rest of her own life.

Shelley's ashes were buried in the Protestant Cemetery in Rome, where his small son William had also found his last resting place. Trelawny purchased a grave adjacent to Shelley's for himself, but almost six decades passed before he, too, was buried there.

Mary Shelley took no active part in the making of these arrangements. She was so dazed that, for a time, all she knew was that her husband and love, whom she regarded as the greatest poet of the age, had died one month prior to his thirtieth birthday. She herself was twenty-five.

XX

On August 15, 1822, Jane Williams and her children left Italy for England, and Mary Shelley sat down to write the story of the tragedy in a letter to Maria Gisborne. After describing the events of the preceding month she wrote briefly of herself, and her comments accurately reflect her feelings:

> Well, here is my story, the last story I shall have to tell. All that might have been bright in my life is now despoiled. I shall live to improve myself, to take care of my child, and render myself worthy to join him. Soon my weary pilgrimage will begin. I rest now, but soon I must leave Italy, and then there is an end of all but despair.

But Mary gave in to neither despair nor melancholy. She remembered what her father had written to her about self-pity in a time of grief, and she would not allow herself to forget she was prone to the dangerous depression she had inherited from her mother. For her child's sake, if not her own, it was necessary for her to live.

There was much to keep her occupied. She had letters to write and new housing arrangements to make; she plunged into correspondence with the executors of Shelley's estate, and also wrote to his father, who made no reply. Her own financial situation was an immediate, urgent problem, as Sir Timothy Shelley abruptly cut off the allowance he had been paying his son.

So Mary went to work with Leigh Hunt, helping him put out the first issue of the *Liberal,* and initiated the arrangements for the publication of her husband's *Posthumous Poems,* which she agreed to edit. Trelawny and Lord Byron discreetly rendered her financial assistance, and she and her son were offered a home by Leigh and Marianne Hunt.

For months the friends of Mary and Shelley marveled at the young widow's strength. She never complained about her situation, and only in her *Journal,* which she believed no one else would ever see, did she record her feelings of desolation. But she never lost sight of the unhappiness her melancholy had caused Shelley, or the harm she had done to herself, and she was determined to overcome her loneliness. She allowed no one else to know of the inner struggle, and she fought the battle alone, realizing that no one could help her.

The departure of Claire Clairmont from Italy a few weeks after Shelley's death marked a major turning point in Mary's life, and thereafter the stepsisters had few real reunions, although they corresponded regularly for many years. Claire went off to Vienna to join her brother Charles, and there accepted a position as a tutor. She was destined to spend the rest of her life as a teacher and governess, living in Austria and Italy, Russia and France.

Pisa had too many unhappy memories for Mary, and when the Hunts proposed a move to Genoa, where living was cheaper, she agreed to accompany them there. Byron was also moving to the neighborhood of Genoa, and promised he would continue to look out for Mary's interests. She saw very little of him after they moved, however, in part because his own interests occupied him, and, in all probability, because Mary made no secret of her dislike for his way of life.

Day-to-day existence under the Hunts' roof was far more

difficult than Mary had anticipated. Marianne proved to be a slovenly housekeeper, and Mary, who demanded cleanliness and order, soon felt she and her child were living in a poverty-stricken factory worker's hovel. Leigh Hunt was the kindest and most considerate of men, but he was so ineffectual, so incapable of dealing with Byron on equal terms, that the failure of the *Liberal* was evident almost from the outset, even though four issues did appear.

The undisciplined Hunt children, who kept the house in an uproar, gave Mary little time to think, and she found the task of editing Shelley's *Posthumous Poems* far more difficult than she had anticipated. The four Hunt children were older than her son, and when they made Percy Florence the butt of their jokes, Mary was forced to intervene in order to protect him, and this complication added to her distress.

She could not afford to move into a place of her own, however, and was forced to tolerate the living conditions. Lord Byron made no move to advance the money he had promised her, and Mary, who knew his niggardliness, was too proud to ask for his help. She wrote again to her father-in-law, requesting that some provision be made for Percy Florence, but Sir Timothy Shelley remained silent.

The failure, critical as well as financial, of the first issue of the *Liberal* in England created new complications. Byron began to quarrel with the meek Hunt, and Mary tried in vain to persuade Hunt that only the independence Shelley had demonstrated would be effective. Unable to stem the drift of the magazine toward ruin by indirect means, Mary intervened directly by writing a strongly worded letter to Byron in which she urged him to give Hunt a freer hand, bolstering her arguments by reminding him that Shelley had placed his complete faith in Hunt.

Byron chose to ignore the communication, but that did not end Mary's relations with him. Shelley had advanced virtually all of the money for the move of the Hunt family to Italy and the publication of the first issue of the *Liberal*, and Byron had promised to pay his colleague his share of the expenses, but had not done so at the time of Shelley's death. The very considerable sum of one thousand pounds was involved, and Mary believed that Byron now owed it to her. Her attitude was strengthened by a letter from her father, who offered her a solution for her financial problems: all she had to do was collect from Byron.

Mary hated to ask anything of Byron, but forced herself to see him, and requested the money. She told the rest of the story herself in a letter to Jane Williams:

> He declared he would regulate all himself. I waited in vain for these arrangements. . . . Byron chose to transact our negotiation through Hunt, and gave such an air of unwillingness and sense of the obligation he conferred, as at last provoked Hunt to say that there was no obligation, since he owed me £1000! "Glad of a quarrel, straight I clap the door!"

Byron dawdled, making no excuse for his failure to pay Mary, and their relationship became distinctly chilly. Meanwhile Byron resented Hunt's interference, even though he himself had insisted on using the editor as his intermediary, and the atmosphere sealed the doom of the *Liberal*.

Mary's own basic situation was clarified by a letter Sir Timothy Shelley sent to her on January 23, 1823. He would be pleased to provide for the living, welfare and education of his grandson, he said in a curtly worded communication, but would do so only on the condition that Mary relinquished the custody of Percy Florence to him. Mary received the letter at the end of the first week in February, and sent an immediate reply. She thanked Sir Timothy for his offer, but made it very plain that nothing would induce her to give up her son. Although her letter was courteously worded, she fumed in private, damning him for his temerity.

At least her own course was clear. Had Shelley's father seen fit to send her an allowance she would have preferred to remain in Italy, but the terms of his offer closed that door. Therefore she would have to return to England and earn a living for herself and her child as an author.

She lacked the necessary funds to ship her books, the piano Shelley had loved and her other household belongings, however, and she could not even scrape up enough for her own passage and that of her child. Swallowing her pride, she spent several months in correspondence with a number of friends, all of whom sympathized with her situation—and none of whom offered her a penny.

Lord Byron was making plans to leave Italy in July with Trelawny, the pair intending to take part in the Greek War of Independence; some of the poet's enemies were unkind enough to suggest that he was making a theatrical gesture in the hope of polishing his tarnished reputation. Shortly before their departure, Trelawny came privately to Mary and offered the sum of two hundred pounds.

At first he tried to pretend that the money came from Lord Byron, but Mary saw through the flimsy excuse, and Trelawny admitted that the offer was his own. She refused the money, knowing that he was short of funds. But Trelawny overwhelmed her. His dignity unruffled, he insisted it was his privilege to be of assistance to her, and that he owed it to her because of his own great love for Shelley. Mary could not refuse an offer made on those terms, and took the money.

Byron and Trelawny sailed for Greece, and Mary did not see the poet before he departed. She wrote to Jane Williams that Byron carried ten thousand pounds, but that Trelawny had only fifty pounds to his name. He regarded the two hundred pounds he had given her as a gift, but to her it was a debt of honor which she subsequently repaid, ignoring the advice of Shelley's old friend Hogg, who had said it was "unwise" of her to send Trelawny anything.

Mary and Percy Florence left Genoa on July 25, 1823, a full year after Shelley's death, on the first overland leg of their journey to England. They stopped in Paris for a week, and Mary hoped to see Amelia Curran, but discovered that the friend she had known in Rome had already left for England. Horace Smith and his wife were in Paris, and dined with her on several occasions. Through Louisa Holcroft, the daughter of an old friend of Godwin's, Mary met John Howard Payne, the dramatist whose plays were financial failures but who achieved immortality through the writing of "Home, Sweet Home." He and his friend Washington Irving, who was regarded by Europeans as the most distinguished of living American authors, saw a great deal of Mary during her brief stay in Paris.

She was still a beautiful young woman, and having stopped wearing widow's black on the anniversary of Shelley's death, she was pleased to discover that men were still attracted to her. She found a kindred spirit in Irving, whom she met on a number of occasions in England, and enjoyed her talks with him. At no time was their mutual interest romantic, and contemporaries who suggested that only Irving's shyness prevented the development of an intimate relationship failed to understand the essence of Mary's appeal. She was one of the few women of her era who was the intellectual equal of any man, and her vast knowledge of literature, combined with her understanding of authors, made her the ideal dinner partner for a man of letters. She and Irving liked to chat, but there is nothing in the correspondence or diaries of either that suggests even the beginnings of an intimate relationship.

Mary's friendship with Payne was a far different matter. Remembered by posterity only because of an incidental song in one of his many plays, he was one of the most popular actors of his day, and his failure as a playwright was caused by bad luck and inadequate copyright laws. Some of his dramas enjoyed popularity for a half-century, although he earned virtually nothing from them, and the vagaries of fortune had embittered him by the time he met Mary.

He had never encountered a lovelier woman, he recognized her as his intellectual peer, and her sympathy, her understanding of his many problems caused him to believe he had fallen in love with her. Mary subsequently corresponded with him, and Payne misinterpreted her warmth, failing to understand that she regarded him as a colleague and friend, but that her heart was still committed to the only man she had ever loved.

When Payne visited Mary in London a year and a half later he proposed marriage to her, and her rejection turned him against her. He struck out at her in his anger, claiming without justification that she had encouraged his attentions because of a desire to establish herself on a romantic basis with Irving, his fellow American and collaborator, of whom he was secretly jealous. Only a few people ever learned of his groundless allegations, which did Mary's reputation no harm.

Mary and her child reached London on August 25, after an uneventful Channel crossing, and were met at the docks by her father and half-brother, William. They took her to their new quarters at 195 Strand, where Mrs. Godwin also greeted her warmly. Mary was grateful for the temporary refuge they offered her, but had no intention of submitting to their authority. In her first letter from London to the Hunts she asked them to write to her in care of the *Examiner,* explaining that "unless you write for Mrs. Godwin's most certain and attentive perusal, do not send any letters" to the Strand.

She was also cautious in her relations with Godwin, finding it impossible to forget the strains of past years. But the training he had given her in childhood made it easy for her to deal with him impersonally, and her admiration of his intellect was renewed. She was pleased and astonished, too, to find that her father treated her with a new respect, and for reasons that had not crossed her mind.

As she wrote to the Hunts, "Lo and behold! I found myself famous!" *Valperga* had achieved a solid success in the three months since its publication, and soon would be going into another printing, the benefits of which would be paid to her. She also learned that a dramatic adaptation of *Frankenstein* was the talk of the town, and soon after her return she saw it performed for the twenty-third time at the English Opera House. It was unprecedented for a contemporary drama to play that many performances, and Mary was not only a celebrated author in her own right, but her royalties from the play made it possible for her to establish a home of her own.

She wrote at once to Jane Williams, who was living in the country, suggesting they share a flat in London. Meanwhile she found it easy to slip back into the routines of Godwin's social life. Hazlitt was still a frequent caller, and treated her with marked courtesy. Charles and Mary Lamb showed her every kindness, invited her to gatherings at their own home, and introduced her to their friends, Victor and Mary Novello, who became members of her immediate circle. Washington Irving came frequently to her father's house, as he had agreed to do what he could to arrange for the publication of Godwin's works in the United States.

The visitor whose presence delighted Mary more than all others was Coleridge, whom she had known since childhood. He was still a fascinating conversationalist who could hold an audience spellbound, and she forgot her own troubles as she listened to him. Later, writing in her *Journal,* she could not help wishing that he and Shelley had met.

Mary's sudden rise to eminence was embarrassing to Sir Timothy Shelley, who was destined never to meet his daughter-in-law face to face. He unexpectedly got in touch with her through his London attorneys, and offered her an allowance of one hundred pounds per year for her son, provided she neither write nor make any substantial contribution to a biography of her late husband, nor allow any of his work to be published. Mary knew her own income was uncertain, and as she was just starting to work on a new novel, she accepted the offer. But she intended to circumvent these restrictions.

Jane Williams was happy to set up housekeeping with Mary, and the two young widows, cherishing the memories of the association that had brought them together, rented an apartment for themselves and their children near Highgate Hill. It was there that Thomas Jefferson Hogg called on them, and was so attentive the Hunts wrote from Italy a few months later that they had heard Jane and Hogg were becoming involved in a romance. Mary denied the story, writing an indignant defense of Jane in which she swore that her friend was true to the memory of Edward Williams.

Shelley's publisher was eager to bring out his *Posthumous Poems,* so Mary bore down on the editing of her husband's work, and also spent two to three hours each day on an outline of her new novel, in which she conceived of a somewhat disguised Shelley as the protagonist. Her one love was still ever-present in her mind, but she was winning her private battle against melancholy. The proof was made evident in a long poem she wrote, called "The Choice," which was not published until 1876, a quarter of a century after her death. It was undated, but was included in her

Journal for 1822–1824, and in the latter part of that period
she sent a somewhat revised version of it to Leigh Hunt.
The first of the poem's eight verses is indicative of the
victory Mary won over the depression that threatened to
engulf and destroy her after Shelley's shocking death:

> My choice!—My Choice, alas, was had and gone
> With the red gleam of last autumnal sun;
> Lost in that deep wherein he bathed his head,
> My Choice, my life, my hope together fled;—
> A wanderer here, no more I seek a home,
> The sky a vault, and Italy a tomb.
> Yet as some days a pilgrim I remain,
> Linked to my orphan child by love's strong chain;
> And since I have a faith that I must earn,
> By suffering and by patience, a return
> Of that companionship and love, which first
> Upon my young life's cloud like sunlight burst,
> And now has left me, dark, as when its beams,
> Quenched in the might of dreadful ocean streams,
> Leave that one cloud, a gloomy speck on high,
> Beside one cloud in the else darkened sky;—
> Since I must live, how would I pass the day,
> How meet with fewest tears the morning's ray,
> How sleep with calmest dreams, how find delights,
> As fireflies gleam through interlunar nights?

By early 1824 people who had known Mary all of her
life, as well as the friends she had made during the years
she and Shelley had been together, were applauding her
courage. She was so successful in creating a new life for
herself that there were a few who secretly believed she was
merely posing for their benefit.

They were mistaken, however, because she had evolved
a new philosophy that was uniquely her own. She would
not allow her irrevocable loss to interfere with the joys,
intellectual and personal, of daily living, because a dim-

ming of her perceptions might interfere with the twin goals she had established for herself. First, she intended to rear a son in a manner worthy of his father's name, and at the same time she would do everything in her power to enhance the reputation of Percy Bysshe Shelley, who was still regarded as a minor literary figure by all but a small handful who knew and appreciated his work. She would not rest, she told everyone from Coleridge to Jane Williams, until Shelley was universally recognized as a poet of the first rank.

There were still major obstacles to be overcome, and not until 1824, or "the second year after 1822," as Mary called it, did she find the courage to pay her first visit since her return to England to Maria and John Gisborne. Even then she found it necessary to take Jane Williams with her, but the tact and unexpressed sympathy of the Gisbornes helped her to overcome her own emotions, and thereafter her recovery was swift.

An entry Mary made in her *Journal* late on the night of June 8, 1824, after she and Jane had spent the evening entertaining a group of literary friends, revealed the new spirit that enabled her to live in the present and to look forward with joyful anticipation to the future:

> I have been gay in company before, but the inspiring sentiments of the heart's peace I have not felt before tonight—and yet, my own, never was I so entirely yours —in sorrow and grief I wish sometimes (how vainly) for earthly consolation at a period of pleasing excitement— I cling to your memory alone, and you alone receive the overflowings of my heart. Beloved Shelley, good night. . . .

XXI

THE YEAR 1824 OPENED on an unhappy note. The *Posthumous Poems* appeared in print, together with Mary's notes on them, and several hundred copies were sent out to prepublication subscribers. But Sir Timothy Shelley was outraged, and notified Mary through his attorneys that she was violating their agreement. Unless she withdrew the remaining copies, he said, he would cancel his allowance to her of one hundred pounds per year.

Mary was forced for financial reasons to bow to his demand, and withdrew the unsold copies of the book. But Sir Timothy's stand in no way altered her determination to make the poetry of her husband available to the public. In 1829, for example, she played a major role in the editing of a one-volume edition of the works of Coleridge, Keats and Shelley, and a decade later, after Sir Timothy had a partial change of heart and altered his ban so that the publication of his son's works was no longer forbidden, Mary brought out a new edition of his poetry, cleverly adding long notes that, in effect, constituted a biography.

Her father-in-law's actions in January, 1824, made Mary more determined than ever to write the novel she had been planning. For a period of two or three months she had been thinking of putting it aside in order to write a play, but she was forced to agree with her father, who had just written to her:

> It is laziness, my dear Mary, that makes you wish to be a dramatist. It seems in prospect a short labor to write a play, and a long one to write a work consisting of volumes. . . . But as there is no royal road to geometry, so there is no idle and self-indulgent activity that leads to literary eminence.

Mary conceived of the new work as a contemporary novel that would include elements of fantasy in order to satisfy the readers who were clamoring for another *Frankenstein*. She would write about the sole survivor of civilization, "the last relic of a beloved race, my companions extinct before me," and would call it *The Last Man*. Her protagonist, whom she called Adrian, was a Shelley so superficially disguised that no reader would be fooled. Another character, whom she called Lord Raymond, could have been no one but Byron.

The Last Man was her third major work, and Mary discovered that her pen did not glide across the pages with the ease and facility she had displayed in doing her earlier books. "Writing has become a task," she scribbled in her *Journal*, adding, "My studies are irksome, my life dreary. In this prison it is only in human intercourse that I can pretend to find consolation." As so many friends who wrote for a living could have told her, she had become a professional author.

Certainly it was not easy for Mary to find relief from the demands of her manuscript. She had already spent the royalties earned by the dramatic version of *Frankenstein* and the new edition of *Valperga,* and she could count on no more than one hundred pounds per year from the continuing sales of both books. This sum, added to her father-in-law's allowance, would force her to live in genteel poverty. Victor and Mary Novello often asked her to dine with them, and other friends extended frequent invitations, too, but Mary felt she could not afford to return hospitality extended to her, so she seldom accepted. The theater, opera and concerts were beyond her reach, too, but her pride would not allow her to admit the real reason she saw so few plays, and she told friends that she lived too far from the theatrical district to attend many performances.

In the spring of 1824 she received a long letter from Trelawny, who revealed to her that Lord Byron had become mired in the tribal feuds of the Greek leaders. Trelawny himself had been fighting with distinction, and had married the daughter of a Greek chieftain, apparently on impulse, but they would separate and be divorced some months later, after the birth of their daughter.

Late in April England was startled to learn that Byron had died in Greece on the nineteenth of the month after a short but painful illness. His body was returned to London, where the liberals joined with the Greek people in hailing him as a hero. He was refused burial in Westminster Abbey because of the scandalous life he had led, and his remains were interred in the graveyard on his ancestral estate.

Mary had no reason to love Byron, but his death caused her to forgive the sexual promiscuity that had outraged her, as well as his financial dealings with her after she became a widow. Thereafter she never again attacked him, and was careful to emphasize only his good qualities when she referred to him in her correspondence. Her portrayal of Lord Raymond in *The Last Man* softened, becoming three-dimensional, and contemporaries regarded the portrait she painted of Byron as compassionate as well as accurate.

Later in 1824 Mary received a letter from Tom Medwin, who told her he intended to write a biography of Byron, and asked for her help in remembering various anecdotes about him. She declined to have any part in the project, and sent an indignant letter to Marianne Hunt, saying:

> Have you heard of Medwin's book? Notes of conversations which he had with Lord Byron (when tipsy); every one is to be in it; every one will be angry. He wanted me to have a hand in it, but I would not. Years ago, when a man died, the worms ate him; now a new set of worms feed on the carcase of the scandal he leaves behind him, and grow fat upon the world's love of tittle-tattle. I will not be numbered among them.

The Mary Godwin who had cared nothing about world opinion and had eloped with a married man had been transformed into a lady of modesty, dignity and decorum. No longer the adolescent who thumbed her nose at society, Mary behaved with a dignity that impressed Shelley's sisters, whom she met in 1824 and 1825. She devoted herself to her son, worked hard on her new book and saw friends infrequently.

She continued to insist, as did Jane Williams, that she would never marry again. Jane suspected her of entertaining a lively interest in Trelawny, and there may have been some substance behind the charge, as Mary had admitted, previously, that the adventurer had fascinated her. But she believed his personality was better suited to mating with a woman of Claire Clairmont's temperament, and in her correspondence with Claire, who was holding a position with a noble family in Russia, she expressed her thoughts freely. With a novelist's insistence on arranging a happy ending for a story that had been steeped in drama and tragedy, she imagined Claire being married to Trelawny and making him the perfect wife, just as he would become the perfect husband. Claire was not averse to the idea, but life had forced her to become practical, and she did not dwell on the theme in her replies.

Thomas Jefferson Hogg was a frequent visitor to the flat occupied by the two widows, and it did not cross Mary's mind that he came there as anything but a friend. Hogg, however, was developing a sharp romantic interest in Jane Williams. At one time or another he had imagined himself in love with each of Shelley's wives, and now, having read Shelley's poems written to Jane, he began to pay court to her. He took care to behave decorously in the presence of Mary, later writing that she would have shown him the door 'had she been aware of his developing sentiments toward Jane.

By 1826 Mary's situation improved appreciably. *The Last Man* was published early in the year, and was greeted by the press with reviews that, with one or two exceptions, were glowing. The book was actually a feeble literary exercise, and posterity has judged it accordingly; the only present-day interest in it stems from the portraits of Shelley and Byron that Mary painted. In 1826, however, it was regarded as a literary triumph, and not only greatly enhanced Mary's reputation as a novelist, but also filled her empty purse. She earned more than six hundred pounds from *The Last Man* in its first year of publication, and thereafter it brought her an additional one hundred pounds annually for at least five years.

Mary's dignified behavior since her return to England also paid unexpected dividends. Shelley's sisters had been deeply impressed by what they heard of her devotion to her son, and even Sir Timothy had not failed to notice that her conduct was faultless. Much as he would have hated to admit it, he was also influenced in her favor by the success of *The Last Man,* and although he did not bother to read it himself, Lady Shelley and their daughters assured him that it was a book of great moral values.

So Sir Timothy was amenable to a discussion when Peacock, acting on his own initiative, approached him on

Mary's behalf. It is curious that Peacock should have acted as an intermediary. Mary long had been convinced that her late husband's friend and one-time pensioner actively disliked her, and she had heard on a number of occasions that he had been very fond of Harriet Westbrook Shelley. This was true, but his love for Shelley impelled him to overlook the faults he saw, or thought he saw in his friend's widow. During the course of several visits to Sir Timothy he assiduously referred to Mary as "my very dear friend."

Not until he became convinced that his mission would succeed did Peacock tell Mary his secret: he had good cause to believe that Sir Timothy was softening, and would consent to increase the allowance he was paying her. The reviews of *The Last Man* that appeared in the conservative press tore away the remaining bastions of Sir Timothy's resistance, and in the spring of 1826 he agreed to double Mary's allowance. Although he had already paid her the sum of one hundred pounds for the year, he handed Peacock a bank order for an additional one hundred pounds.

Mary's circumstances were so much improved that she was able to afford new wardrobes for herself and Percy Florence, and she bought a large number of books she was eager to read. She could entertain more frequently, and was in a position to attend the theater and opera when she wished. She also came to her father's assistance when he was stricken with one of his chronic financial catastrophes, and "loaned" him one hundred pounds, which he never repaid.

The sharing of a dwelling with Jane Williams was becoming complicated, and although there had been difficulties for some time, Mary apparently had been unwilling to recognize them. She regarded Jane as her closest friend and felt bound to her by the tragedy they had shared, but her affection was not completely reciprocated. Mary was content to associate with men on a basis of friendship, but

Jane's need for male flattery and attention was deeper, even though she insisted Edward Williams had been her only love and that she could never care for anyone else.

Living with Mary bored Jane, little daily frictions marred the peace of their household, and the atmosphere was similar, although milder, to that which Mary had endured in her relationship with Claire Clairmont. Thinking that a holiday atmosphere might clear the air, Mary invited Jane and her children to accompany her and Percy Florence to Brighton in the summer of 1826. Jane accepted, and they spent the month of August at the resort, swimming and enjoying the sea air. Mary loved the serenity of the visit, and was shocked, as she confided in her *Journal*, when Jane expressed relief that the ordeal had come to an end.

By this time Mary had become aware of Hogg's strong interest in Jane, and feeling no sense of jealousy, hoped her friend would see fit to marry him. Although she regarded Hogg as weak and something of a pseudointellectual, she nevertheless knew he could well afford to support a wife and children, and was obviously fond of the Williams youngsters. Jane continued to insist, however, that she could never love again, but in the next breath she admitted her need for a husband and a home of her own.

Early in 1827 Jane finally gave in to Hogg's entreaties, and "married" him. Since she was still married to her long-abandoned husband, her union with Hogg was as informal as that with Williams had been; in other words, they lived together, she took his name and was faithful to him, becoming his common-law wife. Mary wished the couple well, and was sincere when she expressed a desire for their mutual happiness. Within a short time, however, she was no longer on speaking terms with her former dearest friend.

Apparently Jane told Hogg what he wanted to hear, and

told him stories about her relationship with Shelley that had no basis in fact. Using Shelley's poems to her as proof, she invented outrageous tales by the score. Shelley had been madly in love with her, and had begged her to have an affair with him, but she had held back for Edward's sake. Shelley had persisted, however, and had given her many gifts, of which her guitar was the only one still in her possession. Shelley had also written songs to her, she claimed, and she played several for Hogg.

The gullible Hogg, happy that he had finally succeeded where he believed Shelley had failed, repeated the stories in person and in his correspondence with virtually every member of the Shelley circle he had ever known. He could not refrain from boasting, and Jane continued to feed his vanity by telling him more lies.

Eventually the stories made their way back to Mary, who was stunned, then saddened, and she wrote in her *Journal* that her principal reaction was a feeling of regret that she and Shelley had wasted their affection on someone who was unworthy of that love. Unable to put the matter out of her mind, she wrote to Trelawny about it, and he replied with typical bluntness, saying he had enjoyed Edward's company, but had disliked Jane from the time of their first meeting.

Mary had been drawing close to Thomas Moore and his wife, who had long been friends of Godwin's, and feeling the need for practical advice, she went to Moore. He was a poet and satirist whose reputation declined sharply after his death, but in his own time he was the most celebrated author in England, commanded enormous fees from publishers for his work, and lived on a prodigal scale. For a time he had been closely associated with Byron, on whose biography he was at work, and had become friendly with Mary because of the Shelleys' association with Byron.

Moore, a forthright man, urged her to bring the matter into the open by writing to Jane and demanding that she retract the lies.

Mary followed his advice, and wrote Jane a strongly worded letter. After a silence of several weeks, Jane sent a reply in which she made no mention of the charges against her, but instead described at length how sorrowful she had been because of Mary's harshness.

Long accustomed to Jane's tears, Mary ignored them and demanded an apology. Jane was cornered, and Hogg, who still believed her stories, convinced her that Mary was fighting for her late husband's good name, and had no choice. Therefore, he said, Jane should make a gesture to her former friend; it would cost little, and would end the feud.

Jane begged Mary for forgiveness, and Mary realized she would gain nothing by keeping the dispute alive, so she extended her hand. On the surface, at least, that ended the matter. The friendship was resumed, and when Jane gave birth to Hogg's daughter, Prudentia, Mary became the child's godmother.

But the damage had already been done. There were many who believed Jane's tales, and others who, even though skeptical, wondered if there might not be some basis for her claims. Mary never really forgave the woman to whom she had given her undiluted friendship, nor did she recover from the hurt inflicted on her. As late as November 23, 1833, she wrote in her *Journal:*

> I am copying Shelley's letters. Great God, what a thing is life! In one of them he says "the curse of this life is that what we have once known we cannot cease to know. . . ." Life is not all ill till we wish to forget. Jane first inspired me with that miserable feeling, staining past years as she did—taking the sweetness from memory and giving it instead a serpent's tooth.

XXII

THE YEAR 1826 WAS IMPORTANT to Mary for reasons she would remember as long as she lived. Harriet's son Charles, who was a sickly boy, fell ill and died, and Percy Florence became the heir to his grandfather's baronetcy and the Shelley fortune. She wrote without delay to Sir Timothy Shelley, expressing the hope that, under the circumstances, he would provide the funds for her son's education, adding that her husband had hoped Percy Florence would attend a public school.

Sir Timothy, who still refused to deal directly with his son's widow, replied to her through his solicitors. They invited Mary to visit their offices, and a tacit understanding was reached. Sir Timothy would pay for his grandson's tuition at public schools, although he would not accept responsibility for the boy's room and board. He would guarantee that the child received the education of an English gentleman to which his future rank entitled him provided that Sir Timothy became acquainted with Percy Florence. Mary agreed to allow her son to visit the Shelley estate for reasonable periods and at reasonable intervals.

Thereafter the boy dutifully paid three visits a year to his hard-shelled, unforgiving grandfather. Percy Florence already bore a strong physical resemblance to his father as a boy, and Lady Shelley's heart went out to him at first sight. Her daughters made a fuss over the child, too, but Sir Timothy's attitudes were unchanged. Still gruff and overbearing, he made it plain to the boy that he had no use for poets, despised scandal and felt only contempt for those who failed to treat money with the respect it deserved. Percy Florence learned to exercise tact and diplomacy very early in life.

He was a healthy child, far more robust than his father had been, and very early in life showed signs that the intellect he had inherited from both of his parents would mature rapidly. Like them, he was artistically inclined, but showed relatively little interest in the written word, and instead displayed talent with a drawing pen and paint brush.

Mary took pains not to spoil him, and although it required an effort on her part, she refrained from hovering over him. She took a realistic view of his character and talent, and tolerated no nonsense from those who wanted to think of him as perfect because he was the son of Percy Bysshe Shelley. Maria Gisborne, after paying Mary a visit in 1834, wrote to her in glowing terms about the boy, but received a blunt reply: "He is not all you say; he has no ambition, and his talents are not so transcendent as you appear to imagine. But he is a fine, spirited, clever boy, and, I think, promises good things."

The realization that her son was not endowed with genius comforted Mary. Shelley's experiences and her own had convinced her that society demanded the payment of too large a penalty by those who were different, those who rebelled, those who tried to establish their own codes and standards. Repeatedly, in her *Journal* and correspondence, she expressed her pleasure in watching the development of a son whose mind and talents were better than average, but who did not stand too far apart from his fellow man. Shelley's lot and her own had been hard because their own inner natures had compelled them to defy the world, but

Percy Florence would be spared the agonies his parents had been forced to endure.

Those who were closest to her in the late 1820's and early 1830's, among them Tom Moore and Trelawny, who returned to England a bachelor after his exploits in Greece, applauded Mary's sensible attitude. Mary's friendship with Moore grew rapidly, and thereafter remained constant. He reminded her, delightfully, of the past, and she liked him very much, she wrote in her *Journal*. There was "something warm and genuine in his feelings and manner which is very attractive, and redeems him from the sin of worldliness with which he has been charged."

Moore admired her, too, first learning to appreciate her early in their acquaintance when they were discussing Byron. As he later wrote in his *Memoirs,* Moore said that she "always winds up her account of Byron's bad traits with 'but still he was very nice.' "

Moore was much in Mary's debt in 1828, when she wrote to Teresa Guiccioli on his behalf to obtain material for his forthcoming biography of Byron, and the Countess generously obliged. By 1829 he was consulting her so frequently about the book that his publisher, John Murray, suggested that Mary be paid a fee for her help. She refused with an indignation touched with humor. She refused to be guilty of an act of incivility to Mr. Moore, she declared, adding, "Besides, it would make me break a vow I made, never to make money of my acquaintance with Lord Byron. His ghost would certainly come and taunt me if I did."

Mary and Tom Moore maintained a lively correspondence from 1827 to 1841, both appreciating quick intelligence, wit and a detailed knowledge of the contemporary literary scene. There was no truth whatever in the malicious rumors spread by Jane and Thomas Jefferson Hogg to the effect that Mary became Moore's mistress, presumably because she so loved the limelight that she wanted to be closely associated with the literary celebrity whose company at dinner was sought by every hostess in London.

In her relationship with Moore, as with others, Mary was undeviatingly loyal to Shelley's memory. Tom Moore was devoted to his wife and children, often referring to them in his correspondence with Mary as "Mrs. Moore and her little etceteras," and there are no hints in his letters or Mary's of any personal intimacy.

Mary passed the milestone of her thirtieth birthday in 1827, but was as beautiful as she had been when younger. Mary Cowden Clarke, the daughter of the Novellos, offered a glowing description, in her *Recollections of Writers*, of Mary's appearance at the age of thirty-one:

> I looked upon her with ceaseless admiration for her personal graces as well as for her literary distinction. Her well shaped golden head, almost always a little bent and drooping,—her marble white shoulders and arms statuesquely visible in the perfectly plain black velvet gown which the custom of that time allowed to be cut low; her thoughtful earnest eyes; the short upper lip and intellectually curved mouth, with a certain close compressed and decisive expression while she listened and a relaxation into fuller redness and mobility when speaking; her exquisitely formed, white, dimpled, small hands, with rosy palms, and plumply commencing fingers, that tapered into tips as slender as those of a Vandyke portrait . . .

Many women of the period failed to share Mrs. Clarke's appreciation of Mary Shelley, and chief among them were the advocates of women's rights. The rapid expansion of the Industrial Revolution, which forced tens of thousands of women in Great Britain, the United States and Canada to work long hours in sweatshops at low pay had spurred the revival of a vigorous campaign in behalf of women's rights on both sides of the Atlantic. Never before had so many women worked so hard for freedom and equality, and most members of the inner circle expected the daughter of Mary Wollstonecraft and William Godwin, the widow of liberty-loving Shelley to assume public leadership of their semiorganized movement.

One of these ladies, the extraordinary Frances Wright Darusmont, who had spent several years in America, where she had been active in the campaign to abolish slavery, became Mary's good friend after writing her the nineteenth-century equivalent of a fan letter. And it was thanks to her influence that Mary made her brief, ill-fated lecture tour in 1828.

A majority of Fanny Wright's colleagues, however, regarded Mary as a traitor to her sex and their cause, and were shocked by her repeated refusal to participate actively in their movement. What they did not understand was that Mary Shelley who was in her thirties and had suffered because of her beliefs was a far cry from the crusading, teen-aged Mary Godwin who had been so eager to change the world.

Mary best expressed her feelings in a succinct statement that she wrote in her *Journal* on March 8, 1831:

> If I had raved and ranted about what I did not understand—had I accepted a set of opinions and propaganda with enthusiasm; had I been careless of attack, and eager for notoriety; then the party to which I belonged would have gathered round me, and I would not have been alone. But since I lost Shelley I have no wish to ally myself to the Radicals—they are full of revulsion to me—violent without any sense of Justice—selfish in the extreme—talking without knowledge—rude, envious and insolent. I wish to have nothing to do with them.

One of those who shared Mary's approach to life was John Murray, the distinguished publisher who had gained an appreciation of her after he had been offered and had rejected the right to publish *Frankenstein*. Murray was the publisher of Tom Moore, through whom Mary received her first invitations to take part in the literary-social discussions that took place in Murray's Albemarle Street drawing room.

It was thanks to Mary's associations under Murray's roof that she became friendly with some of the leading magazine editors and publishers of the period, and blossomed into a prolific writer for their publications. Fred Reynolds, editor of *The Keepsake*, not only published a number of her crisp short stories, but also printed a number of Shelley's hitherto unknown poems. It was also through Murray that she became friendly with Samuel Rogers, the poet and man about town, and attended a number of his renowned literary breakfasts. By this time she was recognized in her own right as a personage of consequence in the arts, rather than as William Godwin's daughter, and she associated with many people who, until they met her, had never read any of Percy Bysshe Shelley's poetry. She soon corrected this deficiency.

The *New Monthly* became a regular outlet for Mary's fiction and travel articles, and accepted so much of her work that she tried to persuade Claire Clairmont to write for the magazine, too. Claire agreed, but her habitual laziness caused her to procrastinate indefinitely, so Mary herself wrote a series of pieces on Italy. Others who bought and published her work were Sir John Bowring, editor of the *Westminster Review,* and Frederick Marryat, editor of the *Metropolitan* and himself a novelist of note, who not only bought fiction and nonfiction from Mary, but through her became Trelawny's friend and editor.

Mary's influence was sufficiently widespread that, in 1828, she was able to obtain a government pension for her father. Even the philosophers and scholars who found little merit in the ideas of William Godwin accepted him as their dean, and almost every English writer considered him the country's foremost man of letters. But he was crippled by advancing age and failing eyesight as well as his ever-present financial problems, and his daughter quietly let it be known that it would be a national disgrace if he starved to death. Others agreed and discussed his plight with Members of Parliament, and Mary continued her unremitting campaign until both the Commons and the Lords passed into law a bill granting him a generous pension.

In the late spring of 1828 Mary went off to Paris, accompanied by a friend, Julia Robinson, to begin a brief lecture tour. Almost immediately after her arrival, however, she contracted smallpox, and was forced to cancel the tour. The infection was slight, fortunately, and did not permanently mar her appearance. Mary bore the trial patiently and in high spirits, and referred to herself as "the monster" until her pockmarks became less pronounced. After spending two weeks in Paris she returned to England with Miss Robinson, and acting on the advice of her physician, went to Sandgate for a month of sea bathing and sunning, which removed the marks of her ailment.

Returning to London in July, she learned that Claire Clairmont was expected at any moment for a visit, and planned to stay with her. She also discovered that Trelawny had already returned to the country and was visiting friends and relatives in Cornwall. His letters showed little of his customary ebullience, and instead he lamented on the "pain, disappointment and sorrow" he saw on every side.

Claire arrived on the heels of her letter, and at first Mary was delighted to see her. Never particularly attractive, Claire had aged rapidly, and her tongue had become even sharper. She ridiculed her mother and Godwin, complained that England was provincial and London a bore, and found fault with virtually everyone she met under Mary's roof.

But the two women had shared so many vicissitudes that, in spite of her constant carping, Mary enjoyed her company.

That situation changed abruptly two days before Claire's departure, when she revealed that her brother Charles, who still lived in Vienna, was in desperate need of a loan of two hundred pounds. Mary could ill afford to advance that large a sum, but Claire begged and wheedled, stormed and became hysterical, and eventually Mary weakened and gave her the money for Charles.

Mary had to increase the pace of her own writing, turning out a number of short stories and a series of articles on the art treasures of Paris in order to compensate for the loss. Thereafter a new chill appeared in her relations with Claire, whose letters indicated that she felt little gratitude and accepted the loan as a matter of course. Mary finally saw that her family regarded her as they had Shelley: she was a convenient source of income when all others failed, and the borrowers did not bother to think about the inconveniences or hardships she might suffer as a result of her attempt to help them.

Over the following years Mary insisted, at intervals, that Charles Clairmont repay the loan. Each of her dunning letters brought an angry response from Claire, but each time Charles responded by sending a small portion of the debt, which took him a full decade to pay. The unpleasant incident did not come to an end until 1845, when Charles wrote Mary a formal, hurt letter, in which he accused her of coldness after doing him the "little favor," an obligation which he had "most punctiliously fulfilled."

Edward Trelawny stormed into London shortly before Claire's departure, as tanned and energetic as ever. He saw enough of Claire before her departure to convince Mary there was no possibility he and her stepsister would become romantically involved. Then, after Claire's departure, he saw old friends, made new ones, launched a variety of projects, quarreled with a retired naval officer and almost was forced to fight a duel. He ate prodigiously, drank to excess yet remained sober, and charmed scores of people in high places. Whatever time was left he spent with Mary.

In February, 1829, he returned to Italy, and immediately sent Mary a letter:

> Come away, dear Mary, from the climate you are in; life is not endurable where you are.
>
> Florence is very gay, and a weight was taken from my mind, and body, too, in getting on this side of the Alps. Heaven and hell cannot be very much more dissimilar.

In the same letter he told her of a plan long simmering in his mind. He wanted to write "a tribute to the memory of Shelley," and asked her to help him by sending him material, including anecdotes, opinions, impressions and documents. The project, he said, could not be completed without her cooperation.

Mary had no intention of helping him, much less acting as an unofficial collaborator. She was still very fond of Trelawny, but could see many of his weaknesses, and did not regard him as any more a biographer of her husband than Hogg, who also spoke of writing such a book. As a matter of fact, she was hoping to write a definitive biography of Shelley herself, after she edited his poems, a task on which she worked whenever she could spare the time. The *Poems of Shelley* was not ready for publication until 1834, as it happened, and Mary rejected an offer of six hundred pounds from a publisher for the book. Her patience was rewarded, and in 1839, when the *Poems* finally appeared, she received an advance payment of fourteen hundred pounds.

In 1829, even though she could not look into the future, she knew that she didn't want to work with Trelawny, and told him in so many words that she was unable to accept his offer. He exploded in self-righteous anger in his next letter, demanding an explanation, professing to be hurt and railing at her in lurid page after page.

Mary elected to ignore the outburst, and soon thereafter Trelawny sought her help in the preparation of his autobiography, which he wanted to call *A Man's Life,* but which his publisher wanted to bring out under the title, *A Discarded Son.* Mary conducted the negotiations for him, and was shocked when she read his manuscript, which contained language that no post-Renaissance author dared to use.

She suggested cuts, which Trelawny resisted, but she held her ground, and he was finally forced to give in, thereby making it possible to publish the book. Mary may have been responsible for giving the book the title under which it appeared in 1831, *The Adventures of a Younger Son.* Trelawny gave her credit for it, but later recanted and insisted the title had been his own. The book was an exaggerated account of his exploits, and no reader knew where fact ended and fiction began, but the story was so entertaining that Trelawny became famous overnight.

Trelawny was in Florence when his book came out, and his overnight success prompted him, in a letter he wrote to Mary in early March, 1831, to hint at marriage: "I should not wonder if fate, without our knowledge, united us; and who can control his fate? I blindly follow his decrees, dear Mary."

Whether Mary had ever given serious thought to the possibility of marrying Trelawny is unknown, but her temperament makes it unlikely. Certainly by 1831 she was aware of his instability and ignored the broad hint in her bland reply.

Trelawny wrote to her again, and apparently he spelled

out his proposal. Unfortunately for posterity, this letter is lost, the only document in his entire correspondence with Mary Shelley that has not been preserved. It has been suggested that Mary, after reading the blunt proposal of marriage, elected to consign it to the fire burning in her drawing room hearth, although there is no proof that she committed this act.

On April 8 she replied to his proposal, her tone light and her approach teasing, so that he would not be offended by her refusal. She said:

> My name will *never* be Trelawny. I am not so young as I was when you first knew me, but I am as proud. I must have the entire affection, devotion, and, above all, the solicitous protection of any one who would win me. You belong to womenkind in general, so Mary Shelley will *never* be yours.

Trelawny seemed to accept her position and showed no obvious resentment, but thereafter the relationship changed. He began to criticize her personal standards of propriety, her tastes in literature and her friends, and Mary, trying without success to reply in the same vein, became self-conscious and shy.

He returned to London a short time later to compete with Moore for the honor of being the author most in demand at dinner parties and other functions. He and Mary saw each other frequently and remained friends, but the gloss had worn off their friendship, and was never replaced. Mary remained firm in her resolve to refuse him her cooperation on his book about her late husband. That work, which was partly autobiographical, and was called, *The Recollections of the Last Days of Shelley and Byron,* was not published until 1858, seven years after Mary's death.

A letter Trelawny sent to Claire on March 23, 1836,

illuminates the changed nature of his friendship. Claire, who now corresponded infrequently with her stepsister, inquired about her in a letter to Trelawny, who replied:

> Oh, you want to Know about Mary—I was at a party with her last night—or rather met her there. She lights up very well at night—and shows to advantage in society —for there she is happy—detesting solitude—in the country she does nothing but complain. She is now determined to fix her head quarters in Town—has a lodging near the Regents Park, and is seeking a small house to call her own. In the daylight the faded colors and chinks of time are observable, but not disproportionate to her years; my bronzed visage is battered and weather-stained. Women are made of softer stuff—and she shows it—some things harden by time and exposure, such as stones and bones—but not beauty's cheek.

The correspondence dwindled to an end in 1837, when Trelawny made plans to marry Mrs. Augusta Goring. Mary went out of her way to be kind to Augusta, and the two women struck up a lasting friendship, although Trelawny did nothing to encourage any intimacy between them. As the years passed Trelawny became increasingly and more openly critical of Mary, accusing her of becoming narrow-minded, stuffy and conventional. He offered no details to substantiate his charges.

But Mary had the last word, and her estimate of his character has been remembered by posterity, and has served as his epitaph: *"He is* a strange, wonderful being, but destroyed by *being nothing."*

XXIII

In November, 1832, Percy Florence would be thirteen years of age, so the preceding spring Mary applied to Sir Timothy Shelley for funds to send him to public school. Remembering how much her husband had hated his years at Eton, she was determined to send him to Harrow, where she would be charged one hundred and eighty pounds per year for his room, board and tuition. Her father-in-law, as usual, replied through his attorneys, ungraciously increasing her annual allowance to three hundred pounds per year and observing that he hoped it would be "practicable" to give the boy "a good education" out of that sum.

Mary literally could not afford the expense. Her fourth novel, *The Fortunes of Perkin Warbeck,* a historical romance, had been scheduled for publication in 1830, but the size of the book, which consisted of three thick volumes, had created problems, and was one of the principal factors in the postponement of publication until the autumn of 1831. Mary had placed great hope in the book, which was based on English history, but the critical appraisal had been lukewarm at best, and the popular reception had been disappointing. Not only had *Perkin Warbeck* failed to enhance her literary standing, but readers showed little interest in it, and it did not go beyond one printing. A French edition achieved a somewhat better record, but the Paris publishers were notorious for their carelessness in sending royalties abroad, so Mary had gained little from the French sale of the book.

Sir Timothy's reply and the increase in the allowance he paid did not reach her until the late summer of 1832. But in the winter of 1833 she realized there was only one way she could afford to send her son to Harrow, and in April she acted accordingly, moving to Harrow herself and enrolling Percy Florence as a day student.

The move forced her to give up the life in London that she enjoyed, and also entailed a financial sacrifice, as she could no longer write regularly for the magazines, since such work required frequent meetings with editors and publishers. Percy Florence was delighted with the school, made friends easily and did well in his studies, which pleased his mother, who was also relieved because the hazing of newcomers was less severe than at Eton, where Shelley had suffered torments.

Claire, who was now living in Pisa as a companion to Mrs. Mason's daughters, expressed her opinion of the move in no uncertain terms, writing in a blunt letter:

> I am very glad to hear that Percy likes Harrow, but I shudder from head to foot when I think of your boldness in sending him there. I think in certain things you are the most daring woman I ever knew. There are few mothers who, having suffered the misfortunes you have, and having such advantages depending upon the life of an only son, would venture to expose that life to the dangers of a public school. . . .

Claire's fears proved unwarranted. Percy Florence enjoyed his school life, made friends easily and conformed to the standards of his peers. Mary found him a "fascinating, strange mixture" of his father's personality and her own, as she wrote to Maria Gisborne. Although he wanted and needed the company of others, as his mother did, he sometimes withdrew into isolation in a manner reminiscent of Shelley, and behaved with stiff shyness in the presence of strangers. He had a stubborn streak similar to that of both his parents, and, Mary told Mrs. Gisborne, his manner was sometimes arrogant, which caused her concern, although he showed her the greatest consideration at all times.

With little to entertain or amuse her in Harrow, Mary was able to concentrate on her work and her reading. She completed the editing of Shelley's poems, a task of considerable delicacy, as she sometimes had to determine which of four or five versions of a work was the last he had written. She had been engaged to write a portion of the biographical section of an encyclopedia, the *Cabinet Cyclopaedia,* and this effort required considerable study. In all, she contributed the sections on the lives of "Eminent Literary and Scientific Men" of Italy, Spain, Portugal and France.

She also went to work in earnest on a new novel. Stung by the critical reaction to *Perkin Warbeck,* she sought to retrieve her reputation as a literary figure of stature, and decided she could best achieve that goal by combining it with another objective, that of winning recognition as a great poet for her late husband. Her new book, *Lodore,* was fiction in the sense that much of the plot was her own invention, but her principal character was Shelley in an almost transparent disguise.

She presented him to the world as she had known him, a man of almost unbelievable brilliance and sensitivity, of inviolable integrity, and, although devoted to intellect, of many moods. It is not surprising that no other writer was ever able to capture as many facets of Shelley's extraordinarily complex character.

Lodore was lacking in the supernatural aspects of *Frankenstein,* the desolation of a world totally destroyed by war that she pictured in *The Last Man,* or the semiscientific fantasizing about inventions of the future that appeared in these two novels, which are her only works still read a century and a half after their publication.

But *Lodore,* which came out in 1835, created a sensation in its own day, and was hailed as a masterpiece of fiction. The reviewers called it one of the finest novels of the era, although only a few commented on her employment of a lightly veiled Shelley as her protagonist. Sales were slow at the outset, but the book had a solidity and integrity that impressed readers, and over a two-year period the sales mounted steadily, earning Mary an impressive fifteen hundred pounds in that time.

Claire, to be sure, expressed an intense dislike for *Lodore* because Mary once again based a principal character on Lord Byron. It was the moral duty of someone endowed with Mary's genius to present the beautiful in human nature, Claire scolded, and remarked that she preferred *Frankenstein* because the monster in that story was less odious.

Mary was saddened in 1835 by the deaths of both John and Maria Gisborne, and in the spring of the following year she was stunned by the death of her father. She long had realized that her admiration for his intellectual attainments had been too great, her emotional attachment to him too intense, and this knowledge cushioned the blow, at least to some extent. In a letter to one of his old friends, who had also been one of Mary Wollstonecraft's few intimates, she wrote about his last days in crisp but moving terms:

> . . . You will be glad to know that one whom you once knew so well died without much suffering. His illness was a catarrhal fever which his great age did not permit him to combat—he was ill about 10, and confined to his bed 5 days. I sat up several nights with him,

and Mrs. Godwin was with him when I was not—as he had a great horror of being left to servants. His thoughts wandered a good deal, but not painfully—he knew himself to be dangerously ill but did not consider his recovery impossible. His last moment was very sudden —Mrs. Godwin and I were both present. He was dozing tranquilly, when a slight rattle called us to his side, his heart ceased to beat, and all was over.

Mary displayed the fortitude of a mature woman after her father's passing, and did not dwell morbidly on the event. Returning to Harrow, where Percy Florence would spend another year, she went to work at once on what would become her last novel, *Falkner*. In it she returned to the form of the historical, but only her backgrounds were real, and all of her characters grew out of her own imagination.

Its theme was marital fidelity, and it was directed almost exclusively to a feminine audience. Published in three volumes, it appeared in 1837, and was pleasantly received by the critics, who made it plain that the book was no masterpiece, but was done with competence and was worth reading. Although almost forgotten within a decade, it earned Mary substantial sums for a number of years; her publishers paid her an advance royalty of seven hundred and fifty pounds, and the novel earned her no less than five hundred pounds per year until 1842.

Mary could afford to send Percy Florence to Cambridge University herself, and was not forced to undergo another humiliation by applying to Sir Timothy for additional funds. She returned to London in 1838, after her son went off to Cambridge, and finally bought herself a small house off Regents Park, which she had so long wanted. Her proprietorship of a dwelling in one of London's most fashionable districts was a symbol of the status she had gradually achieved. No longer regarded as an immoral, atheistic radical by any segment of society, she had won universal acceptance and respect.

Among her friends were prominent nobles, Cabinet officers and Members of Parliament, regardless of party affiliation. Whigs and Tories alike held her in high regard, as she demonstrated soon after her return. The private bill under which William Godwin had been paid a pension protected his widow for two years, but the law was scheduled to expire in 1838, which meant that payments to Mary Jane Godwin would be halted. Mary went to work on her stepmother's behalf, and commanded enough influence to insure the passage of a new bill safeguarding the payment of the pension to Mrs. Godwin.

Mary's motives in protecting the woman she had disliked since early childhood were far from pure. She was the only member of the family who could afford to give financial assistance to her father's widow, and she had no desire to assume that burden. Claire, showing unexpected concern for her mother's welfare, dropped a strong hint in a letter that Mary could solve the problem by taking the old lady under her own roof. This was asking too much, however, and in a firm reply that faced the issue without subterfuge, Mary declared that nothing could persuade her to share her home with Mrs. Godwin.

England's poets, novelists and essayists were virtually unanimous in their acceptance of Mary Shelley as one of the leading authors in the country. William Wordsworth, perhaps the greatest of the Romantics and certainly the most influential member of the school, renewed his earlier friendship with her, and although they never drew close, they nevertheless met fairly frequently and talked at length. Members of the younger generation of poets paid intellectual court to Mary, the most prominent of them being Robert Browning, who had been profoundly influenced by

Shelley's work in his student days. For a time Browning had emulated Shelley by becoming a vegetarian and calling himself an atheist, but now, as he matured, he began to understand that Shelley had not really denied the existence of a Supreme Being, but had been attacking the anthropomorphism of organized religion.

Mary was pleased to be able to move freely in literary circles, but drew the line at the formation of one association. Southey, whom Wordsworth would succeed as poet laureate in 1843, made indirect overtures to her, but she spurned a friendship with him. She vividly remembered, if he did not, that he had long been opposed to Shelley as a man and a poet, and had been highly critical of Mary, too, at the time of Harriet Westbrook Shelley's tragic death.

The publication of the poetic works of Percy Bysshe Shelley in 1839 was undoubtedly the crowning achievement of his widow's life. Sales were brisk and steady, and every important newspaper and magazine in England and Scotland reviewed the book. The vast majority of the critics recognized Shelley's genius, and he emerged from the shadows to take his permanent place among the great poets of the ages. The unremitting efforts exerted by Mary and her lifelong friend, Leigh Hunt, who had returned to England after the *Liberal* fiasco, were finally rewarded.

Shelley did not achieve enduring renown overnight following the publication of his poems, to be sure. But his reception by the press and the public response to the book were guarantees that he would not be forgotten, and with each succeeding year his name gained additional luster.

Mary's changed status and the gradual recognition of her husband's genius have been attributed in part to her growing respectability, but this assertion obscures a deeper truth. Mary remained true to the intellectual beliefs she and Shelley had held, becoming more circumspect, even conservative, only in her personal life. What is far more important is that the times were changing, and with them public attitudes were being transformed.

England, seventeen years after Shelley's death, was a complacent nation basking in a peaceful prosperity unknown since the sixteenth-century reign of Queen Elizabeth I. Her influence as a world power growing steadily, the Industrial Revolution producing greater wealth and security, England was fast becoming the secure, middle-class oriented nation she would remain through the better part of the twentieth century.

Many of the ideas Shelley and Mary had held, many of the principles they had espoused were no longer regarded as shockingly radical, but as mildly liberal. The Chartists and other Socialist-tinged groups might hail Shelley as a great poet because of *Queen Mab*, the product of his youth, but the ranks of those who could not digest his more mature works were slowly dwindling. He was increasingly recognized for the purity of his poetry rather than his Godwin-influenced philosophy, those ideals already having become somewhat outdated in a nation whose outlook was industrial rather than agrarian.

The worst stigma Mary had been forced to bear had been her elopement with the married Shelley and her subsequent pregnancy. But she and her husband had atoned for their rash behavior during Shelley's own lifetime, when they had actually lived according to the conventions of the period. Since her husband's death Mary's conduct had been exemplary, the sacrifices she had made for her son had been duly noted, and the only door in the realm that remained closed to her was that of Field Place, Sir Timothy Shelley's country home. Her father-in-law, still stubborn and unyielding, had no intention of asking her to visit his house, any more than she would have accepted such an invitation.

Soon after Mary's return to London in 1838, however, she renewed her acquaintance with several of her husband's sisters, who called on her. She also came to know her husband's younger brother, John, and on several occasions met Lady Shelley, whose husband may have known nothing of any of these gatherings. Thereafter Mary—and her son—saw Shelley's sisters at irregular intervals, and although their relationship never became intimate and no close family ties were established, they were nevertheless friendly. The creation of this rapport was not the least of Mary's triumphs.

Claire Clairmont returned to England in 1840, presumably to stay, and took a position as a governess with a family living in the country. She had few opportunities to visit London, however, and rarely went to the city. It must be supposed that she and Mary met from time to time, but there is no record of any such reunions in their continuing correspondence.

It is evident from her letters that Claire became increasingly crabbed as she grew older, and she could look forward only to a life of hard work. She was caustic in her comments about everyone except Percy Florence, and she demonstrated genuine affection in her letters to him. He did not return her regard, however, and in 1849, when she tried to sell Robert Browning some documents she claimed Shelley had written, he wrote Browning a stiff letter, in which he not only declared that all valuable documents pertaining to his father were already in his mother's hands, but he also made it plain that Claire was "no relation of mine."

The death of Sir Timothy in 1844 literally changed Claire's status overnight. When Percy Florence came into his inheritance, Mary made certain that the terms of his late father's will were honored, and Claire received a bequest of twelve thousand pounds. This small fortune enabled her to give up her hated work as a governess and tutor, and she retired.

She no longer had any ties in England, however, and had formed no new friendships. Experience had taught her, as it had Mary, that neither benefited from a close relationship, and neither wanted to resume the intimacy of their youth. Claire's only blood relative in the country was her half-brother William, but she was not on particularly good terms with him and his wife, although she was fond of their children.

So, early in 1845, as soon as she received her bequest, she left England for the last time and returned to Vienna, where she lived with her brother Charles and his large family. Charles now held a post of some influence, working as the English, French and Italian tutor to the Archduke Franz Josef, later the emperor of Austria-Hungary. A spark of the young Claire appeared in a letter to Mary expressing her eagerness to taste life at Vienna's royal court.

Neither the years nor her difficult life had truly matured Claire, and she squandered her twelve thousand pounds within a few years. She lived well, bought expensive gifts for Charles's wife and children, and apparently gave no thought to the future. By 1849 she was reduced to poverty again, and wrote vaguely to Mary about returning to England and finding employment there. In a significant sentence that reveals her venom and jealousy, she wrote, ". . . one of the reasons I always say disagreeable things to you and Percy [is] because I cannot bear that anyone should think I am paying my court to you and taking advantage of your love of agreeable sensations."

Mary and her son had already treated Claire generously, and did not offer to support her, so she remained on the Continent, where she took a succession of dreary appointments as a tutor and governess. She retired in 1870 at the age of seventy-two, and embracing Roman Catholicism, retired to a convent in Florence, the one city she truly loved. There she died in 1879, alone and bitter, a woman whose carelessness in her youth had ruined her life, in part because she had never risen above her affair with Byron and their daughter's tragic death. Her few surviving relatives, none of whom knew her well, did not mourn her passing, of which the world's press took no notice.

XXIV

In 1840 Mary Shelley knew, beyond all doubt, that the sacrifices she had made for her son had not been in vain. Percy Florence was planning on making a tour of the Continent with two of his friends from Trinity College, Cambridge, and invited his mother to accompany them. Mary protested, writing him that three young men didn't want or need the company of a forty-three-year-old chaperone. She was flattered that he wanted her to make the trip, and the invitation would be one of the most precious of her memories, but she declined.

Percy Florence soon indicated he was in earnest and had not made an empty gesture for the sake of giving his mother a moment's pleasure. He and his friends wrote her a solemnly worded, formal notice to the effect that they would call off the tour unless she agreed to join them. Their letter arrived on a Friday in early May, and that evening, before she could reply, Percy Florence and his friends descended on her in person to add their verbal pleas to the communication. Unable to resist the pressure, Mary capitulated.

The tour, which began in late May, was an unqualified success. Percy Florence surprised Mary by revealing to her that his grandfather had increased his allowance to four hundred pounds per year, so he not only assumed full responsibilities for his mother's traveling expenses, but hired her a maid.

Mary showed her son and his companions Paris, taking care to spend her evenings with old friends so the youths would be less inhibited in their enjoyment of the city's celebrated night life. Then they made leisurely journeys up the Moselle and Rhine rivers, coming at last to Lake Como, which Mary remembered so vividly from her earlier visits with Shelley.

Her son aroused other, far less pleasant memories when she discovered, for the first time, that he was as avid a boating enthusiast as his father had been. But she exercised the self-control of maturity, and managed to smile in farewell as Percy Florence and his friends went off each afternoon for a long sail on the lake. One day, in response to their repeated invitations, she went boating with them for several hours, and Percy Florence did not know how much the effort cost her until, long after her death, he read her *Journal*.

From Como the party went to Milan, where the young men were expecting funds to be forwarded from England for their return journey. When the money failed to arrive in time, Mary advanced them the cash and stayed on, with only her maid as company. But the Milanese had no intention of neglecting her, and she received so many invitations to social functions that she could accept only a small percentage of them.

In all, the trip gave her so much pleasure that her son insisted they take another the following year, and this time Mary needed little persuasion. They made a slow, lazy journey through the German states in 1841, then went on to Prague, which Mary regarded as "the most perfect of medieval cities." Then they went on to Salzburg, and crossed the Brenner Pass into Italy.

Percy Florence wanted to visit Venice, and his mother steeled herself for the ordeal of visiting the grave of her little daughter Clara, which she had not seen for more than two decades. Ever honest, she vividly described her feelings in the last of her books, *Rambles in Germany and Italy, 1840–43:*

> Gathered into myself, with my "mind's eye" I saw those before me long departed; and I was agitated again by emotions—by passions—and those the deepest a woman's heart can harbour—a dread to see her child even at that instant expire—which then occupied me. It is strange, but to any person who has suffered a similar circumstance, that those who are enduring mental or corporeal agony are strangely alive to immediate external objects, and their imagination even exercises its wild power over them. Shakespeare knew this, and the passionate grief of Queen Constance thence is endued with fearful reality. Wordsworth, as many years ago I remember hearing Coleridge remark, illustrates the same fact, when he makes an insane and afflicted mother exclaim,—
>
> "The breeze I see is in the tree;
> It comes to cool my babe and me."
>
> . . . Thus the banks of the Brenta presented to me a moving scene; not a palace, not a tree of which I did not recognize, as marked and recorded, at a moment when life and death hung upon our speedy arrival at Venice.

Percy Florence was sufficiently advanced in his studies at Cambridge to prolong his holiday for several months. His mother insisted on visiting places where harrowing memories might overwhelm her, so he refused to let her proceed alone. First he escorted her to Florence, where they remained for nine weeks, and Mary's notations in her *Journal* became brief, vague and impersonal. She referred frequently to the cold, mentioning how chilly it had been there in the winter of 1819, but she said nothing about the thoughts that filled her mind.

From Florence they went to Rome, where Percy Florence saw the graves of his father and his brother William for the first time. There is no word in Mary's *Journal* or elsewhere that records what she felt when she stood beside the graves of her beloved Shelley and their lost son.

With her son still at her side, Mary sailed up the Italian coast to Genoa, and made a sentimental journey to the Casa Magni, where she and Shelley had spent the last summer of his life. Unable to force herself to approach the house, she viewed it from a distance, then turned away. Later that day she stood for a long time on a hilltop, the wind ruffling her graying hair as she gazed out at the Mediterranean in which Shelley had drowned. Her son is the authority for the fact that she was dry-eyed and silent, but erect and in full command of her feelings.

Mary wrote the *Rambles* immediately after her return to London, and the book was published early in 1844. The combination of her own renown and Shelley's increasing fame guaranteed the success of this relatively slight effort, and the public bought every volume of three large printings.

The most important event of 1844 was the death of Sir Timothy Shelley, whose grandson inherited his title, estates and fortune, and thereafter was known as Sir Percy. Mary's long, unremitting financial struggle was at an end. She had made notes in preparation for the writing of a new novel, and although she intended to put the book on paper, referring to it occasionally to the end of her days, it remained unwritten. Instead she devoted the remaining years of her life to her one remaining goal, the enhancement of her husband's reputation.

Aided by the ever-faithful Leigh Hunt, she scoured England for his letters and anything else he had written. Most of Shelley's old friends gladly gave her their correspondence with him, and she collected many hundreds of his letters. Only one man refused to cooperate with her: Thomas Jefferson Hogg was planning to write his own biography of Shelley.

Sir Percy and his mother moved into Field Place, the ancestral Shelley home, which was Mary's home for the rest of her life. Two of Shelley's sisters were still there, as was his mother, and at the insistence of Sir Percy and Mary they remained. Eventually the sisters found it convenient to move elsewhere; Lady Shelley did not long survive her husband.

Money was no longer a worry, and Mary enjoyed the rest she had earned. Sir Percy developed his talents as an artist, and frequently attended the theater in London, sometimes escorting his mother. Mary's principal concern now was a dread of the day he married a girl with whom she would not be able to establish a rapport.

Those fears proved groundless. In fact, she and the young woman her son eventually married became such intimate friends that it was long believed Mary selected Sir Percy's bride. This was not the case.

In 1847 Sir Percy met and fell in love with Mrs. Jane St. John, the daughter of Mr. and Mrs. Thomas Gibson and the widow of Charles Robert St. John, to whom she had been married only a short time before his unexpected death. Attractive but by no means beautiful, Jane was a warm, sympathetic young woman with a strong mind and will of her own. She had been an ardent admirer of Mary's work long before meeting Sir Percy, and had not only read Shelley's poems many times, but had committed long passages to memory.

"She is my daughter, not my daughter-in-law," Mary said in a letter to Claire a few months after Jane and Sir Percy were married in 1848, and the girl reciprocated her deep affection. Mary still disliked the chores of housekeeping, and happily relinquished the responsibility to the younger woman, who relished the task. Jane enthusiastically helped her mother-in-law collect Shelley's papers, and late in 1849 she intervened in a situation to save Mary embarrassment and pain. Claire had been hinting in a series of letters from Vienna that she wanted to see Field Place, and Mary finally saw no way to avoid extending an invitation, but said to young Lady Shelley, "I beg you, do not leave me alone with her. She has been the bane of my life ever since I was three years old."

Jane took care of the matter in her own way. Acting without Mary's knowledge, she wrote Claire a firm but polite letter saying a visit would not be convenient at that time, and Mary was spared.

No one, however, could make an even more painful predicament easier for Mary. Under the terms of Shelley's will Leigh Hunt received a legacy, but the sum was insufficient for his needs. He was still suffering misfortunes, and required a substantial amount of money in order to become solvent. Marianne Hunt wrote to Mary, asking for a considerable loan, and Hunt subsequently sent several pressing letters of his own. On one occasion he tried to exert pressure by paying a visit to Field Place, accompanied by his solicitor, who had already drawn the papers that would provide for the loan.

Mary hated to turn down an old and dear friend who had been loyal to her and to the memory of Shelley. But she had advanced various sums to the Hunts on many occasions, and never had been repaid. Her experiences with them, as well as the memory of her father's perennial financial needs hardened her, and she told her daughter-in-law that her conscience would not permit her to fritter away her son's inheritance. So, even though she spent a night and a day in tears, she wrote to Hunt, rejecting his request by telling him, "Percy and I have all in common— I have nothing of my own exclusively."

She continued to maintain a warm correspondence with Mrs. Trelawny, but had no direct contact with the adventurer himself. In 1850 she asked him, through his wife, if he would be good enough to return the portrait of her painted in Rome three decades earlier by Amelia Curran. It had come into his possession at the time of Shelley's death, when he had promised to hold it for Mary, and through the years she had tried in vain to persuade him to return it.

Trelawny did not reply in Mary's lifetime. Lady Shelley made another attempt to retrieve it after her mother-in-law's death, but she failed, too, Trelawny writing her a flowery letter filled with his protestations of good faith and love for the Shelley family—but nevertheless insisting he intended to keep the portrait himself.

The few years of life left to Mary after the marriage of her son were as tranquil, in the main, as they were uneventful, and only a few incidents marred the serenity she had never before known. Her attentive, loving son and daughter-in-law anticipated her wishes, took care to insure that she had as few worries as possible and made no demands on her.

Her one abiding concern was Sir Percy's love of boating, so he gave up the sport for her sake in 1849. He did not sail again while she was alive, but within a year of her death he bought a boat of his own, and for the rest of his days was an enthusiastic yachtsman.

In her last years Mary reverted to the regimen she had followed during the brief span of her marriage. She spent her mornings at her desk, writing letters, making notes as friends sent her their correspondence with Shelley and, whenever the opportunity arose, finding new ways to place Shelley's name before the public in the newspapers and literary magazines. Dinner was eaten at two in the afternoon, and thereafter she went on long, rambling walks, often accompanied by two or three of her son's dogs, but rarely straying beyond the spacious confines of Field Place.

She took tea with her son, daughter-in-law and any friends who happened to be present, then retired to her own suite and read until she was called to dinner. As she had done for so long, she kept a meticulous record of her reading. After dinner she sometimes joined Sir Percy, Lady Shelley and their guests for an hour or two of conversation, but as 1851 approached she formed the habit of retiring to her bed and reading for a few hours before she dropped off to sleep.

Mary's health remained good, or so she insisted, but in the latter months of 1850 it was becoming evident that she tired quickly, and her son and daughter-in-law were increasingly concerned. A day or two after Christmas she informed them that she intended to return to her London house, and went there soon after the New Year, attended by several servants.

In mid-January Sir Percy and Lady Shelley came to the city for a few days, and were shocked to find Mary in bed, her left side paralyzed. She informed them she knew she would die soon, and calmly insisted on staying under her own roof, as she refused to be a burden on them.

Her son and daughter-in-law held hurried consultations with Mary's doctors, and a number of specialists were summoned, but all agreed with the initial diagnosis that Mary was beyond medical help. She was aware of her grave condition, and her serenity astonished everyone who saw her. At her request none of her old friends were told of her illness, and she gave Percy and Jane specific instructions: she wanted a private funeral, but did not care whether her last remains were buried in London, Field Place or beside her husband's in Rome.

"I shall join your father soon," she said, "so I do not care what is done with my body."

She made no formal will, but left her property, money and literary rights to Percy. She also asked him to make three bequests, which he subsequently honored: she left one hundred and fifty pounds to Leigh Hunt, one hundred pounds to Claire Clairmont and fifty pounds per year, for life, to Isabel Baxter, the Scottish friend of her adolescence whom she had never forgotten.

Mary's paralysis grew worse day by day, and her son and daughter-in-law stayed at her bedside, rarely leaving her room. She knew she was dying, but remained cheerful at all times and uttered no complaints. On the evening of January 31 she asked for pen and paper, saying she wanted to write a poem for Shelley. Jane fetched them for her, but Mary could no longer hold a pen in her hand, and it fell onto her bed.

"Never mind, my love," she said. "We shall be together now." She smiled and closed her eyes, never to open them again.

At dawn on the morning of February 1, 1851, Mary Wollstonecraft Godwin Shelley died in her sleep at the age of fifty-four.

Burial took place two days later at Bournemouth churchyard. Her instructions were followed, and a private service was held; only Sir Percy and Lady Shelley, William Godwin the younger and his family, two of the sisters of Percy Bysshe Shelley, the Misses Hellen and Margaret Shelley, and a few close friends were in attendance

It was the custom of the day for a funeral oration to be delivered at the graveside, but instead, at the request of Sir Percy, the Anglican clergyman who presided read an excerpt from Mary's *Journal*. She had written it on June 1, 1840, and it is significant that it was the last long, cohesive passage of consequence that she recorded in her own history of her life:

God and good angels guard us! surely this world, stored outwardly with shapes and influences of beauty and good, is peopled in its intellectual life by myriads of loving spirits that mould our thoughts to good, influence beneficially the course of events, and minister to the destiny of man. Whether the beloved dead make a portion of this company I dare not guess, but that such exist I feel—far off, when we are worldly, evil, selfish; drawing near and imparting joy and sympathy when we rise to noble thoughts and disinterested action. Such surely gather round one on such an evening, and make part of that atmosphere of love, so hushed, so soft, on which the soul reposes and is blest.

Principal Bibliography

Angeli, Helen Rossetti, *Shelley and His Friends in Italy*. London, 1911.
A Shelley Library, collected by T. J. Wise. London, 1924.
Baker, Carlos, *Shelley's Major Poetry*. Princeton, N. J., 1948.
Blunden, Edmund, *Shelley*. London, 1946.
Brown, F. K., *Life of Godwin*. London, 1926.
Campbell, O. W., *Shelley and the Unromantics*. London, 1924.
Church, Richard, *Mary Shelley*. London, 1928.
Cowden Clarke, Charles and Mary, *Recollections of Writers*. London, 1876.
Dowden, Edward, *The Life of Percy Bysshe Shelley*. London, 1886, 2 vols.
Grabo, Carl, *The Magic Plant*. Chapel Hill, N. C., 1936.
Gribble, Francis Henry, *The Romantic Life of Shelley and the Sequel*. London, 1911.
Grylls, R. Glynn, *Mary Shelley*. London, 1938.
Hogg, Thomas Jefferson, *Life of Percy Bysshe Shelley*. Ed. by Humbert Wolfe. London, 1933.
Ingpen, Roger, *Shelley in England*. London, 1917.
Kurtz, B. P., *The Pursuit of Death*. New York, 1933.
Marshall, Mrs. Julian, *The Life and Letters of Mary Wollstonecraft Shelley*. London, 1889.
Massingham, H. J., *A Friend of Shelley: E. J. Trelawny*. London, 1930.
Maurois, André, *Byron*. Paris, 1930.
Origo, Iris, *Allegra*. London, 1935.
Paul, C. Kegan, *William Godwin*. London, 1876.
Peacock's Memoirs of Shelley. Ed. by H. F. B. Brett-Smith. London, 1909.
Peck, Walter E., *Shelley: His Life and Works*. London, 1927.
Pulos, C. E., *The Deep Truth*. Lincoln, Neb., 1962.
Rossetti, Lucy Madox, *Mrs. Shelley*. London, 1890.
Sharp, William, *Life of Shelley*. London, 1887.
Shelley and Mary. London, 1882 (the Shelley family papers, privately printed for and circulated by Sir Percy Florence Shelley).
Shelley, Mary, *Letters of Mary Wollstonecraft Shelley*. Ed. by Frederick L. Jones. Norman, Okla., 1944, 2 vols.
——— *Journal*. Ed. by Frederick L. Jones. Norman, Okla., 1947.

———— *Works*. London, 1894, 20 vols.
Shelley Memorials. Ed. by Lady Shelley. London, 1859.
Shelley, Percy Bysshe, *Letters*. Ed. by Roger Ingpen. London, 1915, 2 vols.
———— *Letters from the Complete Works of Percy Bysshe Shelley*. Ed. by Roger Ingpen and Walter E. Peck. London, 1926. Julian edition.
———— *Poetical Works*. Ed. by Thomas Hutchinson. London, 1905.
Trelawny, Edward John, *The Recollections of Shelley and Byron*. Ed. by Humbert Wolfe. London, 1933.
White, Newman Ivey, *Shelley*. New York, 1940, 2 vols.
———— *The Unextinguished Hearth*. Durham, N. C., 1938.

Index

death of her father, 254–55; and
death of her husband, 215–28; and
death of her son William, 131–34;
and Edward Trelawny, 200, 201–2,
203, 246–50, 268; and Edward Williams, 183–84; fatally ill, 269–70;
and financial problems, 107–10,
142–43, 152–53, 222–24, 231–32,
267; and financial relations between her husband and father,
156–58; in Florence, 143–44; and
Frankenstein, 76–84, 88, 102, 106,
108, 130, 142, 155, 185, 186, 199,
226, 231, 244, 254; funeral oration
for, 271; on husband's 29th birthday, 190; influence on husband's
work, 137–39, 159; and Jane Clairmont, 154, 167–68, 213, 245–46; and
Jane Williams, 183–84, 207, 227,
235–38; and John Howard Payne,
224, 225; and John Murray, 243–44;
last pregnancy of, 210–12; leaves
Florence for Pisa, 147; leaves for
Italy, 112; letter to husband on
Hoppner affair, 190–91; letter to
Mrs. Hoppner, 191–94; life at Albion House, 102–5; life after marriage of her son, 268–69; life outlook after her husband's death,
228–29; life in Pisa, 147–48, 154–55;
literary work after her husband's
death, 227–28, 230–31, 244–45; lives
with Hunts after her husband's
death, 220–21; in London in 1818,
110–11; and Maria Gisborne, 117–
18; miscarriage at Casa Magni,
212–13; and Mrs. Mason, 136–37;
moves into Field Place, 266;
moves to Harrow in 1833, 252–53; in
Naples, 125–29; obtains pension for
her father, 244–45; and Paolo's
blackmail attempt, 155–56; on personality of her son Percy Florence,
252–53; physical description of,
242; political activities of, 101–2;
and publication of *Fortunes of
Perkin Warbeck*, 251–52; and publication of *The Last Man*, 234–
35; publishes husband's works,
230, 257; relationship with her
father-in-law, 222–23, 234–35; rents
Casa Magni, 209–10; returns to
London, 225–26, 255–56, 269; and
rumors about her husband and
Jane Williams, 237, 238; secures
pension for her stepmother, 256;
settles in Pisa, 196; social life in
London after her husband's death,
226–27, 256–57; social life in Pisa,
169–72; and Sophia Stacey, 144–45;
studies painting in Rome, 130–31;
and suicides of Fanny Imlay and
Harriet Shelley, 102–5; supports
Princess Caroline, 160–62; and
Teresa Emilia Viviani, 173–82; and
Thomas Moore, 241–42; and Tom
Medwin, 163–65, 166–67, 171–72;
tours Europe with her son in 1840,

262–65; and upbringing of her son
Percy Florence, 251, 252; visits
daughter Clara's grave, 264; and
Washington Irving, 224; and wom-
en's rights movement, 242–43;
writes *Falkner*, 255; writes *Lodore*,
253–54; writes *Rambles in Germany and Italy*, 265; writes *Valperga*, 185–86, 189, 203–4. *See also*
Godwin, Mary Wollstonecraft
Shelley, Percy Bysshe (husband), 23,
188, 252; arrested in Lake Como,
114; attitude toward world events,
65; background of, 26–27; and
birth of Elena Adelaide Shelley,
126–29; and Byron, 115–16, 119,
189–90, 195, 197–98, 199–200, 207–8;
cremation of, 218; critical reactions
to works of, 155; in custody fight
with Westbrooks, 97–101; death of,
216–18; and death of his daughter
Clara, 120–24; and death of his son
William, 132–34; description of,
240; description of his elopement
trip with Mary Godwin, 44; during wife's last pregnancy, 210–12;
early relationship with Mary Godwin, 20–21, 34–41; and Edward
Trelawny, 201, 202–3, 247, 249;
and Edward Williams, 184; elopes
with Mary Godwin, 41–43, 47–48;
and Fanny Imlay's suicide, 88–89,
91–92; on fatal sailing trip, 214–15;
financial problems of, 57, 105, 107–
10, 142–43; in Florence, 143–44;
and Harriet Shelley's suicide, 92–
94; and Henry Reveley's steam engine, 142–43, 165; illness of, 107;
impact of death of, 228–29; influence on Robert Browning, 256–57;
inherits money, 60; interested in
occult, 75; and Jane Clairmont,
86–87, 168, 190–93, 208, 259, 260;
and Jane Williams, 204–5, 207;
leaves England for last time, 112;
leaves Florence for Pisa, 147; in
Leghorn, Italy, 117; life at Albion
House, 102–5; life at Bishopsgate,
65–66; life at Casa Magni, 213–14;
life in London, 54–57; life in London countryside, 63–65; life in
Pisa, 147–48; literary recognition
of, 258; in London in 1818, 110–11;
marriage to Harriet Westbrook,
27; marries Mary Godwin, 96; and
Mary Jane Godwin, 96–97; meets
Mary Godwin, 28; morality of, 69,
70–72; in Naples, 125–29; near
drowning of, 187–88; and Paolo's
blackmail attempt, 155–56; poem
to Mary Godwin by, 36–37; political opinions of, 101–2; premoni-
tions of his death, 213; and publication of *Frankenstein*, 80; publication of works of, 257; reaction to
birth of daughter Clara, 57–58; reaction to *Frankenstein*, 78, 79; relationship with his father, 85;